D1008884

Private Selves in Public Organizations

Also by Michael A. Diamond

The Unconscious Life of Organizations

Also by Seth Allcorn and Michael A. Diamond

Managing People During Stressful Times

Private Selves in Public Organizations

The Psychodynamics of Organizational Diagnosis and Change

Michael A. Diamond and Seth Allcorn

First published in 2009 by PALGRAVE MACMILLAN® in the United States—a division of St. Martin's Press LLC, 175 Fifth Avenue, New York, NY 10010

Where this book is distributed in the UK, Europe and the rest of the world, this is by Palgrave Macmillan, a division of Macmillan Publishers Limited, registered in England, company number 785998, of Houndmills, Basingstoke, Hampshire RG21 6XS.

Palgrave Macmillan is the global academic imprint of the above companies and has companies and representatives throughout the world.

Palgrave® and Macmillan® are registered trademarks in the United States, the United Kingdom, Europe and other countries.

ISBN-13: 978-0-230-61309-6
ISBN-10: 0-230-61309-8

Library of Congress Cataloging-in-Publication Data

Diamond, Michael A. (Michael Alan), 1950–
    Private selves in public organizations : the psychodynamics of organizational diagnosis and change / Michael A. Diamond, Seth Allcorn.
        p. cm.
    Includes bibliographical references.
    ISBN 0-230-61309-8
    1. Organizational behavior—Psychological aspects. 2. Organizational change—Psychological aspects. 3. Corporate culture. 4. Psychology, Industrial. I. Allcorn, Seth. II. Title.

HD58.7.D528 2009
158.7—dc22   2008032406

A catalogue record of the book is available from the British Library.

Design by Scribe Inc.

First edition: April 2009

10 9 8 7 6 5 4 3 2 1

Printed in the United States of America.

For Tova and Simone

Contents

Preface   ix

Acknowledgments   xi

Introduction: Analyzing Organizations as Experiential   1
     and Relational Systems

Part 1: Organizational Insight

1   Layers of Experience: 13
     An Object Relational Model for Organizations

2   Boundaries and Surfaces   31

3   Silo Mentality   49

4   Organizational Change and the Analytic Third   73

5   Organizations as Defective Containers   93

Part 2: Organizational Tumult

6   Moral Violence   109

7   Chaos and Complexity   127

8   Shame, Oppression, and Persecution   135

Part 3: Intervention and Reparation

9   Shared Emotions: Transference and Countertransference   147

10   Perversions of Democracy   159

11   Immersion and Diagnosis   175

Conclusion: Human Nature and Organizational Silos   187

References   193

About the Authors   205

Index   207

Preface

Human nature, essentially changeable, unstable as the dust, can endure no restraint; if it binds itself it soon begins to tear madly at its bonds, until it rends everything asunder, the wall, the bonds, and its very self.

Franz Kafka, "The Great Wall of China"

Organizations are artifacts of human nature. They would not exist were it not for the people who create, imagine, and operate them. They are objectively, subjectively, and intersubjectively conceived relational systems existing inside and outside the human mind. Their experiential nature encompasses their social, economic, technological, and political attributes. These relational and structural tensions, ambiguities, and eccentricities are the essence of the workplace. These human characteristics of organizational life are not particularly accessible to the positivist's approach. Understanding them requires a theory and method that encompasses conscious, unconscious, subjective, intersubjective, group, and organizational psychosocial dynamics. It is our view that contemporary psychoanalytic theory provides this deeper and more comprehensive understanding of human relations in the workplace.

The conceptual framework offered in this book takes into account this collision of social and psychological forces. Let us begin with the idea that those who seek to understand organizations need a theory for making sense of organizations. This theory ought to provide comprehensive and systematic insight into the multifaceted nature of organizational life. It ought to be reflective, relevant, and representative of human nature in groups and organizations. It ought to be constructed and reconstructed from observation and experience with actual organizations. We meet these challenges by applying a psychoanalytic perspective of human nature to discover the meaning of organizational dynamics beyond the surface behavior and espoused practices that are the grist for many empiricists. This perspective blends contemporary psychoanalytic theory (object relational and self-psychology) and psychological anthropology that embraces participant observation, psychoanalytic fieldwork, and action research.

Acknowledging that organizations are relational, experiential, and perceptual requires that we account for organizational cultures and subcultures that have their origins in human nature. Organizational cultures contain sensemaking and meaning creating qualities that are such a fundamental experience of the workplace that they are often taken for granted and over time rendered unconscious to their members. The psychoanalytically informed approach that we explain in this book takes collective and individual workplace memory and critical incidents seriously. These are the data of organizational history and culture that provide valuable clues to why people in particular organizations act and think in peculiar ways.

This engagement between contemporary psychoanalytic and organization theory and practice shapes our understanding and assumptions about life in organizations. It provides a framework for collecting and organizing qualitative data and rendering it meaningful and relevant to organizational participants. In practice, the application of psychoanalytic ideas about organizations requires a lively engagement between researcher and subject (the client system). The pioneer of action research and change theory, social psychologist Kurt Lewin (1946), claimed that if you want to make a positive impact on social problems, then go out and try to solve them by intervening and then observing the consequences of your having done so.

We take the position that organizational culture, identity, and performance are the outcome of the collision between self (psychological structure) and organizations (social and political structure)—private selves in *public* organizations. We stress throughout the book that a contemporary psychoanalytic definition of organization is one premised on the notion that organizations are experiential and relational (intersubjective) as well as behavioral and observable. When one takes this into account, it becomes self-evident that the study of organizations requires that researchers immerse themselves in the organization with methods for extracting meaning through the organizational narrative and, more importantly, through the collective experiences and relational patterns of the organizational culture under observation. In this book, we draw together many of the insights and perspectives that we have arrived at from nearly three decades of research, consultation, and administrative experience in academia.

Acknowledgments

We wish to thank the following friends and colleagues for their support and encouragement over the years: Guy Adams, Gilles Amado, Chris Argyris, Howell Baum, Robert Denhardt, Yiannis Gabriel, James Glass, Larry Gould, Manfred Kets de Vries, Jim Krantz, David Levine, Harry Levinson, Rose Mersky, Shelley Reciniello, Howard Schwartz, Burkard Sievers, Lionel Stapley, Vamik Volkan, and Bart Wechsler. We also thank Chris Awad, Karen Poulin, and Linda Wolzson for their consulting expertise, intellectual curiosity, and insights. One could not ask for better organizational investigators and co-consultants. We also thank our occasional co-author, constant friend, and colleague extraordinaire, Howard F. Stein. Howard's intellect and generosity are beyond words. We also acknowledge the pioneering work of organizational psychologist and friend, Harry Levinson. His conception of organizational diagnosis is a major contribution to the theory and practice of organizational analysis and intervention. Finally, we thank Lindsey Hagglund for her incredible personal, professional, administrative, and organizational support.

Introduction

Analyzing Organizations as Experiential and Relational Systems

The self is paradoxical: it is an enduring structure and at the same time nearly coterminus with an ever-changing consciousness. Furthermore, the private self supports a relative self-sufficiency, whereas from another perspective the self is not at all autonomous but can be seen as vulnerable in its dependence upon others for a sense of coherence and continuity.

Arnold Modell, The Private Self

The theory and practice of organizational change presented here represents nearly thirty years of fieldwork. We provide readers with a structure, albeit a complex one, for analyzing and changing organizations; one that supports paying attention to participants' and participant-observers' emotional, and interpersonal, awareness and attunement. This framework is a method of organizational research and consultation. It is experientially grounded, interpretive, and action-oriented. Our approach is a form of action research, which requires participant-observation and immersion. It is an approach designed for the study of complex organizations such as government agencies and bureaucracies, businesses and corporations, universities and colleges, and hospitals and nonprofit organizations.

Our approach differs from traditional organization theories of behavior and development in that we acknowledge and attend to the nonrational, emotional, embodied, and unconscious (unaware, taken for granted) side of individuals, groups, and organizations. We take workers' feelings seriously since they frequently shape how individuals perceive and experience the workplace. We assume that feelings are collectively meaningful and that they significantly shape and influence organizational culture, leadership, attitudes, conflicts, morale, strategic thinking, planning, and performance.

Emotions, experiences, perceptions, observations, and stories demand our attention when analyzing organizations. They are at the heart of organizational misbehavior, criminality, and inhumanity.

Workers want to be understood and validated as conscious, creative, thoughtful, and passionate human beings. It is our view that workers frequently feel ignored, unrecognized, and simply not listened to by managers and executive leaders. Listening is a powerful tool for organizational change. As Howard F. Stein (1994), in his book *Listening Deeply: An Approach to Understanding and Consulting in Organizational Culture*, suggests,

> To listen deeply is to replace our need to make the human universe static and accept and welcome the flux that is at the core of creativity. To listen deeply is to replace our need for intrusive control with respect for another's autonomy and empathy for that person's or group's experience. In such a capacity an organizational consultant functions less as a strategist and more as a client's or an organization's temporary auxiliary ego. This human instrument of empathy and respect is heir to the mother or other caregiving person as a source of validation from whom the child could reliably borrow in earliest infancy. (p. 2)

The theory and practice for organizational change presented here is in large part a method for making contact with individuals in organizations and *listening deeply* to what they have to say about their experiences as workers, managers, executives, and stakeholders. Our approach is existential and identity based as well as material and interest based. Thus, both individual meaning and interests combine to inform the rationale for individual affiliation and commitment to work organizations. We believe that the value of traditional (experience-distant) empirical methods of organizational research based on surveys and quantitative analyses is limited, if not at times irrelevant, particularly when it comes to understanding and explaining organizational culture, leadership, membership, and performance. Employee surveys, for example, may be useful in their quantification of attitudes and attributions on the surface. They may be useful in a corroborating function and role along side qualitative data collection and psychodynamic methods of field research and organizational diagnosis. However, we have found no substitute for immersion, participant observation, fieldwork, and interpretation if one is genuinely interested in *knowing* the subject-organization, its culture, and its identity.

Learning and understanding through empathy, introspection, and identification goes beyond collecting information and taking the pulse of people's attitudes about work and organizations. It demands communication and language rooted in mutual subjectivities and in the location of *meaning* about oneself in the context of others and their shared community or organization. Harry Stack Sullivan (1953) referred to this maturational, interpersonal, communicative feat as a *syntaxic* mode of experience or the consensually validated meaning of language. Granted, this approach is more demanding of self and participants than studying organizations from afar, yet in our experience, it is a good deal more satisfying and rewarding for the participants and more beneficial in what is learned about organizations and the human condition. By intervening in the ongoing, taken for granted, frequently routine, rationalized, and unconscious dynamics of organizations, we can interrupt destructive and counterproductive defensive routines, which are often automatic and outside the awareness of organizational participants. Like a spinning wheel in motion, one has to slow it down long enough to get a better look at the texture of its surface and the integrity of its materials. Similarly, we intervene and interrupt the organization in motion so that learning, reflectivity, and insight are possible. This admittedly ambitious goal is at the heart of this book.

We hope this book offers insight for readers into the humanity of organizations. It is unique in that it does not define organizations as simply rational, technological structures and networks for organizing people around tasks and services. It defines organizations as relational, experiential, and perceptual systems. What people feel, think, and imagine matters. And, it matters to how we understand and explain organizational performance. Taking into account the experiential and emotional dimension makes a distinctive and profound difference in how organizational scholars and consultants look at and understand organizations as shaped and perpetuated by the people who inhabit (or are inhabited by) them.

Book Organization

We organized the book into three parts that offer insight into organizational dynamics and structure, different aspects of workplace disruption and violence, and organizational intervention and repair. Each section offers something different, and together they provide concepts and tools for knowing and changing the workplace. Each part illuminates what it means to view organizations as experiential and relational systems and as narrative structures of intersubjectivity that produce knowledge of the meaning and identity of organizations. Each part is preceded by a brief organizer that creates a context for the following chapters.

Part 1, "Organizational Insight," is the most substantial section of the book. The chapters in this section explain our theory of organizations. We begin with Chapter 1, "Layers of Experience," which describes three modes of organizing experience drawn from contemporary object relations theory. The three modes (depressive, paranoid-schizoid, and autistic-contiguous) are rooted in individual development and represent the object relational nuances of the emerging self out of its infantile bonds. One's sense of self is in large part shaped by early (infantile and childhood) relational experiences. These experiences are linked dialectically and provide a conceptual framework for considering the nuance and variation of human relations at work, and they are discussed in three workplace vignettes. These layers of experience become the basis for a tripartite object relational model that is used throughout the book.

Chapter 2, "Boundaries and Surfaces," applies object relations theory to common aspects of workplace experience such as organizational boundaries. Boundaries are found to contain individual and collective meaning and to shape the substance of experience more than might be at first appreciated. In particular, at an emotionally primitive level, boundaries contain or represent psychic and sensate (autistic-contiguous) surfaces more like a wall (hard or soft textured) than a line in the sand. One of these more typical experiences of workplace boundaries is articulated by the metaphor of organizational silos. These silos, with their boundary setting surfaces and infantile roots, are then explored using the tripartite object relations model.

Chapter 3, "Silo Mentality," continues the exploration of the significance of the metaphor of organizational silos as important organizational phenomena in their own right. Silos are found to have their origins in hierarchical organizational design, but just as important, they originate as a creation in individual minds of workers. As meaningful metaphors, silos and the boundaries that they signify function in one's mind in part as powerful inhibitors creating forbidden areas and points of transit. They may also be experienced as protective in shutting out threats from beyond. In addition, silos represent the individual's tendency toward cognitively and emotionally discriminating between one task and another as well as one group and another. Organizational divisions and departments are at times productive and at other times counterproductive manifestations of the silo mentality. Case examples are provided to render their presence, significance, and contribution to organizational dysfunctions as more concrete. Suggestions are provided for penetrating silo mentalities.

Chapter 4, "Organizational Change and the Analytic Third," introduces a unique perspective, the analytic third, as a vantage point for viewing and understanding organizational life. The notion of the third has a rich theoretical history in philosophy and psychoanalysis, which is discussed, and various points of view are reconciled. The understanding gained from this discussion of the third is then crossed over to the workplace where we find that it promotes productive self-consciousness and awareness of relational dynamics and the constructive position of intervention for organizational change. This chapter presents the notion of using one's self as an instrument of observation and change. A case example is provided to ground the analytic third in the study of organizations and the processes of organizational change.

Chapter 5, "Organizations as Defective Containers," explores the phenomenon of psychological regression in groups and organizations, which is triggered by a loss of personal autonomy and individuality of group and organizational members. It is suggested that psychological regression and the emotional return to more primitively dependent and merged states of self experience are due in part to the failure of leaders and their organizations to provide emotional containment for members' distress and anxieties. The very design and implementation of organizational change produces distress and anxiety among workers. Thus, an appreciation of these consequences of transition and upheaval leads in this chapter to a discussion of managing and containing psychological regression in support of change. This chapter is also about the unconscious expectations of workers and their organizational leaders and the consequences of failed and disappointed expectation.

Part 2, "Organizational Tumult," explores a shadowy and more taxing side of organizations, where anger and the potential for aggression and violence introduce a sense of threat and fear. Chapter 6, "Moral Violence," begins this exploration by inquiring into the phenomenon of emotional abuse at work. Abusive, sadistic, and aggressive management of workers results in emotional trauma, dehumanization, and demoralization, a capacity to treat others as objects rather than subjects in their own right. Thus, organizations are potentially morally violent climates. Case examples are provided to illuminate the phenomenon of moral violence in organizations. The origins of moral violence are examined for their infantile roots in mechanisms of splitting, projection, and introjection. The creation of potential space at work is discussed as an antidote for moral violence.

Chapter 7, "Chaos and Complexity," confronts the reality of constantly changing, emerging, and evolving organizations for their contribution to promoting distress, anxiety, and psychological regression among workers. Chaos and complexity are frequently experienced by participants as an assault on the comfort of structure, routine, and familiarity. The notion of organizational disorder is presented as framework for considering emergent organizing properties that support goal oriented behavior, reflective practice, and double loop learning.

Chapter 8, "Shame, Oppression, and Persecution," looks at physical violence and aggression in the workplace. In particular, this chapter examines the collision of narcissistic self and oppressive and persecutory organization. In these cases, organizational members feel threatened, intimidated, victimized, powerless, and hopeless. The workplace climate and culture may be a contributor to aggression and violence alongside psychologically defensive actions of splitting and projection triggered by primitive anxieties. These social and psychological processes play off one another and reinforce persecutory experiences at work, which enhance good/bad cognitive and emotional polarizations and the sense of victimization.

Part 3, "Intervention and Reparation," returns to a general theory and method for organizational change based on understanding and responding to the psychologically defensive nature of organizations. Chapter 9, "Shared Emotions," examines the role of transference and countertransference in human relations and the interpretive value of psychological reality in organizations. One has to consider the contributions of transference and countertransference dynamics in shaping members' as well as researchers' and consultants' experiences and the unconscious meaning of organizational life. This emphasis on the interpretive value of psychological reality distinguishes the psychodynamic approach from social psychological and cognitive-behavioral approaches to organization development and is especially important when it comes to intervening effectively in workplace dynamics.

Chapter 10, "Perversions of Democracy," explores the nature of workplace democracy and its prerequisites. Discussions of workplace democracy are but a faint whisper in contemporary organizational literature. Regrettably, workplace democracy in practice possesses considerable fragility, and to the extent that it exists, it may be overcome by psychological regression in the form of splitting and projection. These regressive dynamics divide one's experience of, as well as the people within, organizations into primitive black and white, good and bad objects. Indeed, workplace democracy is easily perverted when stress generates discomforting levels of anxiety accompanied by psychologically defensive thoughts, feelings, and actions. This outcome is illuminated by the tripartite model and its three modes of workplace (individual and group) experience that are held in a dialectical tension relative to each other. Thus, democratic values and practices are rooted in the self as much as they are embedded in the body politic of organization.

Chapter 11, "Immersion and Diagnosis," provides insight into the theory and practice of organizational diagnosis and intervention, which are meaningful to executives leading change and to organizational consultants. The methods described rely upon one's ability to use one's self as an instrument of data collection and learning. In addition to the kind of self-awareness described in Chapter 4 with the concept of the analytic third, this requires being able to maintain self-other boundaries and the management of one's anxieties permitting self-reflection and the ability to conceptualize the psychologically defensive nature of the workplace. The proposed consultation model contains a number of steps such as contracting, organizational diagnosis, intervention, and follow-up. A case example is provided. This method attends to unconscious (automatic, known but not thought of) organizational dynamics. It provides a framework to assist researchers and consultants with the capacity to observe and reflect on the emotional knots, conflicts, and turmoil of typical organizations.

The conclusion, "Human Nature and Organizational Silos," offers reflections on the theme of what it means to assume a contemporary psychoanalytic position in relation to the study of organizations and organizational change. It revisits the framework of organizations presented in this book as rooted in human nature and our defensive proclivity for silo thinking. Finally, the significance of the metaphor of organizational silos is illustrated by a vignette.

Our Application of Contemporary Psychoanalytic Theory

The approach to organizational change that we take throughout this book is predominantly shaped by the post-Freudian theorists and clinicians in object relations theory starting with Melanie Klein. The ideas and concepts represented by Klein, Bion, Winnicott, Ogden, and others are elaborated on throughout this book and more extensively than the following introductory comments. Nevertheless, it may be helpful at the outset to clarify for readers unfamiliar with psychoanalytic theory outside a Freudian context the evolution of thinking that has occurred over the last century. Psychoanalytic theory today is what some call a two-person (relational) psychology rather than a one-person, individual psychology (Modell, 1984; Mitchell & Aron, 1999). The new psychoanalytic framework is more relational, interpersonal, and intersubjective, in contrast to its Freudian intrapsychic precursor, which is a model rooted in mechanisms such as drives and instincts (Greenberg & Mitchell, 1983). The earliest preverbal interactions between infant and mother, which D. W. Winnicott (1965, 1971) calls "the holding environment," is assumed to be as critical as genetics in affecting the character of human bonds and attachments throughout the life cycle. Infant research, attachment theory, cognitive and experimental psychology, and neuroscience have heightened the emphasis placed on self and object, self and other, and relations as key to understanding character and pathology. The assumption that individuals change and overcome emotional anguish in intensive psychotherapies is supported by brain research in the neurosciences. Evidence of changes in the structure of the brain resulting from relational dynamics in talk therapy has support in the scientific community (Stern, 1985, 2004; Vaughan, 1997; Gedo, 1999; Kandel, 2006).

Melanie Klein's (1975a, 1975b) original findings on the infantile roots of adult behavior continue to influence how psychoanalytically informed organization theorists think about individuals in organizations and how these participants respond to stress and anxiety in groups and in relation to peers and supervisors in positions of authority. Psychological regression, and the notion of adults in childlike roles affected by primitive (infantile-like) thinking and aggressive interactions, is a key concept in the application of object relations theory to adults in the workplace.

We take into account the nature of attachment and emotional bonds that individuals form as adults in groups and organizations. We assume these earlier experiences, however, reshaped and reconstituted by experiences throughout the life cycle, are present in the recruit at the point of entry into the organization. Thus, we further assume and have observed many times that the stress of organizational change triggers regressive and childlike behavior among participants. Melanie Klein and, more recently, Thomas Ogden (1989) provide us with a framework for analyzing and better understanding the infantile roots of adult behavior, which we then apply to our observations of people in the workplace.

The capacity for individuals as adults to engage in primitive thinking stems from infancy and early childhood and then persists throughout the human life cycle. The human infant begins life in an attached and symbiotic state. Its primitive awareness is of sensations of surfaces, such as skin to skin contact between mother and infant. This comprises what Ogden calls the autistic-contiguous mode of experience. And, as the brain develops, the baby begins to experience its world in absolutes, such as nurturing or depriving, cold or warm, comforting or endangering. Klein originally identified these experiences as the paranoid-schizoid position in which the baby's world is fragmented and comprised of dedifferentiated part-objects. It is schizoid in that it is fragmented and thereby not whole. It is paranoid in that the experience of anxiety provokes splitting of the world into polarized opposites of good and bad. In the mind and body of the infant, mother is not as yet fully differentiated from baby. She is not as yet seen as a subject separate in her own right from the child. Good-enough mothering (nurturing and caretaking) according to Winnicott provides the baby with an adequate holding environment, interpersonal security and safety, from which the infant can modulate fears and persecutory anxieties. From object relations theory, we learn that the human capacity for psychological splitting and absolutism has its roots in the paranoid-schizoid mode of experience in infancy and early childhood. We assume, based on Winnicott's work, that an inadequate or not good-enough holding environment in childhood can exacerbate the individual's proclivity to engage in psychological splitting when confronted with threats and uncertainties.

Psychological splitting of self and objects (also others) into absolutes of all or nothing, good or bad, and loving or persecuting can be seen and heard among adults in the contemporary workplace. We find these concepts illuminating when it comes to better understanding individuals in organizations under stress and in turmoil. These ideas are also practical in helping us to create better processes and structures for change that help to contain participants' anxieties and sense of emotional loss associated with transition. In this regard, Melanie Klein's notion of the depressive position as a mode of experience in which the child begins to see the other as separate and distinct is critical to our appreciation of psychological and emotional responses to change as triggering feelings related to separation and loss.

It is our observation that the human processes of change in organizations frequently means that participants overcome their typical resistances to change by opening themselves up emotionally to their anxieties about separation and loss. Learning new organizational routines and procedures implies letting go of old routines and procedures. Human beings attach themselves to objects, whether structural or embodied. Thus, organizational change stirs issues and feelings of attachment, separation, and loss. Object relations theory and its application to the workplace enable us to observe, support, and understand these human responses and feelings of participants. It is more constructive to understand and empathize with human nature in these circumstances than to judge and criticize.

We now turn to Part 1, "Organizational Insight," and our study of the workplace using a tripartite model that reveals the true complexity of organizational life.

Part I

Organizational Insight

Contemporary organizations are not simply rational, cooperative systems stemming from individuals pursuing organizational goals. Rather, organizations, much like their human creators and inhabitants, are comprised of manifest and latent, as well as conscious and unconscious, dynamics that make them complex and challenging to comprehend. How these relational and socio-technical systems operate and how frequently they become irrational, dysfunctional, and unconscious, thereby compromising ethics, performance, and ultimately survival, are questions addressed in this book. In the following theoretical and applied exploration of organizations, we return human nature to center stage in organizational studies. Part 1 examines human nature in organizations from the relational perspective of contemporary object relations theory.

Psychoanalytic object relations theory informs our understanding of conscious and unconscious organizational dynamics. The dilemma for students of organization is that the close up experience of studying organizational culture can itself be disorienting. It can result in a diminishing capacity for observation and reflection. Action researchers and consultants must maintain self-awareness, reflection, and the position of the analytic third (see Chapter 4) in order to participate in experience-near organizational studies. It is critical to have a comprehensive and systematic theoretical framework and method for making sense of the nonsense of organizations. To this end, Part 1 introduces a tripartite model for understanding the psychological reality of organizational life. This model is anchored in object relations theory and Thomas Ogden's revision of Melanie Klein's theory and her findings on the infantile origins of adult behavior. The tripartite model and theory provides students of organizations with a richer understanding of the complexity and chaos surrounding psychological regression in organizations. This approach stresses the intersubjective and dialectical nature of human relationships. It is based on a transformation of Klein's description of developmental positions into what Ogden calls modes of organizing experience. The model is as much about what individuals experience as how they organize and make sense of reality. These relational positions include the depressive, paranoid-schizoid, and Ogden's addition of the preverbal, autistic-contiguous. Also, the psychoanalytic concepts of *identification* and *containment* are singled out in Chapter 1 as central to our understanding the processes of organizational diagnosis and immersion in organizations.

This theory and the tripartite model are then applied to explore organizational boundaries and surfaces and in particular a common feature of hierarchical organizations—silos. The perspective of the analytic third is reviewed for its contribution to understanding self and organizational change; the nature and affect of psychological regression in organizations is then explored for its contribution to organizational dysfunction and distress.

Chapter 1 explains Ogden's modes of relational experience and applies them to the unconscious and intersubjective structure of organizations. Chapter 2 begins the process of locating how the theory and tripartite model inform the understanding of unconscious organizational dynamics by exploring the subject of organizational boundaries and the meaning of organizational structure. These structural boundaries often take the form of organizational silos in the minds of organizational members. Silos are a commonly used metaphor among organizational participants to describe inter-divisional and professional conflict and resistance to collaboration, communication, and information-sharing in all kinds of organizations. Chapter 3 focuses on the study of organizational silos by grounding the insights of the object relational model with actual case examples. Chapter 4 introduces the concept of the analytic third to describe the psychological position of the consultant/researcher and, ideally, organizational members in the process of intervening in often unconscious (automatic and taken-for-granted) organizational dynamics. In Chapter 5, we explore processes of psychological regression in organizations under stress. Organizations and their leadership are often defective containers of displacement and projection. Collective regression into paranoid-schizoid and autistic-contiguous modes of experience can lead to groups and divisions of people losing their capacity to differentiate self from other and subject from object. The presence of regression also implies the incapacity on the part of the leader to hold and accept (contain) these differences among participants, resulting in unnecessarily ambiguous, destructive, and dysfunctional operations.

I

Layers of Experience

An Object Relational Model for Organizations

All human experience, including transference-countertransference experience, can be thought of as the outcome of the dialectical interplay of three modes of creating and organizing psychological meaning. Each of these modes is associated with one of three fundamental psychological organizations—the depressive position, the paranoid-schizoid position, and the autistic-contiguous position.

Thomas Ogden, Subjects of Analysis, *1994, p. 139*

In this chapter, we elaborate on the idea that organizations are experiential and relational systems. A tripartite relational model rooted in contemporary object relations theory is presented. The model is based upon the dialectical interplay between Thomas Ogden's three modes of experience—depressive, paranoid-schizoid, and autistic-contiguous (1989, 1994). This dialectical framework stresses the phenomena of dynamically interacting social and psychological structures (psychological versus social, internal versus external, subjective versus objective). This view of human relations acknowledges that individuals join social organizations with self agency and identities in place. It is the interaction, or dialectical exchange, of these realities that shape the psychodynamics of organizational cultures and experience, helping to answer the action researcher's riddle: "what is it *really* like to work here?"

Object Relations Theory and Application to Organizations

Automatic and unconscious relational dynamics between executives, managers, and workers shape organizational cultures and collective experience. We find Thomas Ogden's (1989, 1994) revision of Melanie Klein's theory of object relations (Klein, 1946; Mitchell, 1987) consistent with the contemporary school of psychoanalysis (object relations theory, relational psychoanalysis, and self psychology). This contemporary post-Freudian theory has evolved out of a century of clinical research, experimental and cognitive psychology, social psychology, neuroscience, and infant research (Eagle, 1984; Stern, 1985; Gill, 1994; Ogden, 1989; 1994; Gedo, 1999). This theory of object relations extends Klein's (1946) original (dyadic) positions into three dialectical modes of organizing experience: (1) depressive; (2) paranoid-schizoid; and (3) autistic-contiguous; the latter is a more primitive and pre-verbal position. More specifically, this expanded and updated framework underscores the importance of coming to know the relational patterns, the narrative themes, the points of urgency, and the horizontal and vertical human interactions that are largely the organization.

In order to understand Ogden's extension of Klein's (1946) object relations theory, one must first understand the depressive and paranoid-schizoid positions. These modes of experience are interdependent experiential and relational dimensions of psychological reality. We start by discussing the more integrated and holistic depressive position, one that is developmentally advanced and yet cannot exist on behalf of the self without the presence of the two other more primitive and regressive modes of human nature, the paranoid-schizoid and the autistic-contiguous. Once again, these layers of experience are not mutually exclusive and are intimately linked one to another.

The Depressive Mode of Experience (Subject-to-Subject)

The depressive mode of experience serves to contain emotions and foster differentiation of self and other, subject and object. Central to this operation is the capacity for "symbol formation proper" (Segal, 1988), in which an interpreting subject represents the object as symbol and experiences the symbolized object as other, separate from self. In the depressive mode, a self-interpreting subject is able to generate interpretive space between the symbol and that which it represents. One experiences oneself as a person who thinks and feels her own thoughts and feelings and thus claims responsibility for them.

To the degree that one is capable of experiencing oneself as a subject it is possible to experience others as subjects rather than objects. Others are seen as capable of their own thoughts, feelings, and actions. They are seen as remaining the same people over time despite shifts in affect one may feel toward them. Along with the separateness of whole object relations, this continuity of experience of self and other reflects the capacity to have experience situated in time (historicity)—that which Ogden calls "the presence of a historically rooted sense of self that is continuous over time and over shifts in affective states" (Ogden, 1994, p. 35). For instance, at some point in time during analysis, the patient begins to delineate and better articulate past and present in his or her experience. Previously, this may very well have been absent—as in the lack of historicity inside the paranoid-schizoid mode of experience (discussed in the next section). Eventually, in practice, the patient comes to consciously acknowledge feelings and reactions to people and events in the present that have their roots in the past. The patient becomes more reflective and conscious and less reactive over time.

The depressive mode of experience, as described, provides for self and other awareness as independently functioning subjects that may have desirable and undesirable attributes. The acceptance of what is referred to as whole object relations opens the door to discussions, such as the assumption of personal responsibility and owning one's actions. Ideally, it is within this mode of experience that we realize our interactive and communicative potential, indicative of emotional intelligence and more fully developed object relations. The depressive mode of experience reflects one's capacity for containment as an interpreting subject. This inter-subjective capacity for experiencing others as subjects in their own right is transferable to the workplace and crucial to learning organizations (Argyris, 1990; Argyris & Schon, 1996). The depressive mode of experience provides for the reflective and empathic give and take that makes interpersonal relations productive, creative, and synergistic. Organization members do not feel particularly threatened (polarized, fragmented, or split apart) by the thoughts, feelings, and actions of others or organizational and external events. Whole object relations and emotional containment are sustained in the face of distressing workplace emotions and events. Ideally, individuals can question or disagree with one another and not take it too personally and defensively.

The depressive mode signifies more fully integrated object relations and contrasts with, but is never separate from, the autistic-contiguous and the paranoid-schizoid mode.

Paranoid-Schizoid Mode of Experience (Object-to-Object)

The paranoid-schizoid mode is characterized by efforts to manage and evacuate emotional pain. Part-object relations characterize this mode. Others are experienced as fragmented mental objects that possess different qualities at different times. The primary dilemma rooted in early development is managing the intolerable anxiety related to loving and hating the same object. The resulting primary anxiety is managed through splitting and projective identification from which one separates the loving and hating aspects of oneself from the loving and hating aspects of the loved object. This faulty solution to anxiety is intended, however unconsciously, to prevent the bad (the endangering) from destroying the good (the endangered). Thus, object relatedness is inevitably accomplished through processes of projective identification where a facet of self (either the endangered or endangering) is placed into another person through projection.

In the paranoid-schizoid mode, immediate experience eclipses both past history and future, thereby creating an eternal, ahistorical present. There exists a lack of interpretive space between subject and object and thus there is no capacity for differentiating the symbol from that which is symbolized. Consequently, experience is two-dimensional. The world is concrete. Everything is and can only be the single thing that it is. Absolutism abounds. What could be more primitive than fragmented thinking, which produces a hostile and brutish world view of part-objects and coercive and manipulative relationships?

Workplace experience often contains regressive and defensive routines (Allcorn & Diamond, 1997; Diamond, 1993, 1998; Kernberg, 1998; Kets de Vries & Miller, 1984; Stein, 1994). The paranoid-schizoid dimension, for instance, directs our attention to the defensive and regressive aspects of interpersonal and intra-organizational dynamics. Defensive actions, such as denial, splitting, projection, and projective identification, are common features of organizational life. Organizations are often inhabited by discrete divisions, departments, sections, groups, skill sets, knowledge bases, and professions. One might readily wonder how all of these various "soft components" of organizations are ever joined together to create a functional whole. It is our sense from many years of organizational research and consulting that the successful integration of these many parts is elusive and problematic. A division such as human resources can become a frustrating source of irritation for line managers who either need to motivate, replace, discipline, or remove a worker. A finance department may express serious reservations about publicly admitting a consumer problem with a product such as a tire, whereas the legal and marketing departments may express grave concerns about using cost-effectiveness as the rule for measuring corporate responsibility. In short, it is neither difficult nor unusual to find many sources of conflict within organizations that promote denial, splitting, and projection: for example, "We are right and you are wrong." "They are the evil empire and we the promoters of good." The workplace can indeed become polarized into black and white: an all good or all bad context in which individuals, sections, departments, and divisions conduct intra-organizational warfare. These psychodynamics redirect and eventually remove the productive energy from organizations while consuming organizational resources. In sum, the paranoid-schizoid mode of experience is rather typical of workplace cultures in which people engage in object-to-object relationships, which contrast experientially with the surface-to-surface relations of the autistic-contiguous dimension.

The Autistic-Contiguous Mode of Experience (Surface to Surface)

Without calling it such and despite his emphasis on the oedipal phase of development Freud referred time and again to bodily sensations, surfaces, and boundaries in the ego's engagement with internal and external worlds. The autistic-contiguous dimension consists of the most elemental forms of human experience. Freud (1923) observed in *The Ego and the Id* that the ego is ultimately derived from bodily sensations, chiefly those springing from the surface of the body. Ogden calls this mode of experience the "autistic-contiguous." It is a pre-symbolic, sensory form in which feelings of rhythm and "surface contiguity" shape the core of an infant's first relationship with the external object world (Ogden, 1989, p. 32). Thus, the origins of this experience are primitive, residing in the earliest days, weeks, and months of life. Here, experience is generated by the impression of two surfaces coming together in either differentiation or merger.

One of Ogden's major contributions to object relations theory is the articulation of the autistic-contiguous mode of experience. Human beings experience the world in the manner of surface-to-surface contact. Tactile sensation reveals much about a surface that may contain many qualities, such as hardness or softness, warmth or cold, pattern and shape, and most of all, a sense at the point of surface-to-surface contact of containment. "I am within my surface (skin) and contact with an opposing surface" both confirms the existence of my surface as well as imposes the dimensionality of the opposing surface upon awareness. This self-affirming sensation of surfaces may be contrasted with the loss of spatial and temporal boundaries and the loss of a sense of containing and reaffirming surface within a sensory deprivation chamber. Within the chamber, one is embraced by a timeless, boundary-less context that deprives one of the feelings of surface-to-surface contact.

As Ogden (1989) notes, this experience exposes the person to a formless sense of dread in which the experiential mode may be thought of as the dissolution of self into the pool of body temperature water. Upon initial consideration, it may appear that the depressive and autistic-contiguous modes of experiencing vary in degree of psychological maturity, sophistication, and achievement. Yet, they are similar insofar that in both forms, the primary anxiety relies upon integrative and containing processes. In the case of the autistic-contiguous, containment is sensation-based while in the depressive mode, containment is accomplished through the distance afforded by language and interpretation. Disintegration, fragmentation, and emotional leakage (as manifestations of ego boundary loss or violation), on the other hand, are more typical in the paranoid-schizoid mode. We stress, however, that both disintegrative and integrative processes are necessary in maintaining the dialectical interplay between these experiential positions.

It is also within the autistic-contiguous mode of experience that the sensation of organizational boundaries as surface is located. This notion of organizational boundary is discussed further in Chapter 2. For now, the question that arises is how this mode of experience, the surface-to-surface contact, can be articulated for inspection. Within the workplace, one is confronted with many physical surfaces, such as the surface of a chair, door, or wall. Consider the following example. The door to one's supervisor's office is much more than merely a portal across a boundary. It contains an unconscious potentiality where all manner of subjective and inter-subjective meaning is created. The substance of the door and the boundary that it guards are ultimately of much less significance than the unconscious nature of what is on either side of what we suggest here represents the surface of organizational boundary.

The Dialectical Interplay of the Three Modes of Experience

Ogden's dialectical interplay is the self-organizing dynamic between the three modes of experiencing internal worlds and external realities. Each mode contributes to the richness and fullness of human encounters. The depressive is defined in terms of its relationship to and delineation from the paranoid-schizoid and the autistic-contiguous. The latter two are defined in terms of each other and their respective position in relation to the depressive. One does not exist without the other. Each of the three modes of experience spills into the other. Under normal circumstances, the autistic-contiguous offers a sense of grounding and integrity of experience through sensory enclosure. It provides what Ogden (1989) refers to as a "sensory floor." The depressive mode, in contrast, binds sensations together through symbolic connections and linkages that contribute to a sense of being rooted in time. This sense of historicity allows reflection on the past and future from the point of view of a self-interpreting subject. Together, they contain the fragmenting pull of the paranoid-schizoid mode without which human experience would be lacking its primary source of enlivening immediacy and spontaneity.

Absence of the disintegrative processes of the paranoid-schizoid also renders learning impossible, since new insights require that old linkages be broken. The dialectical interplay between these forms illustrates the nature of personality as a mosaic of self-organization. At any point in time one or another of these modes might prevail. Awareness of these forms of organizing experience and the tension between them is crucial to managing regression and its destructive and creative potential. For example, in the course of organizational diagnosis, organizational stories comprised of historical and narrative data may strengthen the depressive position in relation to the autistic-contiguous and paranoid-schizoid modes by distinguishing past from present and consciousness of past in present.

It is the collapse of the dialectic tension among these modes of experience that leads to psychological and organizational regression as well as destructive and dysfunctional workplace relations. Threats and vulnerabilities inside and outside the system may foster a collapse of the dialectic, leading to the loss of potential space in which organizational tensions are routinely transformed into creativity, continuity, productivity, and play. The collapse and its disintegrative properties break interpersonal and organizational boundaries into fragments disrupting surface containment and evoking primitive defenses such as splitting, projection, and projective identification. Ogden (1989) writes,

> Collapse toward the autistic-contiguous pole generates imprisonment in the machine-like tyranny of attempted sensory-based escape from the terror of the formless dread, by means of reliance on rigid autistic defenses. Collapse into the paranoid-schizoid pole is characterized by imprisonment in a non-subjective world of thoughts and feelings experienced in terms of frightening and protective things that simply happen, and that cannot be thought about or interpreted. Collapse in the direction of the depressive pole involves a form of isolation of oneself from one's bodily sensations, and from the immediacy of one's lived experience, leaving one devoid of spontaneity and aliveness. (p. 46)

In sum the dialectic is understood to contain self-organizing attributes as well as elements of internal tension that threaten its dynamic stability.

The conceptual shift from individual to organizational psychology takes place in the acknowledgement of patterned, repetitive, and collective actions that shape and characterize organizational culture. The three dialectical modes of experience form a relational context that influences a myriad of dynamics and issues between organizational members and their leaders that affect the quality of work and organizational productivity.

Organizational Modes of Experience

Ogden's work may be translated into a tripartite model that applies to the workplace. This model provides new insights into organizational experience and dynamics that enhance our understanding of organizational change. We begin with the depressive mode.

Organizations and the Depressive Mode

The generative influences of the depressive mode surface within organizations in a number of ways. On the positive side, the depressive mode influences leaders and organization members to maintain a competitive edge by enabling acknowledgment of loss across the multiple domains in which it occurs, including unfavorable financial outcomes and market shifts, cultural changes, leadership transitions, reorganizations, and interpersonal loss (to name a few). History is acknowledged but is neither considered a future determinant nor deterrent. A sense of efficacy and competence in units and individuals exists in the context of interdependent relationships that contribute to coherence in organizational functioning. There is a balanced attention to brainstorming ideas and operating pragmatics. The depressive mode of organizations represents an acknowledgement of no simple answers to strategic questions and encouragement of diverse ideas and conflicting positions.

Depressive experience permits conflicting views to exist without threat of compromising relationships. Toxic feelings and aggressive competitiveness are worked through with containment of affect and linguistic, communicative skill rather than with destructive or passive aggressive "acting out." People develop the capacity to assume responsibility for their emotions and actions. Such constructive and reparative contributions of the depressive in the workplace may seem ideal, if not wishful thinking, to many based on their experiences with organizations. Frequently, one observes an imbalance in the direction of the depressive organization that has counterproductive consequences as well. As with all three modes of experience, the depressive mode is not mutually exclusive and requires tension and counterbalance from the other modes of human nature.

When this is not the case, collapse in the direction of the depressive mode is evidenced by a sense of gloom, hopelessness, lethargy, and loss of feelings of being in control or being omnipotent. Coherence gives way to stagnation. Communication structures become stuck. The cultural ambiance becomes deadened. Power is simultaneously concentrated and stuck at the top. Access to those in power is tightly controlled. Those who have responsibility may not have sufficient delegation of authority, which may be a consequence of distrustful and disrespectful executives. Enforcement of cultural norms and values of the status quo may stifle change. Rather than generating opportunity for empathy and understanding, efforts at emotional containment and holding fail. Participants become cynical and tired. Motivation and enthusiasm about the organizational mission deteriorates, and leadership feels absent and direction-less. A gap between the realities that are internal and external to the organization widens and polarizes. Morale, creativity, and effectiveness are compromised.

Upon entering the organization, organizational researchers and consultants might experience a climate of sadness and powerlessness and a sense of not knowing where to go or what to do. This experience indicates elements of the depressive mode. Before moving onto a discussion of the applicability of the paranoid-schizoid mode to organizations, a brief vignette to illustrate the depressive mode in organizations is provided.

Vignette: A Depressive Organization

A newly appointed public agency director asked for help with assessing the agency's potential and readiness for change. Early on in the assessment, it became evident that members had not as yet internalized the new leader. They had not as yet come to view him as any different from their previous director—it was as if he was one and the same. For instance, they assumed he too managed by intimidation and humiliation. Yet, there was no evidence that might have confirmed this view over his short tenure with the agency. New statements of managerial philosophy or vision generated by the director and his staff were rejected outright by employees who referred to director's memos as "noise" or simply "not credible." There was no way to test their assumptions about the new leader and his management style. Organizational members were stuck in the past; one characterized by emotional insults and intimidation. The culture was one of cynicism and negativity. Consequently, they rejected the authority as well as the character of the new leader.

In order to move ahead, organizational members were given the space and containment in a retreat with consultants to mourn the passing of their past leaders. It was time to reflect and consider from where the agency had come so that the present might be acknowledged and articulated. So, they told stories filled with negative emotions of resentment and hostility toward the old regime. These narratives began to separate out, in the minds of participants, the present from the past (historicity). One might say participants developed the capacity to differentiate their past leadership from their present leader. Consequently, the initial sense of dread began to transform into a feeling of hope. Over the course of several days, participants developed the capacity to publicly test the authenticity and distinctiveness of the new leadership as they moved forward beyond the retreat. This left the organizational participants in a better position to judge the new leadership based on his words and actions rather than on their untested assumptions of him as a carbon copy of their previous director. Cognizance of organizational history and its relevance for reality testing returned to the public agency. In contrast, the paranoid-schizoid mode is characterized by an absence of historicity.

Organizations and the Paranoid-Schizoid Mode

As is the case with the depressive mode, the paranoid-schizoid position carries positive and constructive attributes. In dialectical interplay with the depressive and autistic-contiguous positions, the paranoid-schizoid contributes to efficiency, productivity, and the division of labor through differentiation and decentralization of tasks and functions (splitting up work and control). Roles and responsibilities are well articulated and divisional boundaries and their management contribute to effective work flow and good communications. Scanning the environment for opportunities and threats is also present. Executives and managers use discriminating thinking to sort out and evaluate the quality of workers' performance. Organizational learning, diversification, and innovation are promoted by questioning tradition and productive internal rivalries. The time between idea conception and production may be short, facilitated by energized informal lines of communication. Energy, intensity, spontaneity, and a sense of competing at the cutting edge may characterize the culture of some suspicious and paranoid organizations. In sum, it is not "all bad news" when we consider the paranoid-schizoid position and its contributions to the organization and particular strategic challenges.

However, when an organization collapses in the direction of the paranoid-schizoid, losing it links with the other two modes of experience, and idealization (often of the leader), envy, and destructive aggression rear their ugly head and come to characterize working relationships. Scapegoating and blame take precedence over more routine and reconcilable conflicts and confrontations. The psychodynamics of hierarchic dominance and submission may eliminate creative play space for innovation and productive change (Diamond & Allcorn, 2004). Psychological regression and associated primitive defenses eventually foster an organizational culture of unarticulated and difficult to work through polarized disagreements and well defended organizational silos, a subject we explore in Chapters 2 and 3 (Diamond, Stein, & Allcorn, 2002). Efficiency and coordination of resources are poor. Individuals avoid personal accountability to avoid blame. Mistakes are concealed, making it hard for individuals and organization to learn from experience. This outcome is compounded by blinders to past history and critical institutional moments. The organizational climate is clouded by interpersonal mistrust, suspicion, and polarization. The paranoid-schizoid organizational experience is destructive when it is insufficiently bounded by the depressive and autistic-contiguous modes of experience. A brief vignette is provided to illustrate the dynamics of the paranoid-schizoid mode in organizations.

Vignette: Paranoid-Schizoid Organization

A hospital CEO confronts difficulty in scheduling patients for the operating room (OR). OR managers find anesthesiologists and surgeons are not showing up, and patients are left lying on gurneys outside the operating rooms for extended periods of time. The organizational diagnosis reveals a history of deep mistrust and suspicion between surgeons and anesthesiologists in the hospital. Surgeons view anesthesiologists as rigid and uncooperative. Anesthesiologists view surgeons as dictatorial and disrespectful. Each group blames the other for the difficulties in scheduling and the long wait for patients getting into the OR. Coordination is flawed and OR managers do not have authority over either surgeons or anesthesiologists.

Upon entering similar organizations, one might experience difficulty or resistance to moving from one division to another, which might suggest that doing so could evoke suspicion and a sense of betrayal toward those who do. Organizational researchers and consultants might find themselves feeling torn or pulled into splitting and projection in labeling groups as good or bad or significant or insignificant. These experiences would alert the consultants to the possibility of paranoid-schizoid positions, as often represented by silo-like mentality between divisions of the organization (Diamond, Allcorn, & Stein, 2004).

The consultants in this case had as their challenge repairing (part-object) relationships between the two groups. Critical incidents and points of urgency were identified that contributed to the emotional shape of the conflict. History was brought back to consciousness and seen as relevant to present practices. Past injuries and hostilities were addressed as thematic and repetitive. Problems were articulated and then confirmed by the embattled groups. It gradually became possible for the two physician groups to engage each other in problem solving that included adequate authorization to OR managers to set schedules and manage coordination between these specialist groups. In contrast, the autistic-contiguous dimension is more about sensations of integration, differentiation, and isolation as compared to splitting and fragmentation.

Organizations and the Autistic-Contiguous Mode

The primary contributions of the autistic-contiguous experience to organizational functioning are maintenance of a sense of continuity, timing and pacing of work flows, emotional grounding, and authenticity of human relations in the face of problems, challenges, and constant change. There is an inherent tendency toward integrative and systemic linking of working relationships. Intuition and feelings are valued as factors contributing to effective problem setting and good communications.

Collapse of the autistic-contiguous mode produces feelings of isolation and disconnection among organizational participants and between participants and their organizational leaders. Communication skills are severely diminished. Workers are deskilled and feel infantile. Deep psychological regression settles into the organizational culture. One scenario is that these organizations shut down (operationally and emotionally) and become isolated. This generates feelings of aloneness, disconnection and being out of touch, leaving members set apart, and dreading abandonment. Processes, policies, and procedures may become exceedingly bureaucratized as ends-in-themselves, achieving machine-like perfection and predictability in an effort to contain anxiety via automation of people, processes, and operations.

Organizational leaders and followers collapsed into the autistic-contiguous pole may use mimicry in their attempt to secure a surface (identify) or boundary between themselves and their external task environment. The organization may selectively maintain pressure to continually meet deadlines in the service of producing a continuous surface to experience.

The organization may operate in constant crisis mode in order to create a renewed sense of organizational identification and continuity—defending against the fear of becoming out of touch.

The notion of autistic-contiguous—as a dimension of our early preverbal, sensate world—proffers validation for students of organization, such as ethnographers, action researchers, and psychoanalytic consultants, who rely upon the self-as-instrument-of-observation. Awareness of sensations and reactions to intra-organizational dynamics enables interventionists to observe and process these varied modes of experience. The following vignette illustrates the autistic-contiguous in organizations.

Vignette: Autistic-Contiguous Organization

In one company, the bureaucratic nature of operations did not work effectively with the entrepreneurial culture of marketing. In fact, this inability to work together effectively cost the company millions of dollars in product failures. The rhythm of the operations division was slow and confined while the rhythm of marketing was fast-paced and wide-open. Operations felt oppressive, and withholding while marketing felt liberating and chaotic. Both cultures lacked effective leadership and direction. Consequently, both operations and marketing fell into regressive positions where effective communication was absent. It was also the case that the executive in charge of their coordination was narcissistic and out of touch with the peculiar psychological characteristics of the two cultures. He was more focused on himself and how he might impress or intimidate his subordinates. It seemed as if the only way to reach these disparate and out of touch cultures required reestablishing contact between them and their leader. Since these cultures seemed worlds apart, it was not until they were brought together and engaged in a collaborative planning activity that they began to view each other as multidimensional human subjects rather than part-objects. Most importantly, their leader was put into a position of listening to these contrasting subcultures, and this encouraged him to question assumptions held about them. The capacity to communicate and develop mutual understanding, however limited at the outset of this constructive confrontation between two opposing cultures, provided a platform for productive change and better coordination. Over several days of collaborative work on a common business plan with cross-functional, cross-disciplinary, and cross-cultural groups representing marketing and operations, we observed a productive shift in their capacity to listen and communicate with each other.

Paying attention to "the feel of the place" offers many insights into organizations. Is it cold, warm, dark, light, thick, heavy, friendly, unfriendly, safe, dangerous, receptive, rejecting, fast-paced, slow-paced, rhythmic, emotionally alive, dead (if so, how so), etc., and, do these sensations change as we move vertically or horizontally around the organization and its divisions? These are sensate data, and they are worthy of initial and ongoing attention. These data serve to shape the development of an overarching picture and narrative of the organization. For leaders of these organizations, awareness of the autistic-contiguous mode has value for inspiring and managing people. Negative feelings that are typically suppressed are acknowledged and attended to as opportunities to articulate and solve problems. In sum, it is a mistake to ignore the efforts of organization members to generate palpable organizational surfaces that feel reliable and dependable thereby providing assurance, comfort, security, and protection.

In conclusion, these three forms of experience comprising the whole of organized experience enable us to take a closer look at the psychodynamic tensions between organizational regression and progression. When linked together in relative harmony, these modes of dialectical interplay facilitate individual, interpersonal, group, and organizational containment of uncanny emotions, tensions, and anxieties. As mutual forms of experience, they enable us to better understand the necessity of transitional and potential space in the culture for reality testing, change, creativity, play, trust, and respect. The collapse of the dialectical tension in the direction of any of the three forms of experience produces identifiable outcomes that are considered in the attempt to restore the balance between differentiation and integration so critical to group and organizational functioning and well-being. These responses invariably require those leading change to hold and contain participants' anxieties so that psychological regression, splitting, and fragmentation are minimized. In more fully understanding these psychodynamics, we consider the concepts of identification and containment in organizational diagnosis.

Identification, Containment, and Organizational Diagnosis

Exploring the psychodynamics of identification and containment in organizational research and intervention differentiates psychoanalytic organizational diagnosis from other more traditional social psychological approaches to organizational studies.

Identification

Identification refers to the psychodynamic process of gaining understanding by making sense of how am I being used, manipulated, and experienced in my role, and what effect is it having on me? Identification is a multi-dimensional concept. Identification is frequently used in a generic sense to refer to all the mental processes by which an individual becomes like another in one or several aspects, and so its meaning overlaps with that of other terms (primary identification, introjection, incorporation, and identification with the aggressor) that imply a very real sense of fusion and merger between self and other. More recently, psychoanalytic writers tend to reserve the term for a process of internalization. For example, the case presentation in which staff could not differentiate the present director from the past, resulted from the absence of internalization of the new leader by staff members and the persistent and unresolved emotional attachment to their previous leader. When absent grief and mourning of a prior leader occurs, it becomes problematic for followers to establish a relationship to a new leader with a modicum of reality testing. Internalization involves greater subject-object differentiation, and the process is more selective of the traits internalized. Various attitudes, functions, and values of the other (object) are integrated into a cohesive, effective identity and become fully functional parts of the self, compatible with other parts (Loewald, 1962).

Containment

Containment refers to the facilitation of a "good enough holding environment" for organizational members and clients (Winnicott, 1971) and the manner in which participant-observers and consultants take-in and eventually give back the thoughts, feelings, and experience of others. It is hoped that the return of this (affect-laden) content will be accepted and understood in a meaningful and potentially transforming way. Riesenberg-Malcolm describes Wilfred Bion's theory of containment as "the capacity of one individual (or object) to receive in himself projections from another individual, which he can sense and use as communications (from him), transform them, and finally give them back (or convey back) to the subject in a modified form. Eventually, this can enable the person (an infant at first) to sense and tolerate his own feelings and develop a capacity to think" (Bronstein, 2001, p. 166). Organizations are collectivities of human cooperation, which are vulnerable to emotional leakage (e.g., violation of psychological boundaries or past trauma triggered by current events), particularly in cases where leadership and organizational culture fail to adequately contain participant fears, anxieties, and hostilities about the uncertainty and potential loss inherent in change. Defective containment produces psychologically regressive and primitively defensive engagements of psychological splitting and projective identification between workers and management, executives and professional staff, and clients and consultants. This phenomenon of psychological regression and containment will be discussed further in Chapter 5.

Organizational Diagnosis

When it comes to organizational diagnosis, there are several ways one can think of the notion of identification. First, one can consider the extent to which organizational members form attachments with their institutions. Individuals naturally form transference relationships (mirror hungry, ideal hungry, twin-ship hungry, and persecutory) through their associations with their organizations and leaders (Kohut, 1977; Diamond, 1993). Individual expectations, desires, fantasies, hopes, and ideals are transferred onto organizations (Schwartz, 1990). Second, we may consider the notion of identification as a representation of how psychoanalytic organization consultants work with their subjects (clients), what is referred to previously as internalization and the development of greater self-object differentiation. This differentiation of self and other and subject and object carries with it the historicity of the depressive mode and the capacity for containment of uncanny emotions inside organizations and within their members. Organizational consultants take inside themselves, among other things, toxic emotions, which are unavoidably projected by organizational members.

Rather than impulsively reacting to these uncanny projections, one must take inside and "chew over" the so-called emotional material, digesting their texture, shape, and content, sorting out what belongs where (subject or object) and what these feelings mean in the context of observed and experienced organizational dynamics. Eventually, these communicated affects are returned via language, psychological distancing, and the establishment of potential space, so that organizational members can do something more productive with them. From this perspective, identification and containment are objectives of psychoanalytic organizational diagnosis in that consultants strive to more deeply understand, without over-identifying with, the subjective dimensions of experiences of organizational participants. This process of internalization and identification is part of the act of containment.

A Method to the Madness

Treating organizations as an experiential and relational context might sound rather abstract in that it encompasses the chaos introduced by human nature. It can be frenzied and disordered when there is no method to madness. The tripartite model provides an important framework for understanding organizational experience and dynamics and therefore serves as an instrument of sensing and understanding, which allows for containment that minimizes anxiety and promotes awareness, insight, and reflective practice. The model, when incorporated into a process of organizational change, becomes a road map that offers subjects an ability to sense and understand and in so doing locate a guiding and comforting framework for what they are about to embark upon together.

Chapter 2 continues this discussion by further exploring how the tripartite model informs sensing, knowing, and understanding organizational experience and the effects of change upon organizational members. As evidenced in the vignettes of this chapter, a common attribute of organizations is how they are divided up along lines of specialization and many times geographically into sections and divisions ostensibly organized into a rational hierarchy. The personal experience for workers of the resulting organizational boundaries may not in fact be so rational at all.

2

Boundaries and Surfaces

The nature of one's relationship to one's objects is determined to a
large degree by the nature of the subjectivity (the form of "I-ness") that
constitutes the context for those object relations. In the autistic-contiguous
position, the relationship to objects is one in which the organizations
of a rudimentary sense of "I-ness" arises from relationships of sensory
contiguity (i.e., touching) that over time generate the sense of a bounded
sensory surface on which one's experience occurs (the beginnings of the
feeling of "a place where one lives" [Winnicott, 1971].

Thomas Ogden, The Primitive Edge of Experience

In our studies of organizations, we discovered that individuals experience organizations as having a characteristic rhythm, shape, and feel.
As members and researchers move from one organizational culture to
another and from one subculture to another, they often come into contact with diverse experiences of organizational surfaces. The valuable
insights derived from a study of these sensate and affect-laden dimensions
of organizational life direct us to the ultimate psychological meaning of
organizational structure—what might be called the embodied nature of
organization. This appreciation led us to examine the unconscious nature
of one of the fundamental building blocks of organizations, organizational
boundaries and surfaces.

Our exploration of the surfaces of organizational life has taken us into
a study of the primitive, pre-verbal, pre-symbolic, and pre-subjective
characteristics of boundaries. We find that silos are a common metaphor
produced by organizational participants to describe the cognitive and
emotional quality of their often fragmented and constrained personal (and
interpersonal) engagements at work. Silos described participants' experience
and perception of organizational boundaries. In this chapter, we expand
upon the silo metaphor by exploring its association with boundaries and,
more specifically, with organizational surfaces. The concept of surfaces

adds psychological and affective texture and dimensionality to our under-standing of organizational boundaries. We also apply the tripartite model discussed in the previous chapter and apply object relations theory to par-ticipants' organizational impression of boundaries.

Before proceeding, it is important that we clarify our position on understanding and analyzing organizations (whether public agencies, pri-vate companies, healthcare delivery systems, or non-profit institutions). Our reliance upon a psychoanalytic (object relational) view of organiza-tions means that we view these systems as organizations-in-mind (Dia-mond, 1984, 1993; Shapiro & Carr, 1991; Stein, 1994). Thus, we come to understand organizations and groups as existing predominantly, but not solely, as an outcome of dynamic and changing individual and collective projections rooted in unconscious fantasies and emotions. These fantasies and sentiments are given collective meaning and identity through a com-bination of intrapersonal and intersubjective object relational patterns and modes of experience at work. Organizations, despite their many artifacts and physical objects, are given meaning as a result of what participants (executives, workers, clients, customers, etc.) project via their individual and collective unconscious fantasies. To know an organization requires more than observation, traditional behavioral, and empirical and positiv-istic methods of analysis. It requires eliciting unconscious patterns of rela-tions between individuals and their image of the organization-in-mind. It also requires linking internal processes of organized experience and mean-ing with external patterns of behavior at work.

As noted in Chapter 1, we view organizations as experiential and rela-tional systems governed by unconscious processes whereby much thought and activity takes place outside of conscious awareness (Diamond & All-corn, 2003). Our understanding of organizations locates the meaning of the "interface" between human nature and organization—a collision of content and meaning across the boundary between self and object. We begin our task by clarifying the concept of boundaries as found in the psy-choanalytic and systems-oriented organizational literature.

Spatial/Temporal Organizational Boundaries

Contemporary discussion of organizational boundaries as implied by the use of the word "boundary" tends to have a conceptual concreteness that belies their ultimate experiential significance for organization members. Our review of the literature has encouraged us to examine the nature of the conceptual concreteness of organizational boundaries. This discussion of boundaries implicitly includes a quasi-scientific quality as is alluded to by the popular science fiction phrase, "the space/time continuum." As a result, we examine the psychological underpinnings of organizational boundaries that include the subjective and intersubjective experience of these same boundaries. This sensibility contains a sensate quality, which is best understood from a psychoanalytic object relational perspective. In what follows, we depict this experience by exploring the meaning of organizational boundaries and what we call organizational surfaces that contain the multidimensional intrapersonal and intersubjective experience of organizational life.

The notion of boundaries delineates between that which exists inside the organization (internal processes, operations, structures) and outside the organization ("task environment"). Theorists influenced by systems theory (Churchman, 1968; Lawrence & Lorsch, 1967; Rice, 1963; Rice & Miller, 1976) view organizational boundaries as providing a way of articulating the organization as an open system. Boundaries demarcate points of entry into the system or inputs. These inputs include material and human resources that are transformed by internal operational processes, creating outputs in the form of products and services. From a systemic framework, there exist multiple points of contact within and between organizations and their task environments (Lawrence & Lorsch, 1967). "Boundary maintenance" is therefore seen as crucial to the success of organizational goals and strategies.

From a psychodynamic and systems perspective, William Czander (1993) writes, "The boundary functions as a point of entry for all of the systems inputs, members, materials, information, and so on. It is also where the organization meets its environment, including those constituents and significant others who formulate impressions and views of what occur within the organization's conversion process" (p. 204). He then goes on to note, "The boundary is often the only point where nonmembers witness what goes on inside and obtain information about the organization's ideology, culture, and member preference" (p. 204). In other words, boundaries are the spatial and psychological location from which organizational researchers can decode the peculiar identity of the organization and its inherent characteristics.

It is at this point in time and space that the self becomes an instrument of observation for those researchers interested in understanding what makes one organization unique and what it might mean to work in a particular organization. Similar to earlier systems theorists such as James Thompson (1967), Czander suggests that effective boundary maintenance is crucial to protecting the technological core of any organization and maintaining its integrity and standards of effectiveness and efficiency. Boundary maintenance as performed by management is a crucial indicator of successful organizational adaptation and effective task accomplishment. Also to be appreciated is that boundary maintenance can become filled with unconscious and defensive responses to members' anxieties stimulated by boundary crossings such as with efforts to enhance integration and collaboration across structural and professional divisions.

Ralph Stacey (1992) writes about the managerial challenges of establishing and maintaining functional boundaries to create systemic order relative to workplace chaos.

> These boundaries affect the formation, activity levels, and degree of stability of the networks. At one extreme, managers may tighten the boundaries so much that networks become either relatively inactive and thus stable or active in a covert way and thus unstable. At the other extreme, managers may loosen boundaries so much that networks become hyperactive and produce organizational anarchy. The best choices of intervention produce states of chaos in which instability is constrained and organizations can function creatively. (p. 179–180)

Thus in states of chaos and complexity, bounded instability replaces stable equilibrium as the governing assumption of effective, strategic thinking for managers and leaders. Stacey's notion of bounded instability requires a new executive mindset rooted in the reality of unpredictability and uncertainty. This new mindset stresses the strategic benefits and limitations, as well as questions the plausibility, of tightly controlled boundaries. Given the unpredictability of the future and the reality of chaos and complexity in task environments, managers will have to maximize flexibility and creativity. And, according to Stacey, creativity and innovation are derived from chaos and complexity, which need to be bounded and contained for constructive exploitation. Organizational structure and culture are different forms of boundaries that may or may not contribute to adaptive and productive responses to chaos and complexity. For instance, "hierarchy and the distribution of power provide one boundary around self-organizing processes [while] organizational culture provides another [and] top management can affect each of these boundaries" (Stacey, 1992, p. 180). In the best of circumstances, it is as if structure, and in particular boundaries, serve to trap and productively sublimate collective psychic energy in a manner consistent with a depressive dimension of organized experience. Implicit in this preoccupation with boundary maintenance and management is an acknowledgement of the importance of understanding the psychodynamics of integrative processes such as boundary crossing within and between organizations. In particular, Stacey's concept of bounded instability exemplifies the notion of boundary as a perceptual and experiential phenomenon. Boundaries, if consciously acknowledged by management, proffer a vehicle for shifting one's mindset toward thinking of management positioned at the boundary from where one holds and supports the tension between order and chaos.

While Czander (1993) views organizational boundaries as a point of delineation and reference for contrasting the internal dynamics and external constituencies, Stacey (1992) focuses on boundaries as the location from which management, via the tool of organizational structure, embraces the reality of chaos and complexity. Stapley (1996) adds to our understanding of the meaning of boundaries with the work of anthropologist Leach (1976). He suggests that there exist three types of boundaries: spatial, temporal, and psychological.

> The nature of a boundary is that it separates two zones of social space-time that are normal, time-bound, clear-cut, central, secular, but the temporal and spatial markers, which actually serve as boundaries are themselves abnormal, timeless, ambiguous, at the edge, sacred. Consequently, the ambiguity that exists at the boundary is a source of anxiety, and it is the boundaries that matter. We concentrate our attention on the differences, not the similarities, and this makes us feel that the markers of such boundaries are of special value, or, as Leach (1976) has observed, "sacred" or "taboo." (p. 69)

It is at the so-called "interface" or point of "contact" "where the boundaries of the individual meet other boundaries, such as those of social systems. The boundary is then the location of a relationship where the relationship both separates and connects" (Stapley, 1996, p. 69). Thus, one can say that boundaries (or the edge of boundaries) are the location from which roles, power and authority, and horizontal and vertical relations are potentially defined in organizations and simultaneously signify social and psychological meaning.

Boundaries are essential constructs in that they denote markers of differentiation between self and others and self and organization. Temporal and spatial dimensions of boundaries are often points of ambiguity and anxiety because they include an unconscious and unarticulated nature, what we suggest is an autistic and contiguous surface. It is at the spatial/temporal boundary that relationships are engaged and where individuals are simultaneously separated and connected. And, it is out of these unwitting processes of differentiation and integration that social structures emerge. The location and conscious articulation of spatial and temporal boundaries becomes a basis for understanding particular dimensions of organizational experience, culture, and identity. A deeper comprehension of the respective meaning of boundaries for groups and individuals assists in the resolution of conflict between parties on either side of the boundary.

This discussion of the spatial/temporal nature of organizational boundaries has underscored the transactional, observable, measurable nature of one's sensibility of self, others, groups, organizations, and society. At the interpersonal level, the meaning and experience of boundary crossing is best represented by the following simple thought: "I am here; you are there." Much can be made of the two-dimensional nature of this conception of organizational boundaries. We, however, find that there is a much greater sensate texture to participants' experience of boundaries as surfaces of experience.

The Surfaces of Organizational Experience

In his book, *The Culture of Oklahoma*, Howard Stein (1992) writes of boundaries:

> The nature of cultural boundaries is far more problematic than many social scientists and native peoples everywhere contend. What is a cultural boundary? To begin with, although cultural boundaries might be demarcated by political borders, they are not limited to these. It might be better asked: Where is something located in existential space? We take boundaries, "thereness," for granted yet they first and foremost exist in the imagination, built from our sensation of our own bodies and those of our early caretakers. Projected outward and subsequently reincorporated, boundaries come to "exist" in reality by the strength of group consensus (literally "sensing together") on what a group is and where it is located "out there"—where it begins, where it ends, how to recognize it. (p. xxii)

Organizational boundaries may, therefore, not have entirely concrete qualities that are created and modified by management in the service of control and achieving operating efficiency. They may, in fact, exist in the mind in a manner that is created and shared by others. Shared psychic artifacts and taboos can create just as clear and inviolate boundaries as might an electrified fence topped with razor wire. One may simply not go there. Organizations are filled with many types of boundaries that serve, in large part, to determine the functioning and ultimate viability of the organization as a cooperative system reliant on integrative processes.

Explaining Organizational Boundaries and Surfaces

Psychoanalyst Thomas Ogden (1989), as noted in Chapter 1, identifies three primary modes of organizing experience. He departs from Melanie Klein in conceptualizing modes of psychological organization not as developmental phases, but as processes through which perceptions are imbued with meaning. Ogden begins with recognition of the depressive and paranoid-schizoid positions suggested by Klein and describes them in terms of five interdependent dimensions, including the primary anxiety and associated defense(s), the quality of object-relatedness, degree of subjectivity, and form of symbolization. We summarize the three modes of experience as follows.

The depressive mode of experience functions primarily in the service of containment of experience. Central to this operation is the capacity for "symbol formation proper" (Segal, 1957), in which an interpreting subject represents the object as symbol and experiences the symbolized object as other, separate from self. In the depressive mode, a self-interpreting subject is able to generate interpretive space between the symbol and that which it represents, and comes to view oneself as a person who thinks one's own thoughts, and feels one's own feelings. One experiences a sense of responsibility for one's own thoughts, feelings, and behaviors.

The paranoid-schizoid mode is characterized by equal efforts to manage and evacuate psychic pain. Insofar that this mode is characterized by part-object relations, the primary dilemma is managing the intolerable anxiety related to loving and hating the same object. This primary anxiety is managed through splitting, through which one separates the loving and hating aspects of oneself from the loving and hating aspects of the loved object in order to prevent the bad (the endangering) from destroying the good (the endangered). Object relatedness is accomplished through projective identification. A facet of self (either the endangered or endangering) is placed into another person through projection. The recipient, who may fully or partially integrate the projected content, may be encouraged to integrate the content by being treated in a manner consistent with the content. Instead of feeling ambivalent, one senses as a result of splitting and projection an ongoing series of polarized, affective reversals. With each reversal, one has the experience of unmasking the truth as if for the first time.

As noted in the previous chapter, Ogden posits a third mode of experience known as the "autistic-contiguous." Extending the work of Bick (1968), Meltzer (1975), and Tustin (1980, 1984), Ogden suggests that in the autistic-contiguous mode the most elemental forms of human passions are generated. This is a pre-symbolic, sensory mode in which sensations of rhythm and "surface contiguity" arise from the core of a person's first relationships with the external object world. Put simply, feelings are generated by the sensation of two surfaces coming together in either differentiation or merger. There is a fundamental difference between this form of relatedness and the subject-to-subject relatedness of the depressive and the object-to-object relatedness of the paranoid-schizoid. In the autistic-contiguous experience there is, instead, a sense of "pattern, boundedness, shape, rhythm, texture, hardness, softness, warmth, coldness, and so on" (Ogden, 1989, p. 33). The primary anxiety of this pre-verbal mode resides in the terror generated by the disruption of the continuity of sensations, what Ogden (1989) calls "formless dread." In this instance, individual defensive efforts are directed toward reestablishing a feeling of continuity and integrity of one's surface.

Upon initial consideration, it may appear that the depressive and autistic-contiguous modes of experiencing are most different in terms of degree of psychological sophistication and achievement. Ogden (1989) points out, however, that they are similar insofar that in both modes, the primary anxiety depends upon integrative, containing processes. In the case of the autistic-contiguous mode, continuity is sensation based, whereas in the depressive mode, containment is accomplished through the distance afforded by language and interpretation. In contrast, the paranoid-schizoid mode is characterized by disintegration and fragmentation. Both disintegrative and integrative processes are required to maintain the dialectical link among the positions. And, in dialectical fashion, they simultaneously "create, negate, and preserve" one another.

An Illustration

An unexpected request to report to the supervisor may contain a formless dread not ameliorated by the spatial and temporal boundary of the office door. In order to avoid dissolving into a formless pool of liquid at the door, one creates an opposing surface, namely, the supervisor in mind. Denial, splitting, and projection make their contribution to creating self-experience less threatening. For instance, "I am good and the supervisor is bad for making this unexpected request," or perhaps, "I have been a good employee and will receive a reward for my performance." Of course, there is also the possibility of "I will be downsized and out-placed." These are but some of the possible responses that serve, in the absence of surfaces but in the presence of boundaries, to drive out the formlessness and replace it with an experiential surface. The surface we create in fantasy may be hard or soft, warm or cold, or life-sustaining and life-threatening, as may be the case with a fantasized termination. One, therefore, fills the formless void with experiential surface, one's own and the other. One is comforted by this containment that avoids the affect of formless dissolution much like the sensibility of the infant by the touch of the mother upon the baby's cheek and the rhythm of her heartbeat where formlessness is replaced by the life-giving reassurance of sensate surface-to-surface contact.

The example is an effort to allow the reader to locate self-experience in terms of relations with remote powerful authority figures. A child may feel small, deficient, and insignificant when confronted by a parent regarding unacceptable behavior ("just wait until your father comes home"). These combined descriptive terms are "felt" as terror, fear, threat, panic, falling apart, out of control anxiety and self-experience, self-dissolution ("running down the drain"), and so on. "What will happen?" There is a sensate nature to this experience. It might be described as palpable from the encounter with the door that represents more than a conceptual boundary. The door becomes a threshold signifying one's encounter with the "primitive edge of experience" located intrapsychically in the dialectical tension (or collapse) among autistic-contiguous, paranoid-schizoid, and depressive modes (Ogden, 1989). In this instance, the door symbolizes a surface. Its surface does not validate one's surface. It, thereby, tends to dissolve, damage, and penetrate one's surface. One's insides flow out. Experience of self as integrated and possessing self-integrity (dialectical tension) are lost down the drain (via collapse of the dialectic).

The Dialectic of Surface and Experience

Ogden's three modes of experience are ideally held within a dialectic whereby each component contributes to our sensibility to know and find meaning in that experience. These discrete sensations, when taken together, create self-integration as represented by the dialectic. Available to one is an ability to locate experience and find meaning through each mode and then merge this unconscious knowledge into a self-conceptual whole. For example, one may fill the formless void of the supervisor's request by creating surfaces that contain paranoid imagery and objects. Regardless of the combination of responses that create the surface, one enters the office with abated anxiety and a self-awareness, self-assurance, and self-integration that permits one to stand, albeit uncomfortably, before the supervisor. This example points out the dimensions of workplace experience where the many parts of self are present, the forces of disintegration and integration are momentarily bound, and one is not threatened by formless dissolution or disintegration, although these experiences are present and available to oneself as an interactive whole.

In sum, this discussion of the dialectic provides insight into the nature of its collapse in which the physical nature of the situation combines with the situation in mind to create anxiety, dread, and fear. One's actions are observed at one level but not halted or redirected. Fear or dread may fill one's experience, leading to the collapse of self-integration and intentionality. The anxiety-ridden subordinate visiting his or her dreadful supervisor's office must have a capacity for emotional containment if he or she is to successfully manage a potentially discomforting encounter. Encounters such as these provoke containment and the creation of surfaces, personal fragmentation and partial object relations, or possibly, containment and self-integration in the form of the depressive position. What is important to appreciate is that the collapse of the dialectical interplay between the three modes of experience produces psychological regression and defensive actions that distort and fragment human relations. A sense of historicity breaks down and delineation of past and present experience seems momentarily lost. These defensive and psychologically regressive actions compromise ego integrity, authenticity, and personal responsibility. They jeopardize competent and effective performance while reinforcing fragmentation of self and others. This experiential and behavioral phenomenon is typical when organizational boundaries are described and imagined by participants as "silos."

Organizational Boundaries, Horizontal Fragmentation, and Silos

The horizontal structure of intra-organizational communications is often inhibited by fragmentation that is symbolized by participants as organizational silos. Understanding the metaphor of "silos" as an organizational boundary in the minds and narratives of participants is critical. Silos (as metaphors) are produced by autistic and subjective processes that generate the image of the silo as an invisible barrier as well as a container of collective sentiment (Diamond et al., 2002). At the imagined point of contact, silos seem to be constructed by a multidimensional experiential surface, which by analogy might seem like standing in a glass cylinder. One cannot see it, but it is there. It invisibly restricts mental and physical mobility. However, unlike the glass cylinder, silos are not physically present. Rather, they create a shared impression of their existence, one that is known to organizational participants. For instance, organizational participants may not reach beyond the confines of the silo without assuming personal risk. Organizational artifacts and metaphors such as silos are more meaningful when viewed with the object relational lens of Ogden's (1989) three primary modes of organizing experience.

The imagery of silos as organizational boundaries underscores the psychodynamics of this experience. On the one hand, silos provide safety and comfort, a soothing surface for organizational participants. Organizational silos are also experienced as fragmenting and often signify disintegration of horizontal and vertical relationships between workers (Diamond et al., 2002). Boundary crossing is experienced as surface-to-surface contact; it is a physical (bodily) sensation, which also exists in one's mind (possibly in the form of metaphor or image). Contact at the surface may provide the life-giving containment that avoids the loss of one's sensation of mind and body, or it might be experienced as similar to dissolving into a liquid pool. Boundary crossings at the surface of silos are critical junctures for the observation and experience of organizational structure from which one can determine the presence of a dialectical tension between the three dimensions of organized experience and the potential collapse of the relational dialectic (three modes of experience).

The silo metaphor signifies (1) a near absence of depressive whole object features, (2) a predominance of paranoid-schizoid, part-object experience, and (3) many of the primitive sensate features of the autistic-contiguous mode. Metaphors such as silos provide students of organizations with a means for more deeply understanding and attuning themselves to the emotion of organizational members. Stein and Hill (1988) note, "Cultures and ages leave their footprint through the metaphors their members live by. To know what it was like to have lived at a particular time and place, inquire first into its chief organizing metaphors" (p. 149). The same is true for organizations. The workplace-as-silo image and metaphor is frequently mentioned in management and organizational literature either explicitly or implicitly (Diamond et al., 2002). However, even in the absence of this knowledge, members of organizations spontaneously locate the autistic sensation of silos.

Silo Experience

The experience of the workplace as containing invisible silos is very real. Organization members, when interviewed frequently, volunteer silo-like images when questioned about the functioning of their organizations, particularly in public bureaucracies although not exclusively. Participants often raise their hands up and down to form a silo in the air (Diamond et al., 2002). These hand gestures have their origins in the hearts and minds of many employees. Efforts to communicate the autistic nature of their feelings arise from structural boundaries that delineate different parts and functions of an organization. The nature of these boundaries is often signified by the cylinder-like images of organization charts.

For some workers, the silo metaphor evokes a feeling of "isolation and powerlessness": it is as if they are stuck deep inside the silo. Others may speak of "the left hand not knowing what the right hand is doing": it is as if they felt the silo as a disembodied fragment, disconnected from a larger system. Still other workers associate silos with a lack of collaboration, collegiality, mutual respect, and trust between organization members: it is as if people in one silo were in opposition to people in other silos. Often, the silo metaphor is used to denote the highly specialized knowledge and practices within highly trained groups of professionals. Here, workers often believe that they could not possibly understand what their colleagues in other specialties, divisions, or units were doing or appreciate their everyday practices, and they believe that their counterparts in other specialties, divisions, or units could not possibly comprehend them. Within this context, silos are used to rationalize the technical and functional specialization of people and subsystems within their wider organization. In many corporations, this is reflected in management's apparent inability to cross product-lines or functional divisions.

Workers often mention commonly accepted organizational attributes, such as "following the chain of command" and "organizational turf" or "turf battles." During consultations, as we delved further into why the silo metaphor seems to accurately reflect work impressions, organization members frequently speak of the "us versus them" mindset. This viewpoint can permeate a workplace. For example, when asked about their fellow workers in other units or divisions, many have proclaimed to us, "What I [or we] do is more important than what they do; what I [or we] do has more value than what they do." Others have said, "Our division deserves additional resources and their division does not" (regardless of the lack of valid information about the other division); or "They (other division, profession, or specialty) are to blame for the lack of teamwork" (or are to blame for whatever was espoused to be wrong at that time). Therefore, the language of silos represents a social and psychological structure of "us versus them" and inter-silo chauvinism.

In sum, abstract notions of vision, mission, strategic plans, mindsets, tools, and skills within silo-type workplaces become inseparable from what it feels like to work within a silo. Workers often perceive themselves as "inside" silos, which are in turn "inside" workers. These experiences of organizational silos speak to a profound sense of organizational fragmentation, one that, although clearly present in horizontal relationships, is equally present in vertical relationships, where the many layers of organization do not appear to function in a fully articulated and rational manner. Things, it seems, do not run like a clock. Vertical and horizontal fragmentation is often fused in the minds of workers. This becomes more apparent as workers are challenged to articulate their experience. The dynamics of the two organizational dimensions are frequently mixed together, where it may be that observed fragmentation on one axis reinforced fragmentation on the other. Beyond "vertical tunnel vision," silo thinking (symptomatic of the silo metaphor) fosters horizontal "Balkanizing" and polarized black and white, all or nothing, all "good" or all "bad" images among subcultures within organizations that promote prejudice and narrow-mindedness. While the silo metaphor reflects many negative and certain positive or constructive attributes, it is ultimately an artifact of the unconscious mind and thereby experienced as a boundary with a sensate surface.

The Psychologically Defensive Nature of Silos and Surfaces at Work

Silos are vast psychological spaces that perform the affective-perceptual-organizing functions of putting, evacuating, and storing anxiety-evoking inner mental content "out there." Through reification, the silo comes to be experienced as the source of the feelings rather than its projective surface. The shared psychic purpose of this reification is to assure group members that the problem is "it" rather than themselves, outside rather than inside. It defends against persecutory and annihilating anxiety. As an intrapsychic way of experiencing others, reification denies separateness and distinctness. The "silo mentality," therefore, fosters a bastion of manic "all-knowing," as if participants are at once both the "container" and the "contained," that is, the surface itself and the body touching the surface. Silos in the organizational mind, therefore, pose a paradox for organizational members. On the one hand, they sense themselves as located within the silo. On the other hand, that which they feel physically inside of is a projection of their own "insides," a projection that acquires greater "reality" as it is shared with others in a group (mutual identification).

Reification may be followed by introjection and projective identification wherein people "inside" the silo take the silo "inside" themselves and begin to think of themselves and their lives as Dilbert-like cubicles, divisions, departments, sub-specialties, parts unaware of whole systems, and other world views. In turn, taking the silo "inside" and thinking of oneself as organizational "silage" cuts one off from seeing the whole system of organization and the importance of horizontal relationships at work. As outside and inside become fused, the silo—the part—"becomes" the whole world. It is not that surprising, in the context of ill-managed and dysfunctional boundaries of knowledge, expertise, and task responsibilities, that paranoia, psychological splitting, and regression to autistic-contiguous and paranoid-schizoid modes of functioning may be readily observed in our twenty-first century organizations.

In sum, organizational silos may be felt as primitive, fragmented structures devoid of the integrative bonds and attachments that are representative of the depressive mode. The most fundamental experience of the silo is one of personal isolation, in which whole subjects and objects for the most part cease to exist. This impression and intrapersonal organization space becomes filled with fantasy; silo members create experience unbounded by reality testing. The silo becomes their reality. "Outsiders" (others, divisions, and departments-silos) are invested with attributes via unconscious denial, splitting, and projection that may then be unconsciously manipulated at will. The fantastic creation of the silos, therefore, represents a containing and confining "hard" surface (autistic object) for members of silos. These constitute simultaneously individual and social defenses. Ogden (1989) writes, "An autistic object is a safety-generating sensory impression of edgedness that defines, delineates, and protects ones otherwise exposed and vulnerable surface" (p. 56). This protective surface is associated with such words as armor, shell, crust, danger, attack, separateness, otherness, invasion, rigidity, impenetrability, and repulsion (Ogden, 1989), terms often used to describe silos. It may be concluded that the ultimate psychodynamic significance of the silo metaphor is its individual and group function as a psychological defense against the flood of anxiety-provoking organizational and group membership experiences. The defense, in turn, assures the further generation of anxiety and reliance upon the autistic-contiguous and paranoid-schizoid modes of feeling and thinking within organizations.

Silos as Condensation in Symbolism

Clearly, silos do not have single, simple story lines. Just as they point to many other features of American culture, they also condense many meanings and feelings into a single symbol. Symbols can be approached as psychoanalytic as well as conventional symbols. Robert Paul writes, "It is true that Freud discovered Freudian symbolism through the study of dreams; but this should not be confused with the assertion that the dream is their proper locus, the only place where they can be encountered. They are not projected from dreams into the culture, at least as Freud conceptualizes the matter; they are, rather, out there in the culture to begin with" (1987, p. 89). He goes on to say, "They [myths, rituals, folklore, and so on] are created with the express purpose of being widely understood by strangers. They may not be consciously understood, of course; but they are designed to be deciphered subliminally by the innate mechanisms of symbol formation which typify the unconscious psyche of Homo sapiens" (p. 89). We submit that this is true of the silo metaphor as well. If the silo is a symbol, then what kind of a symbol is it? Where is this symbol located? Is it deep or shallow, and how do we know?

Central to the psychodynamic meaning of the symbol-choice of "silo" is the concept of condensation—a process wherein a single symbol can embody many fantasies, wishes, and feelings. A symbol can be thought of as a wide river fed by many merging tributaries. In societies, as in dreams, symbols mean many things simultaneously, and at many levels, conscious and unconscious. Members of an ethnic group, nation, religion, or workplace do not necessarily invest equally in all, or the same, facets of the symbol. But many can unite around, and through, the symbol.

For instance, if a silo is a space-like container in which workers perform their tasks, some might see it in a positive way. It provides them a clearly delineated, thoroughly structured, narrow surround in which they feel safe. They might find comfort in the Dilbert-like "cubicle" and its silo. Even those workers who experience silo-like workplaces as constricting or even persecutory might find comfort in the fact that they experience all the badness as coming from the outside rather than from within themselves. For example, where the boss is experienced as inaccessible, intimidating, and humiliating, and where dependency between boss and employees has been cultivated, a narcissistic dynamic might be created similar to that originally explored by Freud. It was in Freud's observation of group psychology that, through processes of identification, the ego ideal of the individual worker is replaced by that of the (idealized) leader or manager. Further, via projective identification and splitting, goodness may thus be ascribed to the boss, while "the place" may feel like a suffocating silo. To use a different language, via displacement, the workplace may come to personify the hostility that cannot be acknowledged between workers and management.

Finally, a silo and its associated thinking may serve also as a container to hold and give outer form to inner wishes, fantasies, anxieties, and feelings. In fact, all other symbolic aspects of silos are subordinate to this containment or "housing" function. None of the above scenarios would "work" were the silo not an emotionally good-enough storage-container.

"Silo" may therefore be understood as a metaphor that signifies the psychodynamics of container/contained. These unconscious processes typify all workplaces, whether the silo metaphor is an explicit component of the institutional language or not. There is always the question of whether a workplace and its buildings can safely house workers' feelings, whether it feels, projectively, as if the place is closing in on them or is about to explode, or whether it feels comfortable or harsh—all of these are issues of what silo-like organizations feel like. We now turn to what might conceivably be done about this state of affairs.

The Significance of Surfaces for Work and Consultation

The sensate nature of organizational life introduces primitive, preverbal, pre-symbolic, and pre-subjective considerations into understanding the nature of organizational life. These primitive processes and sensations not only contribute to organizational life and functioning, but they also may, at times, play a large part in determining organizational performance and decision making. The commonplace metaphor of organizational silo underscores the omnipresence of this aspect of organizational life. Assuming that leadership recognizes the counterproductive nature of silo management as a tool for subordinate control, organizational consultants can work to raise participants' awareness of boundaries and silos and their associated organizational surfaces. The ability to open this autistic experience to articulation, inspection, and mutual validation may be regarded as a first step in terms of recovering the dialectical tension between depressive, autistic-contiguous, and paranoid-schizoid modes of experience and with it greater collective organizational reflectivity. In sum, students of organization can benefit from appreciating the significance of these sensate surfaces. Consultants may, for example, speak to creating holding environments where the surfaces are sufficiently comforting to permit work on threatening organizational problems. We suggest that notions such as holding environments and projective vessels contain a complexity that is best appreciated from the point of view of having surfaces.

In Conclusion: Exploring the Sensory Floor of Organizational Experience

This chapter has extended the discussion of the tripartite model and the view of organizations as experiential and relational systems that include organizational surfaces, in particular, silos. We have argued that behind boundaries are sensate and autistic surfaces. We have suggested that these surfaces are present in many forms. They are a part of the unconscious organization-in-mind and as such, contribute to thoughts and emotions at work that shape organizational strategies and actions. Understanding of the phenomena of organizational boundaries, surfaces, and silos contributes to deeper organizational learning and change.

Chapter 3 continues the exploration of silos in relation to broader organizational dysfunctions. The tripartite model once again provides a basis for creating insight into dysfunctional organizational dynamics and further reinforces the view of organizations as experiential and relational systems.

3

Silo Mentality

All metaphor breaks down somewhere.... It is touch and go with the
metaphor, and until you have lived with it long enough you don't know
where it is going. You don't know how much you can get out of it and when
it will cease to yield. It is a very living thing. It is as life itself.

Frost, "Education by Poetry"

Despite globalization and advancing communications technology, organizations of the twenty-first century still rely on time-tested forms of organizational structure that were perfected during the twentieth century. The most numerous of these organizational forms is the hierarchical organizational structure, where layer upon layer of positions are depicted in the familiar chart of organization. These organizational tables array positions downward from a single position containing the lion's share of organizational power and authority to those with the least. The single position at the top of these charts, the chief executive officer (CEO) position, is understood to contain within it the ultimate responsibility for the organization's performance and with this responsibility, ultimate decision-making power and final authority. It is also understood that as one descends the hierarchy, the amount of decision-making power and authority diminishes to the point where, near the bottom, employees may very well have no formal decision-making power or authority relative to even the smallest task that they perform.

Hierarchical organizations are, however, much more than a multi-layered organization form that arrays positions by their importance, power, and authority on a vertical axis. A second equally important attribute is that positions are divided upon a horizontal axis, as any inspection of a traditional organization chart reveals. Large organizations contain many areas of specialization, such as finance, accounting, marketing, legal and information services, research and development, production, and human resources, to list but some of the most common divisions arrayed on this horizontal axis. Additionally, within some of these divisions there may occur further horizontal subdivisions based on specialization and breaking the workforce down into more manageable subsets based on the size of the work units. A plant, for example, may have many teams of individuals doing the exact same work but on different machines.

Yet another operating assumption of these organizations, in addition to the notion of a presumably rational organizational structure, is the presumption of a carefully designed underlying quality that all work, even in its smallest detail, is rationalized. This effort to logically control everything in the workplace by relying on scientific principles is most commonly referred to as bureaucracy. Twenty-first century organizations are replete with huge policies and procedures manuals, carefully constructed schedules and plans, scientifically designed work flows and processes, and specialized training aimed at producing the same action and outcome every time. Predictability and control are what bureaucratic structure is all about. Unfortunately, the controlling nature of this rational approach, while producing coordination and predictability at least to some extent, is also well documented as introducing stultifying rigidities that are not adaptive to the unique qualities of all situations as well as to gradual changes in the organization's task environment—the marketplace (Blau, 1956; Jacoby, 1973; Merton et al., 1952).

The remainder of this chapter explores in greater depth one of the above three aspects of organizations while not ignoring the other two. More specifically, our purpose here is to peel away the many layers of understanding implicit in creating any organization that is divided up on the horizontal axis into specialized divisions and manageable work groups. After all, many of the change efforts underway at this time in the public and private sectors of the American economy are attempts at transcending this stubborn and persistent dimension of bureaucratic culture and design. We approach this task by illuminating the conscious, unconscious, symbolic, and metaphoric nature of the popular representation of this horizontal feature as "organizational silos," a metaphor popularized by workers themselves.

The Origins of Workplace Silos Within and Without

The workplace-as-silo image and metaphor is frequently mentioned in management and organizational literature either explicitly or implicitly. However, one does not have to consult the literature to learn that members of organizations who have not read the literature spontaneously locate the silos within their experience. Our experience with corporations and public agencies and over several decades of organizational research and consultation have led us to appreciate the origins of these silos within and without. Organization members frequently volunteer the image of silos when questioned about the functioning of their organization. As noted earlier, they may be observed, from time to time, raising their hands to form a circle and moving their hands up and down to form a silo in the air. The presence of this image in the minds of employees at various levels of organization led us to appreciate that while the external silos exist in the form of organization charts operationalized by lines of authority and physical features such as departmental offices, they also exist internally within the hearts and minds of employees. Thus, structural boundaries delineating different parts and functions of an organization may be observed to exist not only as an objective reality, but also as an inner reality and subjective experience. Thus, silos come to take on a unique meaning and significance. Employees often speak of problems of voluntary horizontal or lateral cooperation and coordination where the physical and psychological boundaries of the silos are often breached without one receiving time-consuming approval to do so. Rather than make a request that must be directed upward along the hierarchy and within one's silo and down the hierarchy in the other silo, one simply takes action. This depiction of a slow, cumbersome, unpredictable process of communication that moves up and down silos, facilitated by the building of bridges between silos where their tops are connected by their respective leaders reporting to a single position, is frequently an obstacle to creating a more efficient and effective workplace. Yet the problem is not simply structural and therefore has to be addressed psychologically.

We as organizational researchers and consultants validate the silos within and without by asking questions about them and their function. We also occasionally help organization members articulate their internalized silos, which seem to assume the nature of an autistic organizational artifact. In other words, silos often represent a mode of experience and sensation for organizational participants that is autistic in nature—preverbal and pre-relational (discussed further below). Regardless of whether the notion of silos is volunteered by organization members or articulated by an action researcher in response to an effort by workers to explain how their organization functions, there is invariably a sense of almost magical recognition, as if to say, "How did you know this about our workplace?" or "yes" referring to the silo metaphor, "that is exactly how we feel." In sum, we have been prompted many times to inquire into the associations, meanings, and feeling tones associated with these so-called workplace silos within and without. What do they signify?

The Silos Without: Clues from the Language of Business, Technology, and Agriculture

We begin our approach to silos in this chapter from the outside in. Alan Neebe (1987) captures the silo metaphor in his paper "An Improved, Multiplied Adjustment Procedure for the Segregated Storage Problem" (pp. 815–825). The widespread image of workplace silos is drawn from the immense, white concrete grain silos that mark the great North American plains. We quote from the abstract: "The segregated storage problem involves the determination of an optimal distribution of products among existing storage compartments in such a way that, at most, one product may be stored in a given compartment. A typical example is the 'silo problem' in which different varieties of grain are stored in the compartments of a silo, with no compartment able to simultaneously hold more than one type of grain" (p. 815). The grain elevator, or silo, becomes an apt image or metaphor for a vessel able—and designed—to contain only a single entity or function.

Language use provides crucial clues as to the meaning(s) and degree of the cultural sharing of words. The language of American business, technology, and agriculture attests to the reach of the image and its cultural significance as a metaphoric container of shared emotion. A perusal of organizational and marketing literature over the past decade offers a cultural cluster of silo images. These images include "well-entrenched knowledge silos," "silo commanders (leaders, managers)," "brand silos," "functional silos," "departmental silos," "glass silos," "vertical silos," "data silos," "product silos," "paper-bound silos" (at a publishing company), "giant silos of debt," "credit management silos," "investment silos," "money silos," and so forth.

Based on this partial inventory of the use of the word "silo" in the business arena, one may conjecture that a typology of metaphorical silos exists, one that may include knowledge silos, functional silos, information silos, and so on. Furthermore, just as a silo can be a noun, it can also be an adjective, as in the constricted "silo mentality" of decision-makers within divisions or operations of a corporation or public agency where systemic thinking and the vision of the larger organization is absent. Frank J. Burge (1993, p. 188) provides us with the notion of "silo commanders" in relation to the enterprise-wide vision. Burge asserts that large organizations often became poorly integrated collections of virtually independent silos, each aimed at distinct constituencies or markets. Silo leaders often lead only within the silo and not between the silos of the wider enterprise.

The nature of silo-like organizational fragmentation is further under-scored within a story from the November 16, 1999, issue of *The Chronicle of Higher Education* entitled "Researchers Are Urged to Work toward New Treatments with Health-Care Providers." In discussing the report, "Clinical Research: A National Call to Action," Jeffrey Brainard (1999) quotes from the study: "One barrier to a more efficient and effective research enterprise has been the historical fragmentation of research in a culture built around separate 'silos' of knowledge and expertise." Brainard goes on to say, "Collaboration is crucial, but until now it has meant more talk than action" (1999). Similarly in American medicine, there has long been a call for more equally voiced inter-disciplinary "teams," yet clinical teamwork has in practice been fragmented and hierarchically ruled.

In sum, the use of the word "silos" in the management literature is commonplace and most often taken for granted and lamented. The use of the metaphor has come to connote organizational dysfunction and fragmentation, although, as we note below, this is not necessarily always the case.

Silos in American Culture

Silos, with their built-in "barriers," are more often than not solutions to problems we can scarcely articulate (what we call autistic organizational artifacts)—because they are embedded in American culture and, therefore, unconsciously driven. In their pioneering studies of cultural values and value orientations, Florence Kluckhohn and Fred Strodbeck (1961) and John Spiegel (1971) draw attention to chronic conflicts in American culture—conflicts that set the stage for what later became labeled as workplace "silos." Fundamentally, the term "silo" when applied to workplaces designates styles of human relationships and fantasies of relationships. Kluckhohn and Strodbeck (1961), and Spiegel (1971) posited three basic universal value orientations that organize people's roles and govern their relationships with one another: linearity (hierarchy, vertical authority), individuality (autonomy, independence, separateness), and collaterality (horizontal relationships, interdependence, and often consensus).

All people—all societies structure their lives around specific tensions among these. Officially, American culture rests upon a repudiation of- and revolution in 1776 against—lineal rule, and an affirmation of individuality as the dominant, explicitly favored value. The interdependence and "togetherness" of collaterality that lies at the base of egalitarian work-teams, and of voluntarism (de Tocqueville, 1840), is an occasional afterthought. But it is far subordinate to the conflict between interpersonal dominance/submission and the expression of "possessive individualism" (Benjamin, 1988; Macpherson, 1962). Spiegel (1971) notes that "the tension between democratic slogans and elitist practices" (p. 350) and "the chronic conflict between democratic and authoritarian values in our society" (p. 351) become the implicit individuality-based dominance/submission cultural value orientations of our business and social institutions. The tendency toward hierarchically structured and isolated individual "silos" may, in turn, be understood as having deep roots and precursors in American cultural history.

As we have noted, workers often make emotional and experiential associations to the silo metaphor irrespective of whether they volunteer it or the organizational consultant articulates it. For some workers, it refers to a feeling of "isolation and powerlessness"—as if they were stuck deep inside the silo. Others may speak of "the left hand not knowing what the right hand is doing"—as if they experienced the silo as a disconnected fragment of a larger system. Still others associate silos with a lack of collaboration, collegiality, mutual respect, and trust between organization members—as if associating silos with being in opposition to others within their silos. Often, as mentioned above, the silo metaphor is used to refer to the specialized knowledge and practices within trained groups of professionals. It often signifies their acceptance of the fact that they could not possibly understand what their colleagues in other specialties were doing or appreciate their everyday practices. Here, silos refer to one's acceptance of the rationalizing of technical and functional specialization of people and subsystems within their wider organization.

Other workers mention such commonly accepted organizational attributes as "following the chain of command" and "organizational turf" or "turf battles." During consultations, as we delved further into why the silo metaphor seems to accurately reflect work experience, organization members frequently speak of the "us versus them" mindset. On occasion, this viewpoint can permeate a workplace. For example, as we noted earlier, when asked about their fellow workers in other units or divisions, many have proclaimed to us, "What I do is more important than what they do; what I do has more value than what they do." Others have said, "Our division deserves additional resources and their division does not" (regardless of their lack of valid information); or "they (other division, profession, or specialty) are to blame for the lack of teamwork" (or are to blame for whatever was espoused to be the presenting organizational problem at that time). In sum, the language of silos often signifies the social and psychological structure of "us versus them" and inter-silo cultural chauvinism.

Abstract notions of vision, strategic plans, mindsets, tools, and skills within silo-type workspaces are, therefore, inseparable from what it feels like to work within a silo. The popularity of Scott Adams's "Dilbert" comic strip and workplace humor, with images of "silo-like" cubicles, signifies a need to poke anxious fun at and thereby psychologically distance oneself from the truer feelings of workers. They perceive themselves as "inside" silos, which are in turn "inside" workers. The Dilbert phenomenon is in part a comic defense against the oppressive "silo-like" workplace culture with its underlying persecutory anxieties (Diamond, 1997).

These many experiences of organizational silos share one thing: they speak to a sense of organizational fragmentation, one that while clearly present on the horizontal axis also includes equally distressing fragmentation on the vertical axis, where the many layers of organization do not appear to function in a fully articulated and rational manner. Things, it seems, do not run like a well-oiled machine. In a sense, vertical and horizontal fragmentation is held in the minds of workers. This conception becomes more apparent as workers are challenged to articulate their experience. The dynamics of the two organizational dimensions are frequently mixed together where it may be observed that fragmentation on one axis is reinforced by fragmentation on the other. Here lies the importance of separating out the two distinctly different kinds of experience for examination by organization members, who may also articulate the differences without appreciating their significance. Organization members often speak directly to the presence of horizontal fragmentation of work experience. Those working in silos often acknowledge that they have little knowledge of, and minimal communication with, other groups, professionals, divisions, specialties, or subspecialties (all silos). From an object relational perspective, the prevalence of silo mentality means that workers treat the organization, and those occupying other units and divisions, as part-objects. They imagine the organization as a part-object from the narrow perspective of their own divisional silo. They do not conceptualize of the organization as a whole system. In the corporate world, this often reflects management's inability to cross product lines or functional divisions. The following vignette illustrates this.

A Case for Organizational Change: National Insurance Company

In our first vignette, disruptive change led to the need to bridge silos in an organization and in turn to recognize silos as obstacles to coping with change. A vice president of operations of a Fortune 100 insurance company called for assistance: "Our Company is confronted with substantial change. Six months ago we went through a consolidation and several hundred employees quit rather than be relocated. This is the first time in our company history that employees voluntarily quit," said the Vice President. In fact, this was an unusually stable and conservative patriarchy in which two individual executives (the founder and his successor) had headed the enterprise since the early twentieth century. This stability was challenged by the need to adjust to globalization and advancing technology, in particular, the internet and e-commerce. The company had to change.

Two major divisions, "Agency" and "Operations," have come into conflict. Agency (sales) had been seen as central to the success of the company for nearly eighty years. However, the days of the field agent selling a few insurance products (auto, life, health) and waiting in his or her office for customers to call or stop by were numbered. For this company, adapting to change meant providing more insurance, financial products, and services and greater overall customer service. Agency's success depended on working more effectively with "Operations" as well as retraining and further developing agents within its unit. Hence, all of these changes required better integration and coordination between the functions and services of Agency and Operations—a structural, strategic, and cultural shift without precedent and contrary to the old lines of responsibility and authority. The silo metaphor became a vehicle through which both groups could come to understand each other as well as the nature of organizational hierarchies and the marketplace that were imposing the need to transform how they worked together. Additionally, members of this Midwestern company with rural, agricultural roots found the silo metaphor helpful in bringing them together to work cross-functionally on common problems.

Deeper feelings and prejudices had to be addressed to facilitate change. Silo thinking signified a "vertical tunnel vision" in Operations and Agency that promoted a workplace culture that separated Operations and Agency via a horizontal status hierarchy in which Operations was viewed as inferior and Agency as superior. Policies and practices had long reinforced a fragmented corporate culture by facilitating psychological splitting in the form of "us and them." Senior management presented a friendly and benevolent face toward all employees while also fostering an idealized view of the role and function of Agency and in contrast a despised image of the role and function of Operations. It was as if all mistakes and problems were the sole responsibility and fault of Operations. Although the company had been able to function with these silos in place for many years, the changing marketplace required bridging the "wide spaces" between these two polarized functions.

In sum, the National Insurance Company revealed that even though there were real interdependencies and systemic linkages between these structures, the silo mentality meant that managers and professionals avoided "crossing-over," and they resisted collaboration. This horizontal fragmentation signified for many workers their mental conceptualization of the workplace. Systemic thinking seemed beyond their reach.

The experience of National Insurance is not uncommon. Public administrators, business managers, engineers, architects, physicians, psychologists, social workers, nurses, technicians, and university and hospital administrators, among other professionals, often proclaim, "We work in silos." On the surface this simply means, "We do not work together." Or, it implies, "We are not a team, even though management claims we are"—indicative of their awareness of the contradiction between espoused managerial philosophies and actual practices (Argyris & Schon, 1996). This consciousness of contradictions among organization members often leads to cynicism and mistrust of leaders. Over time, this kind of organizational culture of fragmentation, cynicism, and mistrust often renders self-initiated attempts at integration and cooperation problematic. It is at these times, external intervention is seen to be the only way out.

Just as the commonplace reference to silos has something to teach us about the psychological realities of the workplace and thereby the facilitation of more productive and gratifying human relations at work, the insights derived from exploring the meaning of the silo metaphor are critically important. We now turn to interpreting the significance of the metaphoric silos.

The Silos Within: Silo Thinking

"Silo thinking" is a part of the appeal and persistence of silo structure. As discussed above, silo thinking fosters "vertical tunnel vision" that shuts out the wider horizontal organizational world, thereby fostering narrow-mindedness and prejudice. A "silo mentality" with its bunker-like characteristics may exist in customer relations, in budgeting, in public agency management, in healthcare delivery systems, and in business training. Silos are commonly seen and experienced as "Balkanizing" (a term borrowed from international relations and a world war) departments within large organizations—departments much like ethnic groups feeling threatened and vulnerable alongside their neighboring group. Whenever executives, managers, and employees refer to silos within, they are typically referring to an "us versus them" structure and experience. These experiential, cognitive, and organizational characteristics of the silo image are illustrated by the following case.

The Case of Global Entertainment

The vice president of a Fortune 100 multinational entertainment company called with a problem: "Our marketing division in New York City is not working well with our operations function in the Midwest; the operations unit seems unable to implement many of the marketing concepts. The inability of these two functions to work together has cost the company millions of dollars. What can we do?"

Our work began with an organizational diagnosis (Levinson, 1972, 2000). In brief (discussed at length in Chapter 11), organizational diagnosis is a psychodynamic method of organizational assessment that includes collecting narrative, factual, and historical data on the organizational culture and leadership. Psychoanalytically informed interventionists, much like psychological anthropologists, learn the organization's story and the meaning of work and membership in the organization. An important outcome of this methodology is a more empathic and informed introspective relationship with the members of the organization. Organizational intervention is discussed further below.

During the course of the organizational diagnosis, we visited the operations offices and plant in the Midwest and subsequently the marketing offices in New York City. Workers in the Midwest assumed that the New Yorkers did not and could not possibly understand them, and in particular their need for control in order to process the mailing of millions of direct mail advertisements. Marketers in Manhattan assumed a position that proclaimed that the Midwesterners in Operations were simply incompetent and resistant to innovations. They could simply not understand why the Midwest could not handle last minute changes in the materials to be mailed, changes that in one case required purchasing millions of new envelopes to accommodate a last minute change in the size of the advertisement. In fact, the two groups rarely had face-to-face contact with one another and communicated by telephone only when absolutely necessary. Hence, Operations assumed and fantasized about Marketing, and Marketing assumed and fantasized about Operations. In the meantime, the transfer of marketing concepts into actual products was failing and costing the company money, and there was developing a mutual sense of the other division's incompetence and inability to work together effectively.

The diagnostic work, which included reviewing policies; learning (company) history; conducting interviews; and observing work areas, provided a clear picture of the strikingly different subcultures. Silo thinking had fostered prejudice and narrow-mindedness between the two subcultures. Each group thought the other "just couldn't understand what we do here" (a common mirror-imaging of adversaries and enemies). This lack of comprehension of the other's expertise and functional specialization led to unfounded assumptions and fantasies about the "other." At the same time, it was rarely, if ever, admitted that they lacked an understanding of each other. In fact, at a deeper emotional level, members of each group felt mistreated and persecuted by the other. Bridging the "wide spaces" (mental spaces) between silos, in the interest of eventual problem solving and planning, required sharing their thoughts and feelings in the presence of both groups. The telling of stories and the process of interacting with each other to resolve common problems during a corporate retreat fostered insight and change through bridging the apparent "wide-spaces" between silos. Human contact and common tasks enabled them to transcend silo thinking and narrow-mindedness.

Our discussion of the silo metaphor helped to provide the participants with a language for understanding their dysfunctional proclivities toward silo thinking and Balkanizing relations between the two subcultures. More significantly, facilitated open and honest dialogue in terms of the silo metaphor enabled organizational members to examine their own defensive routines and their tendency to relinquish personal responsibility through projection, projective identification, and psychological splitting.

This case vignette underscores the significance of what is embedded in the silo metaphor. In order to fully appreciate its meaning, we further explore its implicit complexity.

A Note on the Implicit Complexity of the Silo Metaphor

The use of the silo metaphor signifies structural and psychodynamic intricacy in human relations, particularly when understood at the latent, emotional, and unconscious level. There are differences in how people experience vertical and horizontal relations with respect to organizational silos. Inter-silo competitiveness for resources is experienced as different from interpersonal competitiveness for promotions within silos. We have observed that when organization members describe their experience of silos, they are implicitly addressing external organizational and internal cognitive and emotional dimensions. Hence, the vertical and horizontal nature of organizational experiences cannot be spoken of as if they were mutually exclusive (structural) contexts in which actions and experiences occur despite some important differences.

We have found, for example, that the psychodynamics of dominance and submission typify top-down, vertical relationships between superordinates and subordinates. In this context, silos are containers and enablers, at least theoretically, of efforts at control and containment, especially as it relates to regulating and limiting interaction among silos. In contrast with this control, containment, and limiting context of the vertical axis, there coexists an opposing implicit assumption about the nature of horizontal relations and how organizations are assumed to work. More specifically, it is assumed by many that integration and cooperation across silos is necessary for successful operations. However, our observations and experiences of workplace cultures suggest that silo thinking and sentiments, mostly unconscious, often foster worker resistance to integration, which then leaves silo inhabitants feeling helpless, hopeless, depressed, distrustful, and childlike. There often exists frustration and disappointment among organization members around their inability to work effectively across divisions. Consequently, a vicious reinforcing cycle emerges in which workers, by their thoughts, feelings, and actions, end up creating and reinforcing the incapacity to work collaboratively with other divisions and silos, horizontally and vertically. In sum, there are different expectations among adults in these vertical and horizontal relationships that are frustrated and foster regressive dynamics. The balance of this chapter is devoted to explaining the psychodynamics of the silo metaphor using several points of view to triangulate its significance for understanding the workplace.

The Psychodynamics of Silos in the Workplace

Silo workplace cultures and silo language are attributes of contemporary organizational experience as attested to by the literature we cite and the case vignettes. Silo workplaces exist in the hearts and minds of workers where there may be an absence of overt silo thinking (language, metaphor, symbolism). At the same time, silos also represent a more concrete ever-narrowing specialization in the division of labor. Silos, therefore, "have" both an external reality (personal separateness, isolation) and an inner world that leads to the experience of a split of the workplace into "good" and "bad" persons and places. In sum, "silos" denote a distinct way of experiencing and speaking of the workplace and its familiar personal isolation and the fragmentation of work and experience reinforced by mental splitting.

We thus must simultaneously explore the phenomenological (experiential), intrapsychic (internal), and intersubjective (interpersonal, as viewed from the unconscious) aspects of organizational "silos." We must inquire into the reality of intrapsychic organizational space. If workplace-as-silo constitutes a social metaphor, what is its status as a personal metaphor? How does one know that silos and silo thinking are not simply shared turns of a phrase or convenient shorthand? This question takes us to the earliest psychoanalytic thinking on metaphors (Sharpe, 1948) and to current controversies within anthropology (Obeyesekere, 1980).

In her classic paper on metaphor, Ella Freeman Sharpe (1948) argued that once bodily orifices are controlled, the discharge of feeling tension occurs through speech. She wrote, "Speech . . . becomes a way of expressing, discharging ideas" (p. 276), abstractions that nonetheless retain their origin in bodily states. Attention to metaphor can inform us of the shared "body image" (Schilder, 1950) and the "body ego feeling" (Federn, 1952) that make its symbolism compelling. Searles emphasized that "the material objects in one's life are an emotionally meaningful part of it" (p. 388). The methodological issue is how one gains access to these meanings, including group meanings, such as in workplaces. Following Searles, one would inquire into what the workplace and material objects in the workplace feel like and how they are experienced (discussed below as the autistic side of organizational artifacts).

In his paper "On the Origin of the 'Influencing Machine' in Schizophrenia," Victor Tausk (1948) described the psychodynamics of "the marvelous powers of this machine, by which the patients feel themselves persecuted" (p. 33). The delusional content is a projection of the patient's genitalized body. Tausk's observations suggest that, at least in some aspects of its symbolism, the workplace "silo" is experienced as a malevolent "influencing machine." Tausk writes,

> The evolution by distortion of the human apparatus into a machine is a projection that corresponds to the development of the pathological process, which converts the ego into a diffuse sexual being, or—expressed through the language of the genital period—into a genital, a machine independent of the aims of the ego and subordinated to a foreign will. It is no longer subordinated to the will of the ego, but dominates it . . . The machines produced by man's ingenuity and created in the image of men are unconscious projections of man's bodily structure. Man's ingenuity seems to be unable to free itself from its relation to the unconscious. (p. 64)

In the context of Tausk's argument, the tall "silo" would have distinctive phallic properties, which then persecute its inhabitants. This recognition returns us to an earlier discussion of the deeply embedded dynamics of dominance and submission of the vertical axis of organizational life.

"Silo" as a metaphor is a way of conceptualizing intra- and interorganizational conflict that stems from unconscious processes such as introjection (taking the outside into one's inner reality), projective identification (projecting onto the other with the unconscious intent of using, coercing, or manipulating the object), and psychological splitting of whole objects (dividing the external world into good or bad objects). The workplace is a context in which these psychodynamic surfaces have personal, interpersonal, and organizational consequences. When emotionally invested, silos come to serve as vats of members' projections, fantasies, unconscious wishes, and expectations. Beyond "vertical tunnel vision," silo thinking fosters "Balkanizing" and polarized black and white, all or nothing, all "good," all "bad" images among subcultures within organizations that promote prejudice and narrow-mindedness.

Silos are, therefore, psychological spaces that perform the affective-perceptual-organizing functions of putting, evacuating, and storing inner mental content "out there." Through reification, the silo comes to be experienced as the source of the experience. The shared psychic purpose of this reification is to assure group members that the problem is "it" rather than themselves, outside rather than inside. As an intrapsychic way of experiencing others, reification denies separateness and distinctness. Silos turn American "individualism" into a group phenomenon, as if to say, "Our silo is an island. We can do it and have it all to ourselves." The silo mentality fosters a bastion of manic "all-knowing," as if participants are at once both the "container" and the "contained." That is, a narcissistic group culture is one in which members share an attitude of "We have to do it all ourselves," or "We can only trust ourselves," out of a deeper fear of intimacy, acknowledged interdependency, and more developed object (self and other) relationships.

Reification is reinforced by introjection and projective identification where people "inside" the silo take the silo "inside" and begin to think of themselves and their lives as cubicles, divisions, departments, subspecialties, parts unaware of whole systems, and other world views. In turn, taking the silo "inside" and thinking of oneself as "silage" cuts one off from seeing the whole system of organization and the necessity of horizontal relationships at work. As outside and inside become hopelessly fused, the silo—the part—"becomes" the world. It is, therefore, not that surprising that in the context of ill-managed and dysfunctional boundaries of function, knowledge, expertise, and task responsibilities, psychological splitting and regression may be readily observed in our modern organizations. Silo mentality reinforces psychological regression and splitting that is reminiscent of infantile states of dedifferentiation and narcissistic omnipotence rooted in persecutory anxieties and feelings of vulnerability.

In sum, the phenomenon of silos in the organizational mind poses a paradox for organizational members. On the one hand, they experience themselves as located within the silo. On the other hand, that which they feel physically inside of is a projection of their own "insides," a projection that acquires greater "reality" as it is shared with others in a group (mutual identification). In the following section, we take these experiences and psychodynamics that constitute the silo mentality and consider a theoretical framework that helps to further explain the psychologically primitive nature of perceptions, sensations, feelings, and thoughts that occur in and about silos, thus emboldening the meaning and significance of the silo as metaphor.

Silos as Autistic Organizational Artifacts

It is our premise as introduced in Chapter 2 that the meaning of silos is fundamentally rooted in what psychoanalyst Thomas Ogden (1989) in *The Primitive Edge of Experience* calls the "autistic-contiguous" mode of experiencing, sensing, feeling, and thinking. The metaphor may be viewed as a vehicle by which organizational participants express what Bollas (1987) calls the "unthought known." It is as if members find the metaphor and then invest it with their primary subjective and intersubjective experiences of touch, shape, and rhythm associated with the earliest phase of preverbal, infantile attachment and dependency.

For Ogden (1986, 1989), these primary object relations are psychological organizations in mind that determine ways in which meaning is attributed to experience. Ogden's modes are the conceptual basis for his tripartite model. Once again, they include (1) the depressive mode or relationship between subjects; (2) the paranoid-schizoid mode or relationship between objects; and (3) the autistic-contiguous mode, where subject and object are absent and one is left only with experience of enclosing surfaces that may have soft or hard properties (Ogden, 1989). "Each of these three modes of generating experience is characterized by its own form of symbolization, method of defense, quality of object relatedness, and degree of subjectivity. The three modes stand in a dialectical relationship to one another, each creating, preserving, and negating, the others" (p. 10). These modes, according to Ogden, are processes through which perception is attributed meaning in a particular way and thereby have certain implications for more deeply understanding the individual-organizational dimension of the workplace. Borrowing from Ogden and the above discussion, it may be understood that organizational silos are experienced as primitive fragmented structures devoid of integrative bonds and attachments.

In this regard, the most fundamental experience of the silo is one of personal isolation, where subjects and objects for the most part cease to exist and the only remaining experience is that of the silo. This experience and intrapersonal organization space becomes filled with fantasy, where silo members create experience unbounded by reality testing. "Outsiders" (others, divisions, and departments-silos) are invested with attributes via unconscious denial, splitting, and projection that may then be unconsciously manipulated at will. The fantastic creation of the silos, therefore, represents a containing and confining "hard" surface (autistic object) for silo members. These constitute simultaneously individual and social defenses. Ogden (1989) writes, "An autistic object is a safety-generating sensory impression of edgedness that defines, delineates, and protects, one's otherwise exposed and vulnerable surface" (p. 56). This protective surface is associated with such words as armor, shell, crust, danger, attack, separateness, otherness, invasion, rigidity, impenetrability, and repulsion (Ogden, 1989). We assert that herein rests the ultimate psychodynamic significance of the silo metaphor as a psychological defensive mechanism to cope with the flood of anxiety—provoking organizational and group membership experiences. We illustrate this primitive autistic organizational artifact and its accompanying experience in the following vignette, one where silo language does not accompany silo experience.

Silos without the Words: A Case Example

This vignette from Howard F. Stein (Diamond, Stein, & Allcorn, 2002) shows the relevance of the silo as a way of understanding and dealing with the threatening nature of organizational problems created by silos. In this vignette, the participants wish away problems (via processes of denial and undoing) with superficial and expensive artifactual fixes, such as new buildings and massive renovations. When they find their efforts do not alleviate these problems, workers get upset and are perplexed as to why the seemingly elaborate effort to improve things has not made a significant difference in human relations.

A large department of medicine within a metropolitan health science center in the United States is seeking to change. For its first twenty years, the department was situated in several dispersed buildings. Some of these were refurbished homes in the neighborhood of the medical school. In the early 1980s, a new, dynamic, and charismatic chairman was recruited to revitalize the department. His vision and mission from the outset was to build a state of the art internal medicine center that would be a national leader and "to bring the (departmental) family into a home under one roof." His decade of chairmanship was single-mindedly dedicated to securing the funds to build "The Building," as it came to be called. All other departmental functions, such as teaching, medical practice, faculty and student recruitment, were subordinated to this goal.

During the department's first twenty years, its clinics were dispersed into three sections (silos) of the city: South, Central, and North. The South and Central clinics were devoted to residency training and saw mostly indigent patients. The North clinic was a faculty clinic that attracted "paying patients"—that is, those who were amply insured. It was considered to be the preferred clinic at which to work. Although there had been a policy that stipulated equal financial, personnel, and equipment resources for all three clinics, those in the Central and South clinics felt unjustly treated. Their physical facilities were more antiquated, more crowded, and less hospitable. They had to take care of a more difficult and complicated patient population. They believe that they were slighted by the chairman and by the wider health sciences center because their clinics were located in impoverished "inner city" areas and did not generate satisfactory income. As compared to North, these clinics were thought to be the choice of last resort for those seeking health care delivery. They felt that the mostly unavailable chairman, and his inner circle of administrators, tended to play favorites with the "Cadillac" clinic and ignored the "Ford" and "Chevy." Those who worked at North did not so much look down on those at Central and South, as they felt comfortable and happy with what they had. Those who staffed the North did their best to keep their positions at North, while those at Central or South often sought the rare transfer to North.

The fall of 1997 saw the completion of "The Building" and immense preparations for "The Move." Large lapel buttons, three inches in diameter, appeared pinned to the shirts and blouses of the more than one hundred employees: "Everything will be better in the new building," it read. There was Dilbert-like anxious humor in anticipation of the move to what was obligatorily called "The Center" (not merely "The _____ Center"). It was as if primary-process thinking had taken hold and otherwise intelligent adults were engaged in wishful, magical thinking—"The Building" would somehow undo and banish all remnants of the past that contained considerable silo-based pain and suffering as well as aggression. Organizational history seemed to vanish.

It was in the new building that the chairman's dream would come true. The department would finally have the dignity of having a single building (like all other medical departments), and everyone in the "family" would be under one roof. Another dream, held by many faculty members as well as the chair, was that clinical practices would be merged so that there would be no physically distinct faculty medical practice separate from those designated for training residents. All clinical activities would be more integrated. Residents, it was planned, would have a better opportunity than before of seeing what it was like to practice medicine in the "real world." At this point, it must be noted that paradoxically the former clinics were to be moved intact to the new building, thereby threatening to recreate the same organizational dynamics but at a different site.

In "The Center," clinics were named for regionally prevailing tree species: Maple (South), Oak (Central), Buckeye (North), and some specialty clinics (cardiology, gastroenterology, etc.) were Elm, Hickory, and the like.

All of the clinics (Oak, Maple, Buckeye and specialty clinics Elm and Hickory, etc.) were connected by a maze of hallways to labs, pharmacies, X-ray, and other ancillary medical services. During the first months following the move and the official "ribbon cutting ceremony," everyone worked hard to "make things work at The Center." There were many "glitches" to correct, from toilets to computers. As the physical plant began to feel familiar, and routines took shape, many of the "old" problems that "the move" was supposed to have solved irresistibly resurfaced. Even though residents trained and faculty practiced in all of the clinics, those in Maple and Oak became disgruntled at the "special treatment" Buckeye was (supposedly) receiving.

Despite the built-in connectedness, it was the psycho-geography that created the separation (Stein, 1987). Just as some of the "old" battle lines between the "administrative" and "clinical" ("academic" and "real world") floors and zones resurfaced, so did those between clinics. Nurses, medical assistants, and transcriptionists resigned from Maple and Oak, not only as individuals, but also remarkably as groups. A physician or two would bring up the topic of the recent resignations for discussion at faculty meetings and inquire into the "morale problem" in the department. Characteristically, such concerns spoken from the heart were met with dead silence or with immediate countertestimonials about "how much I look forward to coming to work here in the department." When a faculty member described how a departing nurse or secretary had talked about work conditions, others quickly countered that the departing staff member was offered a far better paying position elsewhere or that the staff member was "hard to get along with," and the like. Of all the possible variables considered, any that would cause the discomfort of inward-looking at the Department of Medicine were summarily dismissed—as if to say, "It couldn't be we who are the problem."

At one faculty meeting some three years after the move, one senior physician said candidly, "It often feels like nothing's changed in the move, that what was promised didn't happen. It's like we brought North, Central, and South with us (naturally they had). The only difference is that we now have them under one roof. Morale is the pits, when the morale problem was supposed to have been resolved." Several people nodded in assent, but no one would speak to the point. The external interventionist said something about how difficult this was to discuss, but that the problems were supposed to be over and they were not. No one would continue on this sensitive subject. Another agenda item was introduced.

In sum, although no one explicitly used the term "silo" in describing the old and new buildings and clinic structure, its mood was clearly present. Spaces do not have to be called or labeled "silos" in order to feel like and function as silos. The symbolism of silos and silo imagery in the American workplace may then be understood to reflect the pre-symbolic, sensory impressions and infantile experience of the objects Ogden (1989, 1994) describes in the autistic-contiguous mode. These autistic organizational artifacts help to explain why it is so difficult to accomplish collaboration and integration in the workplace. Unconscious silo imagery influences practice often contrary to what managers and executives espouse. The autistic nature of organizational silos and the importance of understanding them are further underscored by the following discussion that focuses on the silo-like artifacts of the workplace and their significance for self, other, group, and organizational experience and meaning.

In an article that has direct bearing on our discussion of the meaning of organizational silos, Stein (1987) critiqued the design of medical facilities composed of sealed, black glass buildings that were coming to dominate not only medical but also corporate and university campuses, long prefiguring Dilbert's "cubicles." He observed, "One is immediately struck by the extent to which these buildings are designed to be self-contained worlds. In this total environment, temperature is automatically regulated. Windows are sealed and designed to remain shut. Insulated from vexatious life, one can almost pretend to be wholly unrelated to the world outside—until the thermostat fails. Life and season go on as though detached from those inside. The world is an alien, inhospitable place; an adversary from which we seek refuge" ("autism"). He goes on to more thickly describe these artifacts of modernity: "Stone massifs with few portals to the outside; sleek window-buildings, with impenetrably tinted or mirrored faces; and buildings with intricately latticed metalwork that mediate the outside; these are alike insular worlds. Metaphors of our disconnectedness, they encapsulate what they contain" (p. 15)—much like silos in the organizational mind.

Office decor has tended to be on the harsh, angular side since the late 1970s; there is a minimalist quality to it that reminds one of the famous Harry Harlow monkey-experiments, with metallic, wire mothers and food. We have perfected indoor environments that isolate and insulate from the object-world of nature, as if collectively we needed to dispel nature and our connectedness altogether. Lighting tends to be blazing, blaring, and emanating from intense florescent fixtures. It is harsh rather than soft. Since the 1980s, even stereo equipment has had the black finish, replacing earlier wood finishes. There is a cold, ominous quality that long predates the "Gothic" style in modern clothing. One also thinks of the Darth Vader "Star Wars" character. This is not the whole story; there is also an element of the paranoid-schizoid sensation as well, but one is struck by the almost "lunar," lifeless quality of much modern workplace architecture and art.

Silo images and impressions occupy the artifacts of workplace culture as well as the values and assumptions held by organizational participants.

In sum, silo thinking and imagery persist in the external reality of artifacts and in the inner world of organizational participants and their unconscious conceptualization of human relations in the workplace. Silos exist in the culture and workplace and thereby become a part of, and gain meaning through, unconscious processes. This critically important dynamic relationship between the silos within and without, and their fusion in the minds of workers, is further understood with the assistance of the psychoanalytic notion of condensation. Moore and Fine note, "According to Freud, dreaming and the foundation of dreams are results of the dream work, a mental process characterized by archaic modes of thinking, particularly displacement, condensation, and substitution (p. 57).

Thus, given the stubborn quality and characteristics of the silo metaphor, what can be done to address its psychologically regressive and organizationally dysfunctional dimensions?

Defragging Our Organizations

Defragging is computer language for recompiling the content on a hard disk into a more orderly manner to improve performance. Defragging is, therefore, analogous to what must be accomplished in an organizational context to overcome losses of personal integrity and organizational integration. In "The Age of the specialized Generalist," Margaret Kaeter writes that looking toward the twenty-first century, "the challenge for trainers is not to destroy silos of knowledge, but to give specialists the tools that will allow them to bridge the wide spaces between these silos" (pp. 48–53). Specifically, Kaeter argues that for manufacturing organizations to be broader-based and cross-functional, employees will have to have multiple mind-sets, not a narrowly specialized single one. We find this is true for most, if not all, twenty-first century organizations.

The Meaning of Silos for Organizational Change

The metaphor of organizational silos signifies for workers a sensate, embodied experience. This primitive experience of silos as autistic organizational artifacts directs our attention to the consequences of this experience, conscious and unconscious, and what it implies for morale, creativity, human relations, and organizational performance. From a lighter perspective, we might ask, are there characteristics of silos, organizational and personal, which can foster (what Winnicott calls) transitional (or potential) space necessary for organizational integration and repair?

The presence of silo thinking is a barrier to integration and collaboration between disciplines and professions, specialties and subspecialties, in governmental agencies, corporations, universities, and academic health care settings. The answer to the riddle of the paradoxical nature of silos is not simple. Silo thinking and the associated characteristics of "vertical tunnel vision" are produced and perpetuated via the unconscious processes of internalization, introjection, and projection onto the organizational and technological landscapes from which they originate. Once internalized by individuals and work groups and accepted as part of an organization's culture, silo images reinforce the psychodynamics of splitting and regression in the form of black and white dichotomies and absolutes. Thus, the psychic reality of internal silos is externalized symbolically and thereby returned to the workplace to create the all too familiar "us" versus "them" organizational dynamics and the accompanying horizontal organizational fragmentation. The challenge for those seeking organizational change is clear.

In order to locate the potential for organizational change, we begin by acknowledging that silo-like organizations contain the promise of establishing necessary and appropriate anxiety-reducing boundaries. Boundaries, as noted in the previous chapter, are essential to the self and the capacity for distinguishing "me" from "not me" and "self from other." Boundaries are also critical to the organization and its capacity to establish structural divisions of labor and specialization as well as structures of accountability and clarity of authority and responsibility. In this regard, silos can and do have positive, functional, and constructive attributes despite the fact that silo imagery frequently conveys negative and counterproductive workplace attributes. "Good enough" boundary maintenance, as represented by the silos, can be productive and anxiety reducing for their members and is an essential function of management. In contrast, preoccupation and over-reliance on silos and organizational boundaries among adults are rooted in infancy and thus have the capacity to be psychologically regressive and counterproductive, if not dysfunctional.

Silos as autistic organizational artifacts (autistic-contiguous objects) are experienced as cocoon-like and thereby at the minimum proffer the illusion of security and safety. Effective boundary management between organizational roles and relationships (professions and divisions) may, therefore, be understood to be a critical factor in achieving organizational success. Success, however, depends on mediating the more primitive psychologically defensive nature of the silos and the wish for control over interpersonal and group members' anxiety. Herein lays the challenge for executives, workers, consultants, and organizational researchers. Nondefensive boundary maintenance as represented by the potential of silos is challenging and can be riddled with much potential conflict for managers. Yet, it is critical that managers assume the responsibility of boundary management and coordination between and among silos.

In sum, organizational success in the twenty-first century may well hinge on the ability of organization leaders to provide sufficient organization structure and predictability to permit organization members to tolerate anxieties associated with collaboration, creativity, and the development of productive relationships among organizational members within and among the silos. Simultaneously they must avoid too much structure and control that provokes silo-based defensive routines and rigidities and the primitive experience of the autistic organizational artifacts that stifle organizational performance.

The Challenge of Organizational Intervention: A Brief Overview

The challenge of capturing the potential or transitional space/time of the metaphoric silos requires leaders to be able to manage them prospectively. It also requires leaders to create the potential for change in organizations where the silo mentality is resident and compromises individual, group, and organizational performance. The following brief discussion builds upon some of the discussion in the case vignettes.

Intervention begins with an organizational diagnosis (Levinson, 1972, 2000), which is derived from the collection of narrative, historical, and factual data (see Chapter 11 for greater elaboration). These data come from many interviews selected to represent a diagonal slice through the organization as well as from policies and procedures and management reports and communications. This work also includes the development of a consensus history of the organization that reveals patterns of growth, leadership, successes, and failures. The articulation of organizational history pays special attention to critical incidents and the associated managerial responses. In addition, it takes into consideration the interpretation of transference and countertransference dynamics between and among participants and with the organizational consultants. The outcome of the diagnosis is frequently an articulation of the preexisting silos, their inter-relationships, and their history of contributing to deficiencies and conflicts in organizational performance. These findings invariably point not only to how employees relate to each other on the horizontal and vertical organizational axes, but also to many problematic, dysfunctional, and ineffective actions of leaders as mentioned above and as illustrated in the cases.

This organizational story is then transformed into a feedback loop that will be attended to by management and workers. This step takes substantial care in order to avoid dumping a considerable amount of negative information and images into the organization that will, in turn, be processed by the silo mentality as finger pointing. It is, therefore, critical to present a balanced organizational depiction, which adequately represents the organization as a perceptual system and gives voice and empowerment to organizational participants, hence minimizing deeply embedded defensive routines and the human proclivity to scapegoat and assign blame.

Based on participants' listening to presentations of the organizational narrative in feedback sessions and their confirmation of the portrayal of organizational identity, a desire for change may then be nurtured by simultaneously (a) trying to minimize defensive routines of the silo mentality and (b) enlisting management and employees in a shared process of locating and implementing change driven from within to promote ownership. Organizational consultants must focus on engaging management and employees in this work and, in particular, around the assumption of tacit roles of command and control by organization members, which often minimize organizational learning and problem solving. Executives and managers may need to be coached in managing and negotiating between silos so that over time the rigidity and inflexibility of these divisions become less pronounced and more malleable.

Change, once articulated as a strategy for solving problems and improving the quality of work life, is then planned and implemented. A communication and participation plan can also be developed to support management and employee learning about the change effort as well as about the silo-based thinking and action. The nature of the change, plans, and implementation naturally varies on an organization-by-organization basis, and more specific direction cannot be provided here. It suffices to say that a one-size-fits-all approach to organizational intervention is not recommended. Rather, the diagnostic work should lead to a carefully designed intervention that is intended to meet the specific needs of an organization.

Last, we recommend at some reasonable interval that a follow-up organizational assessment be conducted to test and validate the success of the change effort. It is more than likely that reinforcing the positive side of silos and minimizing the negative side will be an ongoing challenge. It is, therefore, important that any silo change effort be viewed more as a process than as a time bounded change effort.

In Conclusion

In this chapter, we have considered the "silo" as a distinctive and characteristic feature of bureaucratic organizations in the late twentieth and early twenty-first centuries. We have described and accounted for the widespread use of the "silo" image in the workplace and employed a psychoanalytically informed perspective to help understand its conscious and unconscious appeal in coping with systemic challenges of external adaptation and internal integration.

We have also provided ideas about organizational change that build upon the positive side of silos in order to avoid unnecessary pathologizing of silo thinking. Based on our experience, we believe that positive, constructive, and healthful change is possible, even "within" organizations built, socially and psychologically, as silos. Insight into organizational silos achieved in a setting of safety often leads to problem solving, greater job satisfaction, collaboration, mutual respect, and understanding among organization members.

The tripartite object relational model informs organizational theorizing, analysis and change. Our discussion of silos has grounded the model and theory in the workplace. Chapter 4 explores yet another way Winnicott's and Ogden's work informs the organizational understanding, intervention and change. In particular, there exists a unique mental space filled with awareness, observation, and reflective thought, what Winnicott, Ogden, and others call the perspective of the analytic third. It is from the position of the analytic third that mutual understanding, recognition, and collaboration between silos otherwise systemically fragmented and dysfunctional is acquired thereby promising repair of these fractures and conversion of silos into functional divisions.

4

Organizational Change and the Analytic Third

> I suggest that the time has come for psychoanalytic theory to pay tribute to this third area, that of cultural experience which is a derivative of play. Psychotics insist on our knowing about it, and it is of great importance in our assessment of the lives rather than the health of human beings. (The other two areas are inner or personal psychic reality and the actual world with the individual living in it.)
>
> *D. W. Winnicott*, Playing and Reality

Understanding the theory and practice of psychoanalytically informed organizational diagnosis and change requires a concept that captures the experiential nature of working in depth with organizations. The analytic third is one such helpful analytic concept. It accentuates the intersubjective dimension of the participant observer of organizational culture.

Introduction to the Third in Psychoanalysis and Organizations

Deep change in individuals and groups, as in psychoanalysis and psychotherapy, emerges out of reflective engagement and the dialectical nature of intrapsychic and interpersonal processes. These interactive processes are comprised of creative and destructive tensions, regressive and progressive actions, paralysis and movement, social and psychological structures, conscious and unconscious motivations, and fantasy and reality. The tensions between these processes are experienced among leaders and followers, therapists and patients, consultants and clients, superordinates and subordinates, organizational participants, subject and object, and self and other. One can say that these social and psychological dynamics are the cognitive and emotional forces of human nature and relational systems—what Winnicott (1971) refers to above as "the actual world with the individual living it" (p. 102).

Regardless of whether we call these forces of human nature dialectical tensions, paradoxes, splits and fragments, or simply conflicts, one observes the emergence of a third dimension of experience, and it is in this interme- diate area that things actually happen, and it is within this psychological space that the deeper work of organizational diagnosis and change occur. This chapter explores the concept of the analytic third (Ogden, 1994) or the third (also referred to as thirdness, triangular space, and the third subject) in contemporary, two-person, object relational psychoanalysis (Winnicott, 1971; Lacan, 1975; Cavell, 1998; Mitchell & Aron, 1999; Benjamin, 2004; Britton, 2004; Gerson, 2004; Green, 2004; Minolli & Tricoli, 2004; Ogden, 1994, 2004; Zweibel, 2004). The psychoanalytic concept of the third repre- sents the focal point for studying and attending to unconscious organiza- tional psychodynamics. It is the location and mental space for witnessing and intervening where we observe, analyze, and consult human relations in organizations. In this spirit, the third may be described as a "position" the student of organization assumes.

There are varied ways in which the third in psychoanalysis is defined. Many of our sources on the subject come from a special issue on "The Third in Psychoanalysis" in the journal *Psychoanalytic Quarterly* (Volume LXXIII, Number 1, 2004). This special issue is remarkable in its promo- tion of a dialogue between relational, Kleinian, neo-Kleinian, and other psychoanalytic writers on the topic of the third. As with many important concepts in psychoanalysis, the third is frequently defined differently by theorists, clinicians, and practitioners of multiple schools of psychoana- lytic thought. Our review is not exhaustive. Yet, it is an attempt to illus- trate without perpetuating more confusion the multiple ways in which one can consider the value of the third in psychoanalysis and psychoanalytic organizational practice. Next, we borrow from this review and propose a way to conceptualize the third in the psychoanalytic approach to organiza- tional diagnosis and change. We conclude with a vignette to illustrate the nature of the analytic third in the processes of participating and observing, analyzing, and intervening in organizations. We preface our review of the literature on the third by discussing our position, which we return to in the vignette and our discussion of the third in psychoanalytic organizational consultation.

The Concept of the Third in Psychoanalysis

The third in psychoanalysis stems from an acknowledgement among theorists and practitioners of the value of reflective action, participant observation, and the nature of intersubjective processes in object relations. It is also consistent with the value placed on transference and countertransference and the self consciousness of the analyst to use the self as an instrument of observation. The introduction of the concept of the third signifies a change in the psychoanalytic paradigm as well from one- to two-person psychology, and more recently, the emphasis among relational psychoanalysts on intersubjectivity—the intersubjective third subject. The purpose of a "two-person psychology" is to emphasize the emergence of what Ogden (2004) calls "the intersubjective analytic third." These emergent properties of the dyad exist in dialectical relation to the individual subjectivities of the patient and the analyst. (Mitchell & Aron, 1999, p. XV)

In our experience, the analytic third is where the productive work of repairing and integrating fragmented and broken human systems occurs. Thirdness materializes when two individuals are engaged in the exploration of unconscious meanings, reasons, motives, and actions. In the history of psychoanalysis, this notion of the production of a third subject surfaces most prominently with the paradigmatic shift from the classical drive model to the contemporary relational model. This is a transition from focusing on instincts to attending to relationships. The former is more preoccupied with intrapsychic structure and the psychodynamics of tension reduction. The latter is more encompassing of intra- and intersubjectivity and object-seeking motivations. The intersubjective third is apparent in the phenomena of transference, countertransference, and projective identification. These are the emotional bonds, or knots, that tie one to another, unconsciously. Thomas Ogden (1994) calls these bonds the subjugating third.

This exploration begins with clarification of our position on the third in psychoanalysis and organizations. We are particularly focused on its application in the "here and now" of psychoanalytic organizational interventions. In our view, the analytic third is established when we make genuine contact with others in dyads, groups, communities, or organizations. It is the location of mutual understanding and recognition between two or more subjects. It is also a position that transcends the individual and the dyad. This is precisely why it has relevance for organizational work. Organizational participants must be aware of mutuality, shared identity, and complex relational systems. The third illuminates the dual position of participation and observation. Britton (2004) points out that it is comprised of ontological subjectivity and ontological objectivity. Thus, the concept of the analytic third enriches our understanding of the psychological processes necessary to produce self, group, and organizational consciousness and reflectivity.

In the case example and descriptions of organizational diagnosis and change, the psychodynamic processes between consultants and organizational members share much in common with object relational approaches to psychoanalysis and psychotherapy. In particular, the approach presented here reflects the analytic practice of moving back and forth between subjective (first person) and objective (third person), or between the role of Oedipal provider of the law ("This is how it is") and that of a containing partner in a process of mutual recognition and creation (Searle, 1995; Britton, 2004).

This review of the third in psychoanalysis includes the contributions of Winnicott, Benjamin, Britton, Ogden, Minolli and Tricoli, Gerson, and Green. Table 4.1 is provided as a summary of their contributions.

Table 4.1. The Third in Psychoanalytic Theory

Winnicott's third as transitional and potential space	• Intermediate area • Culture • Psychic reality (experiential)
Benjamin's thirdness	• Intersubjectivity and mutual recognition • Attending to dominance and submission • Creating relational systems
Ogden's analytic third	• Intersubjective third subject • Subjugating third (projective identification)
Britton's triangular space	• Closure of the Oedipal triangle • Limiting boundary for the internal world • Third position as observer and witness
Minolli's and Tricoli's Hegelian third	• Solving the problem of duality • Third as self-consciousness
Gerson's third as the relational unconscious	• Developmental third • Cultural third • Relational third
Green's concept of the third in psychoanalysis	• Binding, unbinding, and rebinding • Rebinding as third element

In developing the concept of the third for organizational interventions and change, we begin with a brief review of Winnicott's notion of transitional and potential space.

Winnicott's Third as Transitional and Potential Space

The concept of analytic third shares much in common with Winnicott's (1971) notion of the transitional and potential space, the intermediate area where culture, play, creativity and imagination reside. Winnicott (1971) introduces the concept of potential space in *Playing and Reality*, "I put forward for discussion of its value as an idea the thesis that for creative playing and for cultural experience, including its most sophisticated developments; the position is the potential space between the baby and the mother. I refer to the hypothetical area that exists (but cannot exist) between the baby and the object (mother or part of mother) during the phase of the repudiation of the object as not-me, that is, at the end of being merged in with the object" (p. 107). For Winnicott, the emergence of potential space via playing and cultural experience coincides with the baby's earliest acknowledgment of itself as separate from yet attached to the mother. The creation of this transitional space, as Winnicott called it, requires some sense of confidence, safety, and security in the presence, empathic attunement, and nurturing capacity of the mother. Potential space originates with the infant's experience of responsive mirroring and maternal affection grounded in good enough mothering (or good enough holding environment), where the baby develops the capacity to be alone and the curiosity to explore his or her internal and external world (Winnicott, 1965, 1971).

For Winnicott (1971), potential space is where we (adults and children) live and experience living, neither in fantasy nor reality but somewhere between the two. It is essential to maturation and the emerging sense of self. The notion of potential space is at the heart of Winnicott's thinking; Ogden (1994) calls this space Winnicott's intersubjective subject. Winnicott's third is however incomplete and therefore limited in ways that will become evident with the additional views presented below. Winnicott's third as transitional and potential space is a dimension of the analytic third where action researchers and consultants provide containment and foster innovation and creativity in setting and solving problems. In particular, action researchers and consultants become transitional objects for their clients in the process of shifting an organizational culture from an unconscious state of defensive denial and fantasy to one of consciousness and attunement to social and political realities.

In sum, Winnicott's revisions of Kleinian object-relations theory and his concepts of potential and transitional space have influenced a new generation of psychoanalytic writers. It is also the case that Benjamin's concepts of thirdness and intersubjectivity add to a deeper understanding of the psychodynamics of organizational hierarchy, power, and authority by highlighting the sadomasochistic interplay of dominance and submission between supervisors and subordinates and executive managers and workers.

Benjamin's Concept of Thirdness and Intersubjectivity

In her article "Beyond Doer and Done To: An Intersubjective View of Thirdness," Jessica Benjamin (2004) states, "thirdness is about how we build relational systems and how we develop the intersubjective capacities for such co-creation" (p. 7) Thirdness is a quality or experience of intersubjective relatedness akin to Winnicott's "potential space," or his "transitional space" (p. 7). The third is not a "thing" but a "principle, function, or relationship" (p. 7). "In the space of thirdness, we are not 'holding onto' a third; we are, in Ghent's (1990) felicitous usage, surrendering to it" (p. 8).

The third is then that to which we surrender. Thirdness is the intersubjective mental space that facilitates or results from surrender. This nondefensive act of surrender does not refer to submission or compliance. It refers to letting go of the self. It implies the ability to take in the other's point of view or reality. Benjamin explains, "Thus, surrender refers us to recognition—being able to sustain connectedness to the other's mind while accepting his separateness and difference: Surrender implies freedom from any intent to control or coerce" (Benjamin, 2004, p. 8). Thirdness is that intersubjective mental space that emerges from our capacity to surrender. It is the opening up of one's intersubjective field of awareness and embrace of the emergence of the co-constructed third subject.[1]

Benjamin is acutely aware of the challenges of the oppositional nature of two subjectivities and their separate realities as it relates to Hegel's philosophical critique of the master-slave relationship and the relational dynamics of masochism and sadism and dominance and submission. She writes, "the presence of an observing third is felt to be intolerable or persecutory" (Benjamin, 2004, p. 30). The subject may experience the occupying force of the object; unconscious sabotage and collusion may be present. Under such circumstances, the boundaries between "me and you" become confused and inadequately delineated inside the mush of transference and countertransference and projection and introjection. Benjamin (2004) states, ". . . malignant complementarity takes hold, the ping-pong of projective identification—the exchange of blame—is often too rapid to halt or even obscure" (p. 30). Benjamin's notion of thirdness enables participant observers, via their awareness of the transference trap, to untie the emotional knot and thereby enhance their understanding of their own participation in the co-constructed relational system. Similarly, Ogden's position on the analytic third stresses the value of consciousness around projective identification and what he calls the "subjugating third" in transference and countertransference.

Ogden's Analytic and Subjugating Third: Attending to Projective Identification

Ogden (2004) refers to a third subject unconsciously co-created by analyst and patient, "which seems to take on a life of its own in the interpersonal field between them" (p. 169). This third subject stands in dialectical tension with the separate individual subjectivities of analyst and patient in such a way that the individual subjectivities and the third create, negate, and pre-serve one another (Ogden, 2004, p. 189). The third subject (or thirdness) is the product of the dialectical processes of the relational unconscious. The analyst and patient confirm, disconfirm, and reconfirm each other in the sense of mutual recognition of individual subjectivities. The analytic third signifies the analyst's position and consciousness of the intersubjec-tive subject or co-created third.[2]

Thus, our simultaneous surrendering to and awareness of the third position[3] enables us to attend to (without being entrapped by) coercive and collusive relational psychodynamics such as projective identification.[4] Ogden (2004) refers to this dimension of the third as mutual subjugation in contrast with mutual recognition (p. 187). He adds that the analytic third comprises a tension between mutual subjugation and mutual recognition. That is, if the relational processes of projective identification inherent in the dynamics of mutual subjugation between analyst and patient and con-sultant and organizational participant become conscious, recognized, and attended to, then the analyst is in a position to locate him- or herself in the analytic third. The analytic third is the mental space for insight and change. It is also the analytic space for working through resistances to insight and change. And, if there is any possibility of deconstructing the twisted and misplaced relational dynamics under the influence of projective identifica-tion, then it would seem to be more probable from the vantage point of the analytic third.

Figure 4.1 illustrates that analytic third as a position, the intersubjec-tive subject, taken up by the participant-observer (consultant). It reflects the location and mental space of reflexive individual and group processes where one participates, observes, witnesses, analyzes, and consults organizational members. Its focus is on intersubjective dynamics at the apex of the triangle. From this position, one experiences, observes, and articulates the collision and potential collusion of psychological forces between subject and object, including such coercive relational dynamics as projective identification.

Consciousness of the analytic third and that which is co-created between two or more individual subjectivities in a relational system enables us to observe and attend to the emotional whirlwind of transference and countertransference dynamics—the shared emotions of individual and mutual subjectivities. In the midst of a fury of projected and introjected emotions, the analytic third represents potential space from which to articulate and differentiate self and other, me and you, and container and contained.[5] Ogden explains how projective identification operates in the space of the analytic third: "The interpersonal facet of projective identification—as I view it from the perspective generated by the concept of the analytic third—involve a transformation of the subjectivity of the 'recipient' in such a way that the separate 'I-ness' of the other-as-subject is (for a time and to a degree) subverted. In this unconscious interplay of subjectivities, 'you [the 'recipient' of the projective identification] are me [the projector] to the extent that I need to make use of you for the purpose of experiencing through you what I cannot experience myself'" (Ogden, 2004, p. 188).

Ogden (2004) describes the recipient in the subjugated analytic third of projective identification as metaphorically making "psychological room"

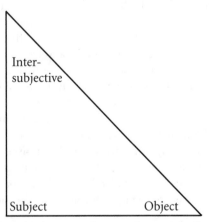

Figure 4.1. The analytic third as triangular mental space for reflectivity and change

for the projector's temporary occupation. The projector turns him- or herself over to the recipient and in effect transfers the disavowed unconscious (part self-object) to the outside other. The recipient then participates, according to Ogden (2004), in a negation of oneself by surrendering to the "disavowed aspect of the subjectivity of the projector" (p. 189). Thus, the recipient is able to open up his or her interpersonal field of experience between the two subjectivities (self and other). It is from this vantage point of the initially subjugated third that the recipient attempts to process and comprehend (via identification and recognition) the other's subjectivity as separate from yet linked with his own.

In sum, in much the same way as Bion's (1967) notion of container and contained is operational in the therapeutic encounter, the analytic third signifies the psychodynamic processes in which the recipient eventually verbalizes and affectively returns to the projector his disavowed subjectivity in a form the projector can receive, reclaim, and find meaningful. Thus, from the position of the analytic third, the projector makes use of the recipient as a container of toxic and nontoxic emotions. In the process of reclaiming split-off and evacuated parts of oneself, self-cohesion is enhanced, along with the capacity to distinguish sensations of "me and not-me." A more unified sense of self comprised of good and bad parts is derived from the psychodynamics of an expanding thirdness.[6] This expansion is precisely what Britton attempts to describe in his notion of the third as "triangular space" rooted in early oedipal relations.

Britton's Subjectivity, Objectivity, and Triangular Space

Britton's perspective of the third rests on the work of Melanie Klein and W. R. Bion. His explicit emphasis on Klein's concept of the early oedipal relations and Bion's theory of containment differentiates Britton's approach. His concept of the third provides a fuller and more nuanced view of the application of the third in psychoanalysis and organizations. His focus on "malignant misunderstanding" in narcissistic and borderline conditions extends Benjamin's exploration of the psychodynamics of dominance and submission, and the invisibility of the other. It also enhances our understanding of Ogden's subjugating third and the collusive and manipulative psychodynamics of "projective identification." In describing the early oedipal triangle Britton (2004) writes,

> The acknowledgement by the child of the parents' relationship with each other unites his psychic world, limiting it to one world shared with his two parents in which different object relationships can exist. The closure of the

oedipal triangle by the recognition of the link joining the parents provides a limiting boundary for the internal world. It creates what I call a "triangular space," i.e., a space bounded by the three persons of the oedipal situation and all their potential relationships. It includes, therefore, the possibility of being a participant in a relationship and observed by a third person as well as being an observer of a relationship between two people. (p. 47)

Britton's application of Klein's theory of early oedipal relations and Bion's theory of containment are present in this quote and throughout his work. For our purposes, it is valuable to point out that the relative success of the individual in negotiating the early oedipal triangle is in part dependent upon the internalization of appropriately limited ego or self-other boundaries. This outcome of self-integrity (integration) is derived from good enough holding or maternal containment. And, as Britton and Searles (1995) point out, the third person (objectivity) emerges as one who is no longer simply a participant (first person, subjectivity). One becomes a witness (third position) as well. The organizational consultant also moves back and forth between what Searle (1995) calls ontological subjectivity and ontological objectivity and between organizational diagnoses and containing interventions. The third position as described by Britton (2004), Benjamin (2004), and Ogden (2004) assumes a Hegelian self consciousness as well as a cognitive and emotional grasp of relational complexities, however paradoxical and dialectical. In this spirit, Minolli and Tricoli (2004) view the concept of the third as a solution to the problem of duality.

Minolli and Tricoli's Hegelian Third as Solution to the Problems of Duality

Minolli's and Tricoli's (2004) view of the expansion of mental space or thirdness comes along with the development of Hegelian (1807) self-consciousness. In their discussion of the concept of the third in psychoanalysis, they remind us that new concepts emerge in the history of ideas when a problem exists that needs to be solved, and according to the authors, psychoanalysis has come up with the concept of the third to solve the problems of duality. Writing on the evolution of psychoanalysis, the authors suggest, "We think that the third was born as an attempt to recall the human being's capacity to grasp [oneself] reflexively. This belief is confirmed by the increasingly widespread use of terms like 'reflexive function' or 'meta-cognition' (Fonagy et al., 1991), 'reflexivity' (Mitchell, 1988), 'self-reflexivity' (Aron, 1998), and many others in psychoanalytic literature" (Minolli & Tricoli, 2004, p. 143). The authors further illuminate our understanding of the third and its function in psychoanalysis by reintroducing the Hegelian (1807) concept of self-consciousness from the philosopher's descriptions of the phenomenology of consciousness in *The Phenomenology of Mind*.[7]

The notion of the third as self-consciousness represents a mental space or position from which one can see and experience the binding and ego distorting affect of projective identification, transference, and counter-transference. The intersubjective third provides the self (or ego) with a vantage point from which one can view the landscape of the relational unconscious dynamics. In Hegelian philosophy, perception, intellect, and self-consciousness are the three levels of consciousness, where perception and intellect are developmental precursors to self-consciousness. Minolli and Tricoli (2004) write that "for Hegel (1807) development of conscious-ness takes place through the 'forms' (Gestalten) of perception, intellect, and self-consciousness" (p. 143).[8]

Perception and intellect are forms of consciousness derived from the subject's infantile dependence on the object. The primitive and emergent self is in part temporarily located inside the object—a form of projective identification. Self-consciousness develops along with overcoming depen-dence on the object. In other words, self-consciousness emerges out of the developmental transition from total dependency to relative autonomy as described by object relations theorists such as Fairbairn (1952), Gun-trip (1969), and Winnicott (1971). It is currently understood from infant research (Stern, 1985), for example, that the sense of self as "I-subject" occurs around eighteen months of age, at the time the child has the capac-ity to carry internalized object representations (pp. 144–145). Hence, "me and not-me" sensations become better delineated along with the subject's primitive sense of subjectivity. At this juncture, it might be said that the nascent form of a developmental, cultural, and relational third takes shape. Gerson extends this thinking.

Gerson's Third and the Relational Unconscious

In his article "The Relational Unconscious: A Core Element of Intersub-jectivity, Thirdness, and Clinical Process," Gerson (2004) identifies three different experiential dimensions of thirdness. First, he refers to the devel-opmental third, which is a position that invokes an oedipal constellation. The oedipal constellation, according to Gerson, represents a third entity (person, institution, or symbol) that disrupts the dyadic. The third subject interferes with the emotional bond between subject and object. Second, the cultural third is a non-intersubjective form of thirdness, according to Gerson (2004), which does not arise from the subjectivities of the individuals in the dyad, but rather "envelops, intrudes upon, and shapes the interactions of the dyad, as well as the subjectivities of each member of the dyad. Exemplars of the cultural third are such forces as the incest taboo, language, and professional standards ..., with each representing a codification, both legal and semiotic (Pierce, 1972), of the possible and the prohibited" (p. 77).

In sum, the relational third for Gerson (2004) is the notion of thirdness that arises from within the dyad and stems from intersubjectivity or the combination of individual subjectivities. In other words, the relational third comprises the collision of subjectivities and the dialectical processes of negation and affirmation. Gerson (2004) writes, "the relational unconscious is not an object, a third, a triad, a field, or a space. Each of these renderings connotes—even if it is not the intention of the author to do so—an entity that can be separated from the two subjectivities that combine to create it. Intersubjectivity and the relational unconscious are better thought of as processes through which individuals communicate with each other without awareness about their wishes and fears, and in so doing, structure the relation according to both mutually regulated concealments and searches for recognition and expression of their individual subjectivities" (p. 81). The relational unconscious is structured out of the developmental processes of separation and individuation, or what Andre Green (2004) describes as binding, unbinding, and rebinding.

Green's Concept of the Third Element: Binding, Unbinding, and Rebinding

In his paper on thirdness, Green (2004) refers to the psychodynamics of binding, unbinding, and rebinding. Binding and unbinding signify respectively the dynamics of attachment and separation, or as Green prefers, Freud's notion of life and love instincts on the one hand and destructive instincts on the other; rebinding stands for the reunion or reuniting of two parts (part-objects) of a broken unity. Rebinding is the third element, according to Green, which refers to reunion after separation. He explains, "In symbolization, two parts of a broken unity are reunited; and the overall result can be considered not only as the rebuilding of a lost unity, but also as the creation of a third element that is distinct from the other two split-off parts" (Green, 2004, p. 107).

Binding, unbinding, and rebinding seem analogous to processes of attachment, separation, and loss in attachment theory and object relations theory (Bowlby, 1969, 1973, 1980; Fonagy, 2001). The third element of rebinding is descriptive of the psychodynamics of change in the depressive position and the notion of change as emotional loss and eventual reparation (Klein & Riviere, 1964; Klein, 1986).

Rebinding is a reparative and reintegrative process. Profound change, individual and organizational, engages the analytic third of consultants and participants alike in constructing, deconstructing, and reconstructing the intellectual, perceptual, and emotional bonds between self and other and subject and object. Table 4.2 summarizes the relevance of the analytic third for organizational intervention and change.

Thirdness as an Emergent Organizational Awareness

Depressive and reparative processes include grief and mourning as a natural yet often overlooked component of change. In reflective work groups, the psychodynamics of grief include denial, anger, aggression, resistance, disorganization, reintegration, and reorganization. Object loss permeates the transitional space (Diamond, Allcorn, & Stein, 2004). The psychodynamics of binding, unbinding, and rebinding foster reuniting broken or fragmented parts of relational systems of people, roles, and organization. These transitional processes signify a shift from paranoid-schizoid modes of experience (where splitting and projective identification abound) to depressive ones (where mutual recognition and reparation are possible). As evidenced in the case vignette to follow, the concept of the third refers to an awareness of an emerging triangular space. This stems from the presentation

Table 4.2 The Analytic Third in Psychoanalytically-Informed Organizational Consultation

Reflective Inquiry about:
• Dialectical tensions
• Subjectivity versus objectivity
• Social versus psychological structures
• Group versus individual
• Fragmentation versus integration
• Dominance versus submission in role
• Change versus resistance to insight and change
• Third as location of organizational identity and change processes
• Triangular space and the organization-in-mind
• Psychic reality and the subjugating third (experience, transference and counter-transference, splitting and projective identification)
• From paranoid-schizoid toward depressive modes of experience
• From fragmenting toward integrative processes
• Change as emotional loss (grief and mourning as reparative processes)

of the organizational diagnosis and consultant's containment of organizational dynamics to foster the development of a good enough holding environment. The consequence of deep listening, trust-building, and empathic understanding in the process of organizational diagnosis (through participation, observation, and structured interviewing) provides organization members with an interpretation (assessment) and a container for unconscious and previously unarticulated emotions and anxieties.

This triangular (or potential) space is the intermediate area of colliding subjects and objects, roles, and divisions that permits the emergence of reflection and change. The third position therefore signifies participants' capacity to occupy the mental space of observation, reflexivity, and double loop learning (see Argyris & Schon, 1978), which enables clients to produce alternative relational structures and more meaningful, productive, and humane organizations.

In sum, during the course of organizational interventions, the third subject emerges through participant observations linking "here-and-now" interactions with those of the organization and its collective past. The analytic third is attended to by efforts to enhance the members' capacity for reflective action (reflexivity) and insight for genuine relational change, and gathering the fruits of these efforts require our intervening in the psychodynamic processes of human relations at work.

Organizational Change and the Analytic Third

The analytic third embraces the organization's relational context. It represents the reflective space and time to inspect relationships between people and their organization, between individuals and their roles and responsibilities, and between units, divisions, professionals, specialists, and disciplines. Locating and attending to these in-between areas or potential spaces is essential in repairing fragmented relationships and linkages between groups and divisions inside organizations. The consultant facilitates the dialogue in the change process at the moment participants seem open to suspending often long held assumptions and beliefs about themselves and their roles in the organization. Typically this occurs following the analysis of resistance to change and a minimization of defensiveness characterized by greater openness to learning from each other (as illustrated in the vignette below).

In sum, the analytic third emerges at the time participants become fully engaged with each other and their consultants in a reflective process of self and other examination—a third position from which it becomes plausible to acknowledge and reclaim projected emotions and attributions.

Vignette: The Analytic Third in Organizational Consultation

Several years ago, we worked with a department of psychiatry (names and certain details have been changed to protect anonymity). Along with a female associate, we provided a comprehensive organizational consultation to a department described by its executive and several executive team members as riddled with deeply personal and frequently vicious interpersonal conflicts. Often, when they met as a group to discuss department business or to engage in intellectual, theoretical, and clinical discourse, their differences and disagreements escalated into hostilities. The leadership and department members were unable to tolerate or contain discord among them. Meetings frequently ended with members destructively personalizing their differences and further fragmenting the department into ideological and embattled camps and unproductive divisions—dysfunctional silos.

The turmoil among members and the frequent dysfunction foreclosed strategic and business planning. Many knew it was time to reexamine their mission, goals, and strategies to turn around decreasing student enrollments, diminishing patient populations for psychotherapy, and depleted institutional morale. Political and economic conditions in health care and the impact of managed care made reimbursement more difficult and discouraged medical students from specializing in psychiatry. Those who did were discouraged from practicing psychotherapy for economic reasons. The department head and her executive team of administrators and clinicians felt something needed to be done. They needed more effective strategies to adapt to an unwelcoming political environment. Yet, they could not accomplish anything of this magnitude until conflicts from within were reconciled and until they had developed the capacity to work more effectively as a team and with a stronger sense of affiliation to the department.

We provided this department with a structured method and process for organizational diagnosis, feedback, and strategic interventions. After several weeks of on-site interviews and data collection, the organizational consultants presented the department with a depiction of the organization. It was during this time, space, and experience of telling the organizational story that a glimmer of thirdness in the group emerged in a context of injured narcissism and broken and distorted relationships.

The department members gathered to hear the story derived from the historical and narrative data of structured interviews, observations, and participation in groups and committees. The organizational text was projected onto a flip chart and the consultants (male and female) read from the text of their organizational diagnosis. In the spirit of a provision of the oedipal law and the establishment of triangular space, the organizational consultants were saying to their clients, "Here it is. This is our best depiction of who you are as an organization based on what we experienced, observed, and heard from all of you." Sometimes, at this point, the consultant can feel people in the group shift their attention off themselves, momentarily, and onto a larger and more systemic image of themselves, an image that signifies "you are more than any one individual in this room, you are a group, an organization, yet all of you share responsibility for your culture and for your collective identity." With this in mind, department members temporarily shifted their attention and expanded their perspectives away from this preoccupation with internal fragmentation, angst, and interpersonal conflicts and toward seeing themselves as a group and as an organization, not simply a collection of individual clinicians and administrators.

In this case, it was as if, in the course of the dialogue and our facilitation of transitional and potential space (the analytic third), members for a short time transcended their own narcissism and their proclivity to be entrapped in dyadic relations. They could move beyond their obsession with interpersonal conflicts. The third becomes then a solution to the problem of duality. By focusing on themselves as a group and organization, they momentarily broke down their own resistances to the process of psychodynamic organizational consultation and their resistances rooted in the belief that the consultants could not change anything since they "could not change members' personalities."

The telling of the organizational story altered group members' awareness. Their attention moved away from themselves as individuals and dyads. They seemed to overcome, at least for the moment, their investment in interpersonal conflicts and psychological splitting into groups of enemies and allies. They came to see themselves as comprising a whole. Movement from relational binding to unbinding, and ultimately to rebinding, occurred with intensive, reflective, and repetitive group sessions. Part-object relationships within the group became more characteristic of whole object relations promoting the capacity to acknowledge, tolerate, and value similarities as well as differences among members.

One incident late in the intervention depicted the value and function of the analytic third and the quality of thirdness. Sabotage is not unusual in organizational change efforts and late in the consultation, one member introduced a letter to the group. In the letter, the author, a member of the department not present in the group at the time, had written a vicious criticism and personal attack on a colleague who was in the group. The purloined letter was shared openly by a protective female colleague. Group members got angry, felt shame, regressed, and retreated into familiar oppositional camps. Some defended the victim of the attack, while others attacked the messenger for bringing it out into the public without the author's permission. The group collapsed into paranoid and schizoid dynamics. A break of ten minutes was called in order to allow time to assess and process what was going on. At the break, several members aggressively lobbied the consultants as "judges" to "deal with" the incriminating letter and the "malicious and cruel person who wrote it." It was as if these members were demanding justice and that the consultants were somehow in a position to proffer justice and determine punishment. Psychological splitting and projected aggression in the group reinforced scapegoating among several members.

We reconvened the group and reminded them of their task as a group. We suggested that what was going on was indicative of the patterns and themes inherent in their organizational story. We continued by suggesting that they had an opportunity to acknowledge it as a painful and critical incident and assume responsibility for their actions. We pointed out that once they could acknowledge it as part of their collective past, they could move forward in a productive and progressive manner. We were giving the group, in the midst of sadomasochistic and paranoid-schizoid dynamics, an opportunity to reflect and assume responsibility for themselves as a group and organization. We also provided them with an opportunity to reflect on what had just happened in the group as evidence of and confirmation for the organizational diagnosis. They were eventually able to see how the introduction of the letter and their reaction to it perpetuated fragmentation and aggression that had rendered them dysfunctional as an organization. They could see how this incident signified their tendency as a group to move into and remain stuck in a fragmented and broken state.

Focusing on the analytic third signified movement into a triangular (potential) space where they could engage in reflective inquiry and participant observation, enabling them to acknowledge their regressive group processes and their own impact on themselves as an organization. It was as if the consultants were asking organization members to join them at the apex of the triangle (Figure 4.1), thereby developing their capacity to acknowledge entrenched narcissistic injury and the subjugating third of projective identification. They could now begin to see themselves as a group with a mission and goals.

In sum, the vignette illustrates a key element of organizational change and intervention. An organizational diagnosis is presented publicly to all the participant subjects in the form of an organizational story. It is an act of storytelling that produces a psychological space, an analytic third to promote reflectivity. This narrative that emerges represents the production of a third subject that is produced by organizational participants with the assistance of consultants.

Conclusion

The concept of the analytic third contributes to contemporary psycho-analytic theories of organizational change. It assumes that organizations are relational systems, and this encourages attending to the perceptual, intellectual, experiential, and emotional lives of their members. Due to its emphasis on relational dynamics, the concept of the analytic third accentuates the psychodynamics of splitting, polarization, fragmentation, projections, introjections, and projective identifications within organizations, and it enables organizational participants to reflectively attend to the emergence of mutual recognition between co-workers and with their capacity to transcend *the problem of duality*, such as that found in the *us and them* structure characteristic of so many regressive organizations.

In Chapter 5, we take a look at the psychodynamic forces of regression in organizations and the often counterproductive emotional pull of individuals into less differentiated and more symbiotic-like positions. Frequently, we have discovered that when leaders and their organizations fail to adequately contain (in Bion's idea of container-contained) workers' thoughts, feelings, and actions, psychological regression occurs and organizations become less rational and more childlike.

Notes

1. This notion of surrender to the emergent third comes closer to what we imagine to be Winnicott's conception of the true and authentic self in contrast to the false and compliant self.
2. You might say that with the concept of the third in relational psychoanalysis $1 + 1 = 3$.
3. The third position may remind some of H. S. Sullivan's (1953) technique of counterprojection, where the projected image is placed momentarily outside the dyad so that it can be viewed with some degree of psychological distance.
4. Projective identification involves the creation of unconscious narratives (symbolized both verbally and nonverbally) that involve the fantasy of evacuating a part of oneself into another person. This fantasized evacuation serves the purpose of either protecting oneself from the dangers posed by an aspect of oneself or of safeguarding a part of oneself by depositing it in another person who is experienced as only partially differentiated from oneself (Ogden, 2004, p. 187).
5. Bion abstracted the model of the relationship "container-contained" from a particular aspect of projective identification, which afforded further insight into this mechanism. According to this model, the infant projects a part of his psyche, especially his uncontrollable emotions (the contained), into the good

breast-container, only to receive them back "detoxified" and in a more tolerable form. (Grinberg, Sor, & Bianchedi, 1993).

6. What we are referring to here as "an expanding potential space" is the depth of experience, insight, and self-consciousness that comes from a good enough holding environment.

7. This has also been true for the study of organizational change from both cognitive and psychoanalytic perspectives. The notion of organizational learning, double-loop learning, reflective practice, and reflective inquiry represent this trend. In particular, see Argyris and Schon (1978) and Diamond (1993).

8. See Freud's essay on "On the Unconscious" (SE XIV, 161), particularly his discussion of the various meanings of the unconscious and the topographical point of view (P. Gay [ed.] *The Freud reader* [1989], pp. 572–84).

5

Organizations as Defective Containers

The rudiments of the sensory experience of self in an autistic-contiguous mode have nothing to do with the representation of one's affective states, either idiographically or fully symbolically. The sensory experience is the infant in this mode, and the abrupt disruption of shape, symmetry, rhythm, skin moldedness, and so on, marks the end of the infant.

Thomas Ogden, The Primitive Edge of Experience

Bion described the consequences for some individuals of a failure of maternal containment as the development of a destructive, envious superego, which prevents them from learning or pursuing profitable relations with any object. He made it clear that the inability of the mother to take in her child's projections is experienced by the child as a destructive attack by her on the child's link and communication with her as the good object.

Ronald Britton, "Subjectivity, Objectivity, and Triangular Space"

Joining, merging with, and submission to a group or organization, while to some degree a part of life in modern society, may be viewed from an object relational perspective as having its emotional roots in infancy and as including the potential for threat and loss of self. The surface of organizational experience may be filled with feelings of constriction, confinement, engulfment, and abandonment. We conjecture that these oppressive feelings often arise in organizations where leaders do not provide effective containment of workers' emotions. Containment here refers to the capacity of one individual to act as a container of emotions of another individual, where bad feelings are evacuated and projected outside the self onto an object outside. We will elaborate on the psychodynamics of containment later in the chapter. For our purposes here, it is important to point out that when leaders cannot provide this containment for followers, workers become distressed and anxious. Consequently, they become reliant on primitive and frequently destructive psychological defenses such as regression, splitting, and projection. This chapter focuses on psychological regression in groups and organizations. It is particularly concerned with the potentially destructive and oppressive forms of collapse into states of collective merger and symbiosis in which absolutist and what might be called fascistic ideologies take root.

Organizational research (as noted in earlier chapters) often assumes decisions and actions are guided by rational (logical and sensible) norms and intentional processes. The positivists' assumption of human nature found in mainstream organization theory is that of a one-dimensional worker void of inner life. And, despite some progress in the field during the last century (March & Simon, 1958; Simon, 1961; Weick, 1969, 1995), there remains a fixation with the "conscious" levels of organization to the exclusion of hidden features of organizational life (Field, 1974; Zaleznik & Kets de Vries, 1975; Diamond, 1993; Gabriel, 1999).

In *The Irrational Executive*, Manfred Kets de Vries (1984) called attention to the notion of rationality in management theory: "The notion of the idealized, completely rational decision maker, comparable to the classical homo economicus of economic theory, living in a world of optimal choices, has never really been abandoned. It appears that most management theorists, like the economists before them, have been reluctant to go beyond the directly observable and pay attention to the determining effects of intrapsychic processes on individual motivation" (pp. xv–xvi). The introduction of psychoanalysis to organization studies has addressed these concerns by challenging the underlying assumptions of the nature of human relationships at work, and these assumptions govern much of management and organization theory. In his article "The Unconscious Organization," George Field (1974) notes, "The basic reasons why we largely ignore hidden levels that harbor the nonrational organizational elements inhere in our American ethos. As a people, we are oriented toward action and efficiency, a trait that has yielded astounding economic output and technological achievement while simultaneously producing pathological social conditions that are an almost inevitable by-product of our preoccupation with mechanical and scientific approaches to problems that do not readily lend themselves to traditional mechanistic solutions hampered by methodological constraints" (pp. 333–334). Interfering with "progress" and production, for purposes of reflection, runs contrary to American customs. The predominance of mechanistic and scientific approaches to the study of organizations has supplanted insight and relevance with method and rigor. The belief of the superiority of rational approaches to organizations has limited American scholars' abilities to understand organizations as human groups and cultures that engage in repressive, irresponsible, destructive, and seemingly juvenile acts.

Our premise for understanding the psychologically regressive and destructive side of organizations emphasizes the presence of a dialectical tension between nonrational (illogical, nonsensible) and rational (logical, sensible) forces in organizational life itself. Accordingly, the field of organizational studies requires a socio-psychoanalytic, object relational paradigm for examining the nature of rational and nonrational actions. Organizations must then be defined as intersubjective, relational structures of meaning, affect, perception, and experience that interact with and, at times, contradict their social, economic, and political structures. Revealing these contradictory and conflicting powers connotes defining organizations as fundamentally human and inevitably flawed. People come to work and fill their roles of responsibility and authority with their private selves that, in turn, influence their perceptions and wishes. Strategy, structure, and technology become instruments of unconscious and nonrational as well as conscious and rational forces. In order to better understand and apply these social and psychological tensions, organization theorists and researchers acknowledge the presence of unconscious defensive and regressive forces at work. Life in groups and organizations is not linear. It has a back and forth, oppositional and resistant momentum.

Organizations are symbolically represented by the self through a variety of artifacts such as posted mission statements, organizational charts, written policies, formality or informality, interior office designs, architecture, and corporate logos. These symbols of organizational culture gain their meaning through a deeper understanding of what the artifacts signify in the minds of members, clients, and customers. This deeper meaning is only accessible through an understanding of unconscious psychological defenses, such as regression, and the psychodynamics of transference and countertransference. Individuals who join organizations transfer conscious and unconscious desires and expectations onto their image of the organization and in particular, its leader. Organizations become psychological containers (Bion, 1959) for members' unconscious projections of aggression, expectations, ideals, anxieties, and conflicts. In particular, the organization-in-mind can be understood to individually and collectively comprise the self created organizational identity. If we take seriously the observations of Freud (1921) and Bion (1959), indicating that whenever individuals join groups and organizations, they experience psychological regression, then we benefit from examining the association between psychological regression and organizational identity.

Regression and the Psychodynamics of Organizational Identity

Organizational identities are reflected in values, assumptions, and unconscious collective desires. These are communicated by affect and experienced via projection of internal self images onto externalized shared images of organization and leaders. Understanding the subjective and interpretive value of intersubjective structures of organizations requires transcending the surface level of artifactual and social data (Allcorn, 1995; Diamond, 1993; Stein, 1994). In particular, understanding the psychodynamics of group membership is helpful to interpreting organizational identity.

Group membership entails an intrapersonal compromise between desires for dependency versus demands for autonomy. The mere presence of a group, Wilfred Bion (1959) observed, presumes a defensive state of psychological regression among participants. Referring to Freud's (1921) *Group Psychology and the Analysis of the Ego*, Bion (1959) wrote, "Substance is given to the phantasy that the group exists by the fact that the regression involves the individual in a loss of his 'individual distinctiveness' (Freud, 1921, p. 9). . . . It follows that if the observer judges a group to be in existence, the individuals composing it must have experienced this regression" (p. 142). When they join a group, adults may experience themselves in infantile or childlike roles. Individual uniqueness has to be reconciled with dependency and group identity (Diamond & Allcorn, 1987).

Anxiety and regressive behavior among organizational participants is frequently provoked by a focal event. A director's mere "thinking out loud" to her staff of her intent to reorganize may be experienced by them as her general lack of confidence in their abilities to manage effectively. Subjectively, her staff experiences this as her withdrawal of support (loss of the good parent). Staff may then feel unjustly treated and, consequently, regress to a primitive and infantile emotional state of totalistic, bifurcated thinking, whereby individuals and objects are categorized (split) into all-or-nothing terms. Staff may further come to view human relationships at work as black or white; good or bad. They may feel like helpless victims and come to perceive themselves as "all good" and others, via splitting and projection, as victimizers and "all bad."

Psychological regression takes hold as a consequence of group and organizational membership and as a response to a stressful focal event. Workers' otherwise mature mental states of cognition become more primitive and immature. Their capacity to solve complex problems in the workplace is diminished. The mention of change or reorganization can induce regressive psychodynamics. Yet, organizational participation may also be experienced as personally gratifying and constructive. Reflective thinking by individuals and groups can promote learning from experience and democratic and less homogenized dynamics.

Acknowledging and valuing the presence of tension between psychological and social structures of the workplace is vital to worker well-being, competency, and to democratic organizational processes. Participants' who can resolve conflict and promote reconciliation and consensus-building will be better positioned to promote mature group and organizational processes that include problem solving, ongoing monitoring of policy implementation, and effective service delivery. Psychological resilience and flexibility is also a prerequisite for adapting to a constantly changing organizational context.

A theory is needed to explain the forces that drag seemingly rational (logical and sensible) participants along emotionally regressive and destructive paths that oppose constructive work. If we take seriously the tension between social and economic forces (politics and markets) and psychological structures (intrapersonal and intersubjective dynamics), we come to realize that members routinely and unwittingly engage in defensive and regressive psychodynamics that contradict rational processes at work. These organizational psychodynamics limit and, in some instances, destroy participants' capacity for collaborative and cooperative action. Nevertheless, psychological regression is a fact of human existence inside and outside of institutions. Can organizational leaders learn how to respond effectively and appropriately to these seemingly counterproductive forces within them and among followers? In order to achieve this significant achievement, leaders (and transitionally consultants) must have the capacity to hold and contain members' anxieties and aggressive feelings.

Organizations as Defective Containers

Participants who feel threatened and anxious about their place in the organization may revert to unconscious defensive modes of oneness, dedifferentiation, homogeneity, and overdependency. These primitive states of regression occur in organizations under stress where individuals fear standing outside the group norm and question the status quo as problematic and dangerous. When self integrity is at risk in a culture, which does not support differences, workers retreat into a symbiotic state of merger with the leadership and their ideas. Observers of groups in organizations attest to the presence of defensive and regressive strategies to cope with anxiety associated with a variety of critical incidents. Workers may avoid making individual contributions as they look toward leaders for simple solutions to complex problems. Under such conditions, it may seem as if any solution will do as long as it is pronounced by someone in a position of authority and rapidly agreed upon by all.

Winnicott (1965) identified two types of regression: (1) a withdrawal into dependency and (2) schizoid withdrawal. The "withdrawal into dependency" refers to a self-object merger (Kohut, 1977) or sadomasochistic relationship (Fromm, 1941), which connotes an internal resignation into a self-object world of fragmentation in which psychological splitting of self and objects occurs. The self and object are perceived in black and white as good or bad, loving or hating, and accepting or rejecting. Fromm (1941) wrote, "I suggest calling the aim which is at the basis of both sadism and masochism: symbiosis. Symbiosis means the union of one's self with another self in such a way as to make each lose self integrity making them dependent on each other. The sadistic person needs his object just as much as the masochistic needs his. Only instead of seeking security by being swallowed, he gains it by swallowing somebody else. In both cases, the integrity of the individual self is lost" (p. 180). Similarly, what we call in organizations with defective containment the symbiotic lure signifies participants' deepest fears of engulfment and self-annihilation. Such primitive regressive tendencies are often triggered by critical incidents and organizational change that challenge the status quo.

In contrast to withdrawal into dependency, schizoid withdrawal refers to the individual moving away from relationships and human contact to avoid feeling coerced and persecuted. This primitive state of regression is akin to Winnicott's (1971) notion of the predominant false self protecting the repressed true self locked away in a metaphorical deep freeze or crypt. Schizoid withdrawal is a form of regression not uncommon at the top of many organizations where executives prefer distance and anonymity from their employees and often from the public.

It is not our intent to argue that these unconscious forces need to be suppressed in a manner that seals them off to member consciousness. We all carry with us the potential and capacity for psychological regression. Rather, these social and psychological forces in human nature demand our awareness of their presence and acknowledgment of their function in everyday work life. What is more, this self consciousness and awareness of the psychodynamic forces of regression are required for democratic work processes in groups and organizations (the subject of Chapter 10). Suppression is certainly not the answer, and when attempted, it results in social denial, distorted communications, and twisted and distrustful human relations at work as well as destruction of creativity, innovation, and consensual decision making. Acknowledging the interplay between conscious and rational, unconscious and nonrational, forces at work is critical. And, in so doing, one needs to understand the significance of emotional containment in groups and organizations. However, leadership may not consistently provide this function of containment.

Bion's Notion of Container-contained in Groups and Organizations

Externalization in the form of projection is an effective psychological mechanism in relocating "bad" feelings and toxic emotions to objects (containers) such as others or institutions. In a simultaneous act of splitting and projection, workers relocate bad feelings to their leaders, managers, and organization. Hence, organizations and leaders often serve containing and holding functions for members' projected aggression and anxieties. When organizational leaders fail to "contain" members' aggression and anxieties over separation and loss associated with change, for example, regressive psychodynamics pull members into symbiotic and undifferentiated relationships. Such regressive actions are a symbolic return to the maternal object. It is as if one is unconsciously living and experiencing the past in the present moment. Thus, this uncontained desire for merger and protection among workers becomes a flight from anxiety that takes the organization and its members down a collectively regressive and potentially destructive path.

In contrast, when organizational leaders and their cultures serve as adequate containers of members' unconscious wishes, desires, and fears, they come to symbolize what Winnicott (1965) called a "good enough" holding environment. These organizational cultures promote safe and secure psychological space for administering to the members' internal world of object relations. These reinforce productive and imaginative dialogue and open exchange of ideas. This holding and containing provision does not, however, require transforming work organizations into therapeutic institutions. It does demand a shift in organizational culture from defective to effective containment of workers anxieties. In so doing, the silo mentality of horizontal fragmentation discussed earlier is minimized and the value of a Winnicottian transitional and potential space necessary for changes is maximized. Organizational leaders who encourage reflective processes for learning, conflict resolution, and change as vehicles for countering suppression, psychological regression, and defensive actions create vital operating culture and context. An organizational culture that acknowledges emotions rather than suppressing them promotes articulation and confrontation between conflicting parties and ideas and encourages productive and supportive democratic processes and effective organizational operations (see Chapter 10). We have to understand the psychodynamics of power, aggression, and regression in groups to achieve this. We have

to confront the oversimplified, one-directional notion of leaders imposing their will on groups. We have to come to understand the reciprocity of
dyadic relations between leaders and followers in shaping group culture.
While leaders influence group culture, groups demand certain leadership
styles and characters.

In *Psychosis and Power*, James M. Glass (1995) views the group as the
agent of unconscious fantasy. Groups, according to Glass (1995), are capable of violently imposing their power on others: "Groups whose identity
derives from collective acts of violence may be auto-engendered . . . evolving not around a central admonitory figure [for example, Freud's primal
father] but around the group itself. The group makes frenzied efforts to
forge an identity by destroying difference and fusing with an omnipotent
maternal ego ideal. In its regression toward oneness, the group may push
its individual members toward less-differentiated and therefore more
totalizing and absolute forms of psychological organization" (p. 120). Paying attention to the dangers and attractions of merger and homogeneous
regressive forces in groups and organizations is critical to confronting and
alleviating oppressive outcomes. Absolutist ideologies and belief systems
may signify the potential dangers of defective emotional containers within
group and organizational cultures. The absence of psychological regression leads to the appreciation that "secondary process mental operations
appear as the values of negotiation, tolerance, and limitation (democratic
values)"; the presence of psychological regression and the pull toward oneness leads to the appreciation that "primary process operations take shape
as intolerance, jingoism, racist and tyrannical appeals to action and repression" (Glass, 1995, p. 15). The incapacity of organizations and their leaders
to contain toxic emotions promotes a predominance of primary processes
(over secondary processes) and psychological regression in groups. These
psychodynamics are a direct threat to democratic practices in organizations and political institutions. More alarmingly, they represent emotional,
ideological, and institutional prerequisites to a fascist (or totalitarian) state
of mind.

The Fascist Self and the Symbiotic Lure

A deeper understanding of what we call "the symbiotic lure" and its psychologically regressive force in groups and organizations is critical to confronting absolutist, fascistic, and totalitarian human proclivities within
hierarchic structures of power and authority. In his book, *Being a Character*, Christopher Bollas (1992) writes of the fascist state of mind and the
potential for genocidal violence: "Whatever the factors that sponsor any

specific social act of genocide, the core element in the fascist state of mind (in the individual or in the group) is the presence of an ideology that maintains its certainty through the operation of specific mental mechanisms aimed at eliminating all opposition" (p. 200). Bollas goes on to say that members engage in a special mental act of binding in which the individual rejects all doubts and counter-views. He explains, "The mind ceases to be complex, achieving a simplicity held together initially by bindings around the signs of ideology" (Bollas, 1992, p. 201). Ideology, then, as a signifier of organizational identity and culture, represents unconscious assumptions and desires of participants. However, an ideology aimed at destroying opposing views driven to maintain the certainty of its righteousness and correctness is a sign of simplicity triumphing over complexity and the regressive withdrawal into a primitive state of oneness and homogeneity—the essence of the symbiotic lure.

In the symbiotic lure, organizational members unconsciously forego their individuality for the group and organizational ideal. Freud (1921), Bion (1959), Chasseguet-Smirgel (1985), Glass (1995), Schwartz (1990), and others explain this as the transfer of individual ego ideal to the ideal of the group (or organization). The observation that organizational members engage in denial and suppression of differences and separateness between and among themselves under these regressive circumstances may be of little surprise. Certainly Bion (1959) observed this collective regression in his *Experiences in Groups*.

This particular form of psychological regression in groups and organizations is emotionally primitive (infantile and pre-oedipal). Self and other boundaries blur. An undifferentiated, schizoid-like emotional state surfaces. Thomas Ogden (1989) describes it as the binding power of symbols and the "collapse of the generative dialectical interplay of modes of experience" forcing participants into a paranoid-schizoid "entrapment in a world of things-in-themselves" (p. 77). An external world of bombarding things and objects (people, ideas, and symbols) are then cognitively and emotionally identified by simple categories of right and wrong and good and bad.

This state of annihilating anxiety and psychological splitting severely diminishes debate over differences of strategy, values, and ideas. Doubt is suspiciously absent. The implicit assumption of absolute positions seems to govern interpersonal relationships and threaten the dialectical tension. Consensual reality seems out of reach (Glass, 1995). Under these conditions, managing organizational change effectively and humanely and promoting participation in the workplace are unlikely. Members' autonomy and relative independence are unconsciously replaced by narcissistic fusion and merger, which forfeits what Argyris (1978/1996) calls "advocacy with inquiry" and the necessary surfacing of conflicts and contradictions required for "double-loop" (second-order) learning and reflectivity. In the final analysis, the eradication of opposition, as Glass (1995) points out, poses a grave threat to democracy, the self, and the group.

The symbiotic lure signifies contagious, primal emotions that pollute otherwise reasonable decision making, strategic planning, and actions taken by organizational participants. For example, the mere mention of structural change by management in the workplace will provoke anxieties and insecurities among members. This reaction is not uncommon and not necessarily alarming in and of itself. However, if ignored, denied, and unacknowledged by leaders and organization members, it can deteriorate into a problem over time. In those instances where management suppresses affective responses and reactions and limits horizontal and vertical participation and communications, a failure to contain anger and aggression may well arise.

In sum, the regressive (symbiotic-like) withdrawal of workers is more likely in situations where mechanical and unreflective "rational" systems suppress worker input at times that policy changes or market forces impose organizational transformation. Individuals may withdraw into excessive dependency relationships typical of what may be called organizational co-dependence (Allcorn, 1992; Goff & Goff, 1991).

The symbiotic lure leads organizational members to seek a safe haven in primitive subjective (pre-oedipal) states of imagined union with the maternal object (the organization and its leaders). Self-object differentiation is limited along with innovation, creativity, and independence. This infantile-like state leads to the development of a schizoid organizational identity in which members come to view relations to others as coercive and potentially annihilating. Successful organizational adaptation is compromised by these unconscious forces.

Managing Change against the Tide of Regressive Forces

Managing change productively requires a state of mind that enables participants to address unconscious regressive forces within the group and organization. These reflective and self-conscious actions require sensitivity to the psychological structure of organization. They demand a heightened awareness of individual and cultural mechanisms that unwittingly promote denial and suppression of differences and conflict. A critical component of a comprehensive organizational intervention is collaboratively analyzing successful responses to past crises and critical incidents. Members develop a heightened awareness of their defensive and regressive routines. They better understand how these routines inhibit learning and successful management of change.

Organizational participants may come to acknowledge that they colluded in social denial that assumed a defensive flight (Bion, 1959). They assume responsibility for the collusion and eventually feel empowered to act to resolve rather than avoid embarrassing problems in the future. Organizational members at all levels come to appreciate how their withdrawal into dependency and resignation jeopardizes conflict resolution, consensus-building, and critical inquiry. In contrast, actions of members seeking quick and simplistic solutions to complex problems are symptomatic of regressive forces at play in organizations. A brief illustration is helpful.

A Case of Workplace Regression

During a consultation with a social agency undergoing change as the result of a shift in federal public policy, consultants found themselves challenged by a subculture of like-minded and seemingly polite and agreeable middle managers and staff. The executive director of the agency wanted to reorganize staff but did so without first assessing the readiness of his workforce to change. Middle managers and their subordinates had no opportunity to provide input into the nature of (and rationale for) this change.

For the executive director "managing the change" meant "controlling" employee "reactions" and resistance to change. This was a strategy partly responsible for the current state of oppressive affairs. It was the director's view that career civil servants are to be excluded from the influence of politics, and that meant his staff did not need to share in the rationale for policy-driven strategic and structural change.

The director was also experiencing anticipatory anxiety about his staff's hostile reactions. He feared their rejection and abandonment. The director was operating on the assumption that, in fact, his managers and workers would negatively react in the manner he fantasized. When a consultant asked him to describe the imagery of rejection that came to mind, the director constructed a violent scene in which he was the victim of attack and found himself perishing in a pool of blood. Similarly, in anticipation of their director's unwillingness to listen to them, agency workers developed a defensive routine to protect themselves from their fears, hostilities, and anxieties about unilaterally imposed change. "Oh, he wouldn't listen to us anyway," several commented to the consultants. "It's never done any good in the past, nothing's changed," others could be heard saying. "Oh, he will do whatever he wants to do anyway," several others indicated.

This collusive behavior concealed and suppressed conflicts and differences of opinion and ideas between organization members. Organizational participants unwittingly constructed a homogeneous culture of like-minded individuals supported by a psychological structure of paranoid-schizoid modes of experience and totalistic thinking. Members were "not themselves," they said to the consultants.

In this example, organizational members became containers of paranoia that fuelled undifferentiated relations and suppression of conflict. This fantasy came to dominate the agency culture. Members acted as if they were of one mind and, therefore, did not provide feedback to the director regarding problems related to the intended change. He was of course not going to listen, and they, mirroring this state of affairs, were not going to inquire. Any admission on their part of problems would fulfill the director's fears of their discontent, anger, and frustration. A negative outcome of their fantasy driven psychological defensive context was virtually assured.

In sum, homogeneous cultures such as this are driven by primitive anxieties based on separation (differentiation), loss, and rejection. Projective identification and collusion between the executive director, middle management, and workers produced unconscious communications in which organizational participants came to share fears and anxieties tied to change. Under these circumstances, members feared being ostracized if they conveyed differences between themselves in how they thought or felt. Differentiation (for these participants) signified a potential disconnection and loss of self, while in the mind of the director it represented the wrath of others' aggression. Change stimulated deeper feelings of uncertainty and loss of control. These feelings were experienced as intolerable. It is as if members feared a severing of the symbolic umbilical cord attaching them to the workplace as a primary source of their identity. Thus, the leader and organization were experienced by participants as defective containers.

Conclusion

Containment and holding require the development of a safe and non-retributive environment. In the above example, middle managers and staff were given an opportunity to voice their concerns and to analyze the organizational paradox. The managers complained about their political director. They asserted that their director did not understand the "real" work of agency employees nor did he appreciate the needs of their clients and constituents. There seemed to be no differences of opinion or contrasting sentiments among them. The group simply targeted the director and established a clearly defined boundary between themselves and their director (and all things political), a boundary that attributed blame by identifying the enemy and shutting down any opposition. The director was also engaged in the same sort of socially defensive system by excluding his staff from participating in key decision making and strategic planning. Bringing the group and their director together with this new awareness enabled them to see how their action had perpetuated a schizoid culture driven by psychological regression and the symbiotic lure. They had taken flight into the withdrawal of dependency, sameness, and alikeness.

It must be stressed that such an intervention does not "fix" the symbiotic lure and psychological regression; rather, it returns the organization to a "normal" state of tension between various modes of experience. This is the strength and relevance of the theoretical framework of the tripartite object relations model of dialectical experience presented earlier. Further, the power of psychological regression in groups and organizations rests in our collective denial and the associated cultural insistence on seeing humans and their organizations as rational economic actors. The unconscious intent of these primitive forces of regression, whether at the group or individual level of analysis, is to repair the fragmented self and other relations triggered by anxieties about change and loss. Through restoration of the "good enough holding environment," an effective container is produced for managing aggression and anxiety among members. The good enough organization can sustain the integrity of self-object relations and the reality of a tension between and among organizational participants. Ironically, the force of psychological regression in groups and organizations, as noted, fosters a flight of withdrawal into dependency and into a paranoid-schizoid mode of organizing experience. Human relations are characterized by mistrust and fragmentation of thoughts, emotions, and relationships. Meaningful self and other boundaries are seemingly obliterated, producing absolutism and totality in the form of extremist ideologies, dangerous belief systems, and fascistic states of mind.

The unsuccessful containment of psychodynamic regression at work renders conflict management and resolution impossible, encouraging unilateralism and top-down, oppressive methods of management that further perpetuate psychologically regressive workplace cultures. This vicious cycle of organized madness, driven by the symbiotic lure, suppresses collaboration and consensual decision making and destroys the democratic spirit at work. Consequently, there is a quality of organizational violence in certain workplaces where organizational regression dominates.

Chapter 6 explores the psychodynamics of emotionally abusive workplaces, what we call moral violence. Moral violence may not be as dramatic as the physical violence discussed in Chapter 8, however, it can be as destructive to the human core of organizational culture and occurs more frequently than the more overt and explicit cousin.

Part 2

Organizational Tumult

Typically, people think of violence in the workplace when the media reports another shooting rampage at an industrial plant, high school, or post office. Images like these, when combined with incidents of assault and harassment, underscore the brutality that is a part of organizational life. This brutality is added to by downsizing, management by intimidation, and, more recently, corporate deception and betrayal of the public trust illustrated by Enron, Arthur Andersen, and WorldCom, to name a few. Given this broad range of suspect, harmful, and unethical actions taken by executives and managers, inquiry into the character of organizational culture and leadership is crucial.

When it comes to these types of workplace violence, we suggest that a combination of oppressive organizational cultures, characterized by unilateral management practices and persecutory organizational experiences and driven by narcissistic injury, rage, and shame, contribute to violence and aggression in the workplace. Typically, this involves workers who feel victimized, taken advantage of, mistreated, and treated unjustly by managers, executives, and often the public (external constituents, citizens, legislators). To this experience is added a sense of marginally controlled chaos that promotes anxiety.

In Part 2, we discuss less overtly dramatic but nevertheless destructive organizational violence that contributes to oppressive and persecutory experience. In particular, we find that irrational and psychologically defensive behavior fuels interpersonal and group dynamics that devolve into destructive actions. Elements of organizations often taken for granted, such as structure and strategy, are found to contain unconscious individual and group motivations and destructive psychodynamics. Dynamics such as these contain elements of moral violence and a subtext of command and control demanding unquestioning submission to authority. To these considerations may be added the implicit violence resident within continuous organizational change where what is changed or eliminated requires organization members to continuously adjust to feelings of chaotic, threatening, and anxiety ridden change.

Defective containment (as previously discussed in Chapter 5) that results in psychological regression often contributes to destructive human relations, particularly where no interventions or reconciliations are attempted or in incidences where they are rejected by management. Whenever organizational members and their leaders resist knowing what is wrong, attempts to promote reflective learning fail and workplace culture collapses into paranoid and schizoid shared experience. This unbounded and uncontained experience in the workplace produces disintegration into moral and, at times, physical violence. The following chapters explore moral violence, chaos and complexity, and violence and aggression at work. We begin by exploring the moral violence of emotionally abusive organizations.

6

Moral Violence

Omnipotence describes a defensive wish, buried in every psyche, that one will have a perfect world, will prevail over time, death, and the other— and that coercion can succeed.

Benjamin, Like Subjects, Love Objects

Human aggression is most dangerous when it is attached to two great absolutarian psychological constellations: the grandiose self and the archaic omnipotent object.

Kohut, "Thoughts on Narcissism and Narcissistic Rage,"
The Psychoanalytic Study of the Child, *Vol. 27*

From now on the subject says "Hullo object! I destroyed you. I love you. You have value for me because of your survival of my destruction of you. While I am loving you I am all the time destroying you in (unconscious) fantasy."

Winnicott, Playing and Reality

In this chapter, we inquire into the routine, taken-for-granted, and even banal qualities of organization experienced by members as emotionally abusive. Following Michael Eigen (1996) in his book *Psychic Deadness,* we refer to emotional abuse in the workplace as *moral violence.* In this chapter we ask: Is the workplace filled with moral violence? Is it dominated by a culture that is emotionally and psychologically deadening, numbing, or brutal? Are there certain attributes and assumptions linked to these experiences, such as the destruction of reflectivity and learning from experience? Do leaders and followers co-produce the sort of organizational culture in which interpersonal and intra-organizational acts of moral violence are tacitly condoned? What role, if any, does power and hierarchy with its implicit values of dominance and submission play in promoting acts of moral violence? We analyze these issues by using a perspective informed by psychoanalytic object-relations theory (Greenberg & Mitchell, 1983; Ogden, 1989) and to a lesser degree self-psychology (Kohut, 1977, 1984).

We begin by presenting three foundational assumptions. First, twenty-first-century organizations (public, private, and non-profit) are stressful places to work. This is particularly the case in countries where stress increases as a consequence of citizens', clients', and customers' demands, financial pressures to "make the numbers," and an increasing emphasis on public accountability alongside deregulation of services and industry. Additionally, organizational change in the form of downsizing and reengineering, serves to create distressing experience. In sum, pressures from without and pressures from within organizations, when combined with ill-conceived forms of organizational change in the service of adaptation, create a stressful workplace. Many organizations and executives, while offering the promise of self-fulfillment to workers, more often present a difficult to understand and manage context, filled with marginally controlled events that lead to the experience of stress.

Second, organizations are comprised of individuals in positions of authority with varying degrees of self-esteem and self-cohesion from "good enough" to deficient and from healthy to excessively narcissistic. We find that the presence of moral violence within the workplace is shaped by a combination of hierarchic social structures of dominance and submission and narcissistic executives who are supported by compliant and idealizing subordinates. These leaders compensate for self deficits and inner emptiness (narcissistic deficits) by striving to occupy positions of inordinate power and authority and by demanding the devotion, admiration, and loyalty of followers. The fact that individual leaders with excessive narcissism (and self-deficits) shape organizational cultures, strategies, and decision making, in often destructive and pathological ways, is well established (Zaleznik & Kets de Vries, 1975; Kets de Vries & Miller, 1984; Schwartz, 1991; Kernberg, 1998; Czander, 1993; Diamond, 1993; Allcorn & Diamond, 1997; Gabriel, 1999; Kets de Vries, 2001; Stein, 2001; Allcorn, 2002; Post, 2004).

Third, the combination of an abundance of workplace stress and individuals in senior leadership positions with excessive narcissism substantially increases the likelihood of psychological regression within these individuals and their organizations (Diamond, 1993; Kernberg, 1998). This regression introduces an array of highly energized and compulsively relied upon psychological defenses that, while serving as coping mechanisms for leaders, create destructive and pathological outcomes that emotionally harm participants and diminish their ability to achieve organizational success. These potentially avoidable and hard to resolve operating problems arising from leaders (and tacitly supported by organizational members) may, in turn, further increase the experience of stress and reliance upon defensive routines and destructive enactments. This toxic mix of defensive strategies and destructive outcomes is well established in the literature (Horney, 1950; Levinson, 1957; Zaleznik & Kets de Vries, 1975; Kets de Vries & Miller, 1984; Baum, 1987; Diamond, 1993; Czander, 1993; Allcorn & Diamond, 1997; Gabriel, 1999).

These foundational assumptions lead us to the following argument: moral violence in organizations is structured around leadership, the particular character of leader-follower relations, and the underlying feature of transference as the shared emotions between them (discussed at the conclusion of this chapter). We explore leadership as a part of a larger issue of power and authority comprised of conscious and unconscious relational dynamics between participants with a shared goal or mission. In brief, moral violence in organizations is a manifestation of leader-follower psychodynamics. These characteristically involve emotional and cognitive processes of defensive splitting of self and other into good or bad, all or nothing, black or white, and for and against categories. Splitting includes the act of introjecting and projecting experiences of self and other, processes of taking-in and putting-out self and other representations. Acts of introjecting and projecting are at the heart of emotional attachment between human beings and with organizations and their leaders. Attachment behavior encompasses the psychodynamics of organizational members in moving to form identifications with the organizational ideal (Schwartz, 1991). These typical psychological processes take a destructive turn toward increased moral violence. We begin by elaborating the concept of moral violence in the workplace.

Organizations as a Context for Violence

We define moral violence as abusive, sadistic, and oppressive treatment that results in the emotional trauma, dehumanization, and demoralization of organizational members. A case in point is organizational reengineering, downsizing, or right-sizing. These management actions are by now universally embraced as standard practices supposedly necessary to save the organization from faltering performance, failure, bankruptcy, and death. Saving the organization from its excesses by "cutting the fat" is seen as necessary and justified and as fulfilling a higher moral and ethical calling as represented by protecting the jobs of the remaining employees, value for stockholders, and even the larger community that draws substance from it. These management acts, while introducing a real sense of dread and threat for employees, are also paradoxically understood, if not rationalized, as a "good." Much the same is said for attacks upon individual employees, who are bullied, threatened, manipulated, intimidated, and publicly humiliated. We, as witnesses to moral violence, might ask: "What did he or she do to deserve this?" Corporate might respond with defensive rationalization such as, "Running a tight ship is important." "Discipline must be maintained." In other words, reminicent of military combat, management must destroy the organization to save it.

Moral violence must be understood to reside within a context that, despite its destructive properties, seems oddly normal and expected. It may be experienced as part of a daily routine that is unavoidable and something that must be lived through and tolerated. Within this context, self-integrity is compromised and depersonalization emerges with its accompanying diminishment of passion, creativity, adventure, and play. To survive, one conforms, becoming compliant and submissive. The organizational culture becomes one that values false self-representation and unawareness over true self, authenticity, and consciousness.

Harmful and destructive assaults on individual integrity are encountered during childhood and prior to joining the workforce. Instances of not good enough or more overtly abusive parenting are emotionally traumatizing. Also, as the previous chapter on organizations as defective containers indicated, membership in groups and organizations is known to produce psychological regression in adults. This observation reinforces the potential for abusive relationships in the workplace. And, while adults in the workforce are not children, the workplace is filled with equally abusive and destructive, but also familiar, patterns of behavior that dehumanize, depersonalize, and infantilize employees.

Workers submit or risk losing their jobs. Rationalizing submission may be, therefore, a prerequisite to maintaining employment (thereby sustaining attachment). In particular, workers who find that sadistic-masochistic relational patterns at work are familiar configurations of childhood abuse and neglect may have well established psychological defenses already in place. For these individuals, love and attachment are fused with abuse and sadism; workplace abuse is not merely tolerated, it may be embraced (Masterson, 1988). Love and hate are forms of object attachment. Our explanation for emotional abuse in the workplace cannot be as simple as solely blaming the leadership of the culture. The followers also seem to reinforce and perpetuate this vicious cycle of what Eigen (1996) calls psychic deadness.

Moral violence in organizations resides with the punishing nature of individual-organizational attachments, what Benjamin (1988) calls "the problem of domination" and the presence of narcissistic and persecutory emotional bonds (transference) between individual members and their organizational leadership (Diamond, 1997; Kernberg, 1998; Kets de Vries, 2001). In cases such as these, narcissistic attachments are organized around unconscious demands for self and other aggrandizement and embellishment, while persecutory attachments are shaped by perpetrator and victim (sadistic-masochistic) experiences. In particular, transference of past experiences and accompanying feelings associated with abuse and parental failures are triggered by the presence of unconsciously familiar organizational dynamics. Also, emotional bonds and transference dynamics are understood as a predominant feature of hierarchically structured human relations. We define transference (discussed at length in Chapter 9) as the "displacement of patterns of feelings, thoughts, and behavior, originally experienced in relation to significant figures during childhood, onto a person involved in a current interpersonal relationship" (Moore & Fine, 1990, p. 196; Diamond & Allcorn, 2003).

Cultures of moral violence are discovered by observing the interpersonal (intrapersonal and intersubjective) relations between participants that comprise dominance and submission. They are also revealed by experiencing transference and countertransference dynamics and by learning from the victims' narratives and stories that often include themes of oppression and persecution. Workers frequently portray their government agencies and companies as cruel and violent. In so doing, they are not, typically, implying that people physically harm or assault one another. They are, however, indicating their experience of emotional assault and the potential for ongoing destructive interpersonal transgressions. More specifically, they are referring to oppressive leadership, management by intimidation, and a lack of mutual respect, recognition, and trust. The result is that victims are conveying a form of emotional abuse, which renders them depersonalized, traumatized, broken and split apart, and psychologically deadened.

Organizations as Morally Violent Settings

Most organizations and their participants move in and out of morally violent phases. Moral violence can take the shape of mass terminations, public humiliations, or simply unplanned and non-participatory reorganizations and change. Actions such as these are often viewed as so routine as to constitute "taken for granted" elements of organizational culture (Schein, 1985). Much can be learned when organization members articulate workplace experiences filled with violent images and metaphors. "It's a jungle out there!" "Keep your head down!" "Watch your back!" "Cover your ass!" Consultants are often referred to as "terminators" and "hatchet men."

These are not mere signifiers of fantasy. Rather they are rooted in collective experiences and observations.

The following vignettes provide perspectives that inform our understanding of moral violence in the workplace. These vignettes share in common the sense that management sees itself as morally and ethically justified in taking these actions. Consequently, emotionally traumatized workers come to share a profound sense of alienation, helplessness, and submission. Minimized and objectified, these workers experience themselves as bullied, threatened, and intimidated. The creative meaning, identity, self-worth, and personal satisfaction of human work vanishes when inordinate power and control coerce subordination, producing anxiety and paranoia among workers.

Vignettes of Moral Violence

An internal consultant to a large health care organization remarked, "My experience at Health West [fictional name] was one of encountering a culture filled with violence. That is, if I said it was dangerous to work there, few [employees] would disagree." The potential for violent outcomes had a pervasive quality, one that filled the organization with a sense of danger. "I was told not to put anything in email or phone messages that I did not want to have forwarded throughout the organization, especially to the highest levels."

A discussion with the administrative assistant who supported the president of a division of this organization was also revealing. She reported that during her eighteen months of tenure, almost everyone else had left. She was, in fact, reporting to a new division president, the third in as many years. People feared and mistrusted each other, yet their task responsibilities were interdependent. One recently departed employee from the same organization wrote, "Most people that work for Paul [the CEO] quit or get fired. Paul can't tolerate anyone smarter than he is and most people are smarter, so he fires them because of his ego or they quit because Health West is one of the most messed up companies on planet earth. Their stock will soon be trading via pink sheets." Apparently many at Health West found that they could not be themselves, particularly if being oneself (maintaining self-integrity and authenticity) meant contradicting Paul's need for security, control, aggrandizement, and omnipotence. However, being compliant and inauthentic has emotional and organizational costs. On the organizational side, shared learning becomes problematic and for the individual the emotional dimension is split off from the real self to create a compliant deadened self-experience largely devoid of creativity, innovation, learning, play, passion and emotion.

In another instance, a colleague shared his experience with a public agency. Fifteen top managers, during a review of the organization's history, described their situation for the last few years as one in which their past director had created a group of favorites who were awarded promotions and generous raises. Those who did not support the director's "larger than life view of herself" did not receive promotions or raises despite their seniority and professional experience. Stories were told about people banished to basement offices and others "living in fox holes." The members of the "out group" were discriminated against and attacked by the director and her "in group" of loyal followers. Paradoxically, it was also mentioned that the director and her "in group" came to feel that they were under attack from the "out group." This intergroup conflict went on for years. It was finally surfaced in a contained setting. The two groups were observed sitting on opposite sides of the table. Efforts to get their historical antagonism out in the open created a cathartic resonance. Group members reached across the table to make contact with each other. This was a humanizing act in contrast to a dehumanizing and depersonalizing historical split between the members of the two groups (in and out groups). The violence that resided within the organizational split created by the director's personal needs had cut both ways. As one worker said, "Everyone it turned out felt beat up and abused."

At DPS (another public organization) the director was known for handing out lapel pins to loyal employees who "worked hard, took directives without question, and never complained." Employees were called into his office where he commended them for their performance and pinned upon them the agency lapel pin. Ironically, workers who received the pin removed it as soon as possible after leaving his office and before being seen by their peers. The pin identified them with the director, and it was generally felt that those who wore the pin were sycophants. The same director was also well known for his style of management by intimidation and humiliation. When employees made "mistakes" or "questioned his authority," he would call them into his office. Upon their arrival, he would ask them to step out into the hallway where he proceeded to openly and loudly verbally abuse them in front of their colleagues. One can imagine how his lambasted victims experienced these assaults. It is easy to imagine that employees at this agency felt oppressed by their compliance and fearful of critical thinking and legitimate self-expression.

In addition, we have encountered instances where oppressive stress and the persecutory experience have manifested in physical symptoms, such as intestinal distress, ulcers, restlessness, insomnia, drugs, and alcohol abuse.

For instance, a police department hired a new chief who began his work with a mandate for radical and immediate change from traditional to community policing. He did not, however, provide his newly acquired police department with a plan for organizational change. Rather, he arbitrarily imposed new rules, regulations, and demands for a radically different culture. Shortly after arriving, he removed the sign that read "Police Department" and replaced it with one that read "Service Department." This left officers in an anxious, alienated, and enraged state filled with ambiguity and uncertainty that, depending upon circumstances, endangered them and their fellow officers. For example, there existed uncertainty around when and in what sorts of predicaments police officers could draw their weapons. Patrol cars were taken away from many officers and replaced by bicycles. Predictably, this arbitrary use of power and authority and concomitant ambiguities about performing policing duties were distressing. Consequences for incorrectly second guessing the chief often manifested in psychosomatic symptoms. Structure and authority can be as much a tool of oppression and terror as it can be a comforting and clarifying tool of leadership. Regardless of whether or not officers were inclined or favorable toward community policing, the abusive and unilateral manner in which it was introduced rendered it unsuccessful and tragic.

What about the stubbornly persistent, repetitive, and impulsive phenomenon of reorganization in governmental institutions? Public agencies are routinely faced with a revolving door of politically appointed directors, each presuming to change the agency. Such seemingly automatic strategy changes are often experienced by staff as an assault. Employees see themselves as being told, "Despite your years of knowledge and experience with the agency, you have been doing it all wrong." It seems worth asking: If institutional change represents disrespect and emotional abuse for individual members, how much change and loss can workers take before they feel numb, broken down, and cynical? These public servants are, after all, human and experience these personally and politically motivated changes as an insult to their self-worth and self-competence. They are frequently committed to the espoused mission and values of their agencies. Their sense of affiliation and purpose is often wound up with the agency's mandate. Over time, these repeated assaults of imposed and unilateral change create an overarching experience of moral violence, a culture (of values, assumptions, and rules) experienced and perceived as abusive and harmful to participants and their sense of work's meaning and their well-being.

Understanding the Origins and Perpetuation
of Moral Violence in Organizations

A psychoanalytic perspective of organizations requires understanding the nature of leader-follower relations, individual-organizational attachments, and the destructive proclivities these relational dynamics contain. These attachments, at times, may be compensatory and defensive and aimed at controlling self-experience by using others in the service of acquiring narcissistic sustenance. In particular, hierarchic organizational structures often contain deeply embedded dominance and submission issues that fuel unconscious (self and other) conflicts centered on autonomy and dependency and recognition and self-assertion that have their origins in infancy and childhood (Winnicott, 1965). Adverse workplace experience promotes psychological regression and transference where past experience enters the collective present in ways that are not simply counterproductive, but also at times destructive.

Individual-Organizational Attachments:
Hierarchic Dominance and Submission

People attach themselves, emotionally and psychologically, to their leaders, professional careers, and organizations. Frequently, the quality of these attachments is positive and generates a sense of satisfaction and gratification that comes from affiliation with a group or institution larger than one's self (Diamond, 1993). Yet the need for affiliation and belonging has to be balanced with sufficient autonomy and independence (Diamond and Allcorn, 1987).

Benjamin (1988) calls this striving for balance the "paradox of recognition," where asserting the self and recognition of the other are experienced simultaneously. An absence of this tension, Benjamin argues, brings to our attention that dominance and submission are the governing pattern of human relations. Thus, subordinates within the hierarchic structure of superior/subordinate relations may be treated as non-persons rather than as persons (Ogden, 1989). This depersonalized treatment of the other represents a collapse of tensions between self and object and an incapacity for mutual recognition. Autonomy and independence are diminished. Submission and compliance take hold and awareness of the self eventually may vanish. In the above vignettes, we find that destructive organizational and individual psychodynamics prevail. Participants experience themselves as under attack by organizational leadership. This predominant pattern of depersonalization in leader-follower relations is perpetuated by an unconscious collusion (transference and countertransference) between organizational participants. Benjamin (1988) writes, "If I completely control the other, then the other ceases to exist and if the other completely controls me, then I cease to exist. A condition of our own independent existence is recognizing the other. True independence means sustaining the essential tension of these contradictory impulses; that is, both asserting the self and recognizing the other" (p. 53).

In organizations, this essential tension is vulnerable to the narcissistic and paranoid proclivities of leaders and their anxiously idealizing and compliant followers. One could say that both the compliant and the resistant employees are symbolically "killed off" in one way or the other. They are psychically dead. In desperation, the resistant employee may leave, paying a personal and professional cost. However, he or she may do so with self-cohesion and dignity intact, while those who remain are consumed by submission.

For Benjamin (1988), "the root of domination lies in the breakdown of tension between self and other" (p. 55). Certainly, it can be argued, these are conditions that occur in many relationships, not simply those in organizations. However, in formal hierarchic organizations, dominance and submission are often implicit, unmentionable values of organizational culture and leadership as well as structures that frequently constrain and define the character of human relations. Consequently, it is taboo to talk about. These oppressive relational patterns are frequently rendered unconscious over time, concealing the values and assumptions of an organizational culture of narcissism in which hierarchic structure is replaced by ideology and the arbitrary abuse of power and authority.

Of course, there are degrees of dominance and submission from one organization to another. Our immediate concern is acknowledging the extent to which dominance and submission prevail in the organizational culture and are practiced by the organizational leadership as exemplified in the vignettes. Dominance and submission are frequently the relational and ideological norm of modern organizations, and where these patterns coexist, psychological splitting and moral violence are not far away.

Psychological Splitting, Projection, Introjection and the Origins of Moral Violence

As we discussed at length in Chapter 5, regressive forces are often at play in organizations. Organizational structure and mission, one might assume, absorb and contain aggression where people feel empowered and authorized to do their work. However, it is also the case that hierarchic structures frequently endow those at the top with inordinate power and authority. This power, given the narcissistic and expansive proclivities of executives, often reinforces dominance and submission as a pattern for human relations. Where dominance and submission prevail, fear, mistrust, and paranoia shape the intersubjective character of self and other relations at work. Consequently, object-to-object relations (the paranoid-schizoid mode of experience) in contrast with subject-to-subject relations (the depressive mode of experience) become the standard configuration. Suspicious black or white and all or nothing thoughts arise from this experience in which one views and treats others as depersonalized and dehumanized objects. Psychological splitting and projection are contributors to this outcome. This is the psychodynamic reframing of Immanuel Kant's (1929) categorical imperative of moral law and pure reasoning. Unlike Kantian philosophy, morality rooted in practical reason is not in opposition to human passions and character. Rather, it is motivated by desire and thereby requires emotional attunement to self and other in order that sufficient psychological distancing can occur in support of "self-interested" and "other-regarding" motives (Wallwork, 1991). Moral violence describes this repressed and unconscious nature of abusive and instrumental treatment of others in a manner consistent with psychoanalytic theory and ethics. Unconscious psychological splitting, dissociation, and depersonalization of oneself and others contradict the capacity for reflection and self-consciousness. Moral violence may then be understood as a form of enactment, whereby one acts automatically and unconsciously on a destructive impulse rather than merely entertaining harmful acts of brutality. The dehumanized object may be acted upon safely and without moral conscience. Reliance upon splitting as a defense also has implications for the perpetrator of moral violence.

Melanie Klein (1975b) described the combined splitting of the ego and of the object as the "impoverishment of the ego" whereby the individual engages in the "dispersal of emotions" through processes of introjection and projection of good and bad part-objects. Similarly, Eigen (1996) warns that excessive splitting fosters "psychic deadness" and the incapacity to process experience. The ability to contain and internally digest ambivalent and contrary emotions and ideas is lost. Splitting of the self and object is therefore ultimately an ineffectual defense against destructive psychic forces and persecutory anxieties. Similar to dissociation, splitting leads to taking leave of one's emotional floor and of the capacity to experience self-contained emotions. This psychic escapism renders oneself emotionally numb and without a core awareness of self and other. The executive may also be destroyed. These phenomena have obvious implications for the workplace culture.

Within many organizations, dominance and submission are a governing ideology and moral violence prevails. The predominant pattern of vertical and horizontal relations comprises a depersonalizing and dehumanizing character devoid of meaning, self-assertion, and recognition of the other. Employees are transformed into numbers, human resources, and organizational "fat." Routine organizational dynamics may conceal human tragedy. Primitive psychic and personal survival considerations dominate intrapsychic and interpersonal agendas. Leaders who remove the "fat" and the individuals who are the "fat" as well as those who remain may suffer psychic deadening for different reasons. Everyone becomes a victim, a loser.

Acknowledging psychic deadness as a manifestation of moral violence and hierarchic dominance at work leads to an inquiry of what kinds of leaders and self-experience contribute to the creation, reinforcement, and perpetuation of moral violence. Kohut's (1972, 1984) self-psychology and his notions of narcissistic rage and disorders of the self that arise from inadequate parental mirroring (or what Winnicott [1965, pp. 43–46] calls a failure of the "holding environment") provide additional insights.

Narcissistic Rage and the Shame-Prone Individual

Narcissistic rage arises from individual and collective histories of abuse, deficiencies of warmth, safety, and love, and injustices and shame. Many psychoanalytic writers on leadership and organizations point to excessive and malignant narcissism as destructive and dysfunctional and as contributing to vindictiveness, hubris, and, in some instances, the short-lived success of organizations (Kets de Vries, 1984, 2001; Schwartz, 1991; Diamond, 1993; Allcorn & Diamond, 1997; Kernberg, 1998).

Heinz Kohut (1972) contributes to our understanding by examining the relationship between infantile narcissism, self-cohesion, and self-esteem. He asserts that narcissistic deficiencies lead to narcissistic rage as if the adult were on an unconscious quest for that which was absent in childhood. Their unconscious search may manifest itself as an expansive and frequently imposing and dominant personality. Kohut (1972) writes, "And the most gruesome human destructiveness is encountered not in the form of wild, regressive, and primitive behavior, but in the form of orderly and organized activities in which perpetrator's destructiveness is alloyed with absolutarian convictions about their greatness and with the devotion to archaic omnipotent figures" (p. 378).

Concealed behind the projection of greatness and omnipotence common to narcissism are mental splits between emotionally charged and volatile, opposing parts of self-experience. And beneath the split and torn apart self are feelings of shame and injustice that become the experiential core of violent attacks. Behind the mask of omnipotence may well reside a face of impotence and insecurity. If colleagues were only to see and know the narcissism of these executives, they would find someone who questions his or her self-worth and capacity for the love of others, along with a deeper sense of shame. Kohut (1972) writes,

> The shame-prone individual who is ready to experience setbacks as narcissistic injuries and to respond to them with insatiable rage does not recognize his opponent as a center of independent initiative with whom he happens to be at cross-purposes. Aggressions employed in the pursuit of maturely experienced causes are not limitless. However, vigorously mobilized, their goal is definite: the defeat of the enemy who blocks the way to a cherished goal. The narcissistically injured, on the other hand, cannot rest until he has blotted out a vaguely experienced offender who dared to oppose him, to disagree with him, or to outshine him. (p. 385)

This description jibes with the motivational force of the executives discussed. Patterns of narcissistic rage, psychological splitting, and projection are observable through the participation and experience of transference dynamics in organizations (Diamond & Allcorn, 2003). These intersubjective patterns of self-object relations are discernible in at least four experiential dimensions: mirroring, idealizing, twinship, and persecutory. These experiences are not mutually exclusive. They are each linked in some way to narcissism and narcissistic processes as a predominant feature of human relations in the context of organizational cultures of moral violence.

Relational Patterns of Narcissism and Moral Violence

Individual narcissism contributes to moral violence in the workplace, where dominance and submission shape horizontal and vertical interactions behind a veil of rational organization. These experiences of emotional attachment are important to understand and contribute to understanding the underlying psychodynamics of moral violence in the workplace.

Mirroring

Mirroring relationships are indicative of directors and executives at the top of many organizations, such as those described in our vignettes. These psychologically defensive executives strive to protect their own grandiosity. They surround themselves with people who mirror their expansive self-image and their insatiable needs for admiration and aggrandizement. Whereas the mirroring affect is absent in the other executive, narcissistic rage may surface and the consequences for fellow workers are usually harmful and dehumanizing. Failure to idealize this leader has its consequences.

Idealizing

Idealizing relationships help to explain follower experience where submission becomes a prominent aspect of work life. Idealizing desires are an essential component of narcissistic transferences. In the case of idealizing transferences of emotion, we observe loyal and admiring subordinates who find safety and comfort in identifying with their narcissistic executive. Often narcissistically wounded, these workers find temporary solace and protection in their proximity to leadership. They have an uncanny sensitivity to the self-serving demands and wishes of the executive. Idealizing followers are, therefore, intimately linked with mirroring leaders, where one dimension of the dyad cannot survive without the other.

Twinship

Another manifestation of narcissistic mirroring is the twinship transferences sometimes referred to as alter-ego (Kohut, 1977, 1984). Twinship relationships generate emotional needs for merger, affiliation, and belonging to groups or organizations of like-minded others. While some level of joining with those who think and act similarly is an avenue for healthy contact and emotional attachment and association, there is a vulnerability to group think (Janus, 1982), homogeneity, and suppression of differences and individuality. As long as twinship dynamics govern interpersonal relations, there will be a minimization of tensions and a limited capacity for containing opposing ideas and feelings within a group or organization. Maintaining the paradox of mutual recognition between participants is unlikely when there are excessive demands for twinship. Similar to mirroring and idealizing exchanges of emotion, twinship supports and perpetuates dominant and submissive patterns of group action that defensively follow the dictates of narcissistic culture and leadership.

Persecution

Finally, persecutory transferences of emotion are particularly common in organizations shaped by acts of moral violence where workers experience a collective sense of shame and unjust and disrespectful treatment. Similar to the above three dimensions of transference, persecutory relationships are shaped by psychological splitting and narcissistic injury out of which arises a perceptual world of enemies and allies and a social structure of us against them. In these cases, narcissistic injuries to self-esteem combine with deeper feelings of shame and self-doubt. These workers experience themselves as unrecognized (by authorities) as contributors and, therefore, devalued and not recognized as individuals, but rather as things or objects. Decisions that directly affect them are made without their input. Hence, they experience powerlessness and feel taken-for-granted, discarded, and treated as objects rather than subjects. In some cases, rage is precariously contained, and for some, psychic deadness and numbing results.

Emotional Bonds at Work

Transference patterns are present in the workplace. Predominance of one or several of these transference dynamics may be found to contribute to distorted communications, conflicts, and various forms of destructive behavior. The psychodynamics of hierarchy, dominance and submission, psychological regression and splitting, and these four types of relational transference constitute the elements of moral violence in organizations. Not wanting to lose their jobs, fearful of retributions, workers of morally violent organizations operate defensively and unconsciously by removing or distancing themselves from their distressing experience of membership. If they could, in fact, experience the emotionally violent nature of these destructive organizations, they might be able to join in reflective dialogue about the destructive elements of their culture and possibly avoid harmful enactments. This, however, is often not plausible unless a crisis emerges in which the institution's survival is perceived to be in jeopardy. What is missing in organizations filled with persistent patterns of moral violence and psychic trauma is sufficient relief from the threat to play and imagination, an intermediate area and potential space for creativity and change. Winnicott's (1971) writings on the "intermediate areas" (transitional objects and transitional phenomena) provide a deeper and concluding insight into moral violence.

All Work and No Play: The Absence of
Potential Space and Cultural Experience

Winnicott's (1971) concept of transitional phenomena acknowledges the essential function of transitional objects in early development and in particular, the early childhood shift from total dependence toward relative independence. Teddy bears, blankets, music, and the like may become transitional childhood objects that cushion the traumatic affect of early recognition of maternal separateness, periodic absences, and loss. Abram (1997) writes, "This necessary developmental journey leads to the use of illusion, the use of symbols, and the use of an object" (p. 311). The use of the object is not left behind as we enter adulthood and careers in and with organizations. On the contrary, it becomes essential to one's emotional wellness, creativity, and quality of life. What would life be like without music, art, literature, humor, sports, and the like?

Play is that transitional area where imagination and creativity exist somewhere between reality and fantasy. It is also in this transitional area that we are able to contain and digest opposing feelings and ideas, something absent in organizational cultures of moral violence. Winnicott explains, "Playing and cultural experiences are things that we do value in a special way; these experiences link the past, present, and the future; they take up time and space. They demand and get our concentrated deliberate attention, deliberate but without too much of the deliberateness of trying" (Winnicott, 1971, p. 109).

Winnicott's (1971) concept of transitional phenomena provides a clue to the riddle of what is missing in the morally violent organization. The absence of transitional space and time leaves no room for workers' play and imagination while institutionalizing either too much reality or too much fantasy (and escape). A workplace without a sense of humor or without the capacity to combine play with work becomes the "facilitative environment" for moral violence. High tech firms, despite the imposing stress of enormous competition and demands for innovation that they face, create a context where one finds employees riding scooters and tossing tiny basketballs into nets. Without the capacity for play, organizations and their leaders are handicapped in their ability to tolerate ambiguity, new ideas, differences of opinion, critical feedback, and worker demands for recognition and respect. As noted earlier, where object-to-object relations (paranoid-schizoid modes of experience) predominate, the absence of transitional objects means that the differentiation between me-and-not-me is at the very least blurred and often missing. As a consequence, the lack of potential space for reflection and holding of complex ideas and feelings results in others becoming frequent containers for projections and projective identifications via splitting.

Conclusion

Moral violence is an underappreciated presence in many workplaces that degrades organizational members and organizational performance. Its basis lies in punishing intrapsychic processes that objectify others and create a fragmented split, a part world of object relations. When organizations are filled with moral violence, problem solving becomes unimaginative and flawed due to the inability to experience the uncertainty of problem setting and assumption testing between participants. Dialogic space is absent as well. Perceptions and experiences are not viewed as worthy of acknowledgment, and learning from experience and reflectivity are unlikely. Defensive routines lead to not recognizing contradictions, tensions, and paradoxical forces. They are denied, disavowed, and suppressed rather than experienced and processed. In particular, empathic attunement seems unavailable to narcissistic leaders whose conscious and/or unconscious view of worker participation and involvement may be limited to their own self-aggrandizement. The lack of "intermediate areas" that contain transitional objects and phenomena where play and imagination exist is a prerequisite for moral violence. Where there is no capacity for the presence of Benjamin's "paradox of recognition," dehumanizing processes of dominance and submission prevail.

We now turn to Chapter 7 where we explore yet another aspect of organizations and leaders as containers for members' emotions and anxieties about unpredictable change and transformation at work. In particular, many aspects of the workplace are constantly changing disrupting workers' sense of form and structure, internally and externally, intra- and interpersonally, intra- and interorganizationally. Beyond that is the more profound experience of organizational chaos and complexity—once again returning to the primitive need for a good enough maternal holding environment and containment in the face of tumult and constant change.

7

Chaos and Complexity

There is no emotional or physical survival of an infant minus environment. To start with, minus environment the infant would fall infinitely. The infant who is held or who is lying in a cot is not aware of being preserved from infinitely falling. In analysis a patient may report a sense of falling, dating from earliest days, but can never report being held at this early stage of development.

D. W. Winnicott, The Maturational Process and the Facilitating Environment

New technologies, such as e-commerce and wireless internet access; globalization; atomization; privatization in the public sector; and natural and man-made catastrophes, are external factors that impact the future of organizations and the meaning of affiliation and employment. This chapter addresses this quandary from the perspectives of chaos, complexity, and psychoanalytic theory. If we accept the premises of chaos and complexity theories on the high level of uncertainty and unpredictability, then what are the psychological and emotional prerequisites for organizational membership? How does one survive the anxieties and potential violence resident in chaotic change? Will individual ego strength and the integrity of the core self permit successful personal adaptation and the maintenance of personal boundaries for leaders standing at the edge of chaos?

In our view, applied object relations theory is well-suited to the task of responding to this ever present sense of threat to self and organization that arises from having to submit oneself to the loss, threats, and challenges of dealing with omnipresent change (Greenberg & Mitchell, 1983; Modell, 1984; Ogden, 1989). An object relational theory of self provides a deeper comprehension of the violence and tumult inherent in chaotic change.

Leaders and their organizations are faced with perpetual adaptation to external and internal threats. This constant need to change promotes for many organization members existential anxiety akin to Winnicott's (1965) description of "infinite falling." "Am I going to be dropped by my organization or leader? Do I have confidence in the leadership's capacity to manage the environment so we do not collapse?" Given these workplace, threats we have to ask: What is the future of organizational membership, affiliation, and belonging? Will the maternal holding function of leadership and organizational culture collapse under pressure?

From the perspective of chaos and complexity theories, organizations are nonlinear adaptive feedback networks that operate far from equilibrium (Stacey, 1996). Yet, these networks are often led and managed as bureaucratic structures as though they exist in stable states. If we are to better understand this contradictory phenomenon, a reconceptualization of organizations as nonlinear, adaptive feedback networks requires a deeper comprehension of individual, group, and organizational adaptive and maturational dynamics. Future leaders and organizational participants need to embrace a new action strategy of organized disorder that requires "good-enough" individual development, maturation, and integrated core self. The ability to humanely and effectively lead and manage organized complexity and chaos will depend upon the authenticity and the capability of leaders to promote "good-enough" organizational cultures.

Observations on the Changing Workplace

As we enter the twenty-first century, many companies and public agencies are experimenting with bottom-up processes for strategic planning and organizational change. In some instances, organizational members who are close to their constituents and customers and further down hierarchic structures are affecting planning and corporate/agency direction. Organizational vision and policy implementation are becoming better integrated via cross-functional teams and bottom-up processes of participation and double-loop learning. The concept of double-loop learning refers to the capacity to change based on feedback contrary to the status-quo despite having to rethink and question previously held assumptions (values, norms, and policies) and practices.

One can, however, increasingly observe countercultural, horizontal, and bottom-up organizational activities that permit a response to chaotic processes of social, political, and economic change. Innovative work processes, such as cross-functional teams and team-based strategic planning, are becoming common. Strategies that foster greater reflectivity and the capacity for double-loop learning create greater adaptation to complex landscapes and unpredictable futures. However, despite attempts at more inclusive problem solving and decision making, organizational hierarchies and divisional silos persist. Vision and policies are continually set at higher levels than where the work with citizens, customers, and constituents takes place. Organization members are many times loosely coupled, and they often work within defended domains that block sharing. Innovative and collaborative planning that comes with genuine delegation of authority and power from the top may ironically exist only as a consequence of draconian executive acts of downsizing, reengineering, and right-sizing. Many workers in public and private sector organizations also resist change, preferring to remain attached to routine and familiar hierarchical structures of power and authority. In some industries, corporate recruiters place increasing weight on psychological testing and rigorous interviewing. They are searching for the best fit with their corporate culture. In some instances, these corporate cultures assume a cult-like quality, tacitly encouraging homogeneity and predictability, sacrificing individual autonomy, creativity, and adeptness.

Chaos and complexity are phenomena that exist both inside and outside of self and organization. However, at an intrapersonal level of experience, these states are more often associated with primitive anxieties and emotional disorder. Not surprisingly, psychological regression and associated anxieties over loss of control and uncertainty are often linked to these personal experiences of chaos and complexity. The notion of organized disorder best exemplifies the psychological challenge and contradiction of living and working with chaos and complexity. This concept signifies the human experience of disorder in an organized context.

Adaptation to and planning for change become a collective struggle of making sense out of the non-sense of complexity. Complexity and chaos theorists characterize organizations as adaptive feedback networks that are (1) nonlinear, such that there is no proportionality between cause and effect; (2) fractal, such that measurement is scale dependent and concepts are indeterminate; (3) recursive between scale levels, such that it is easy to get lost; (4) sensitive to initial conditions, such that the system is experienced as volatile; (5) replete with feedback loops and potential bifurcation points; and (6) subject to emergence (Lissack, 1999).

These new assumptions include a recognition that creativity and innovation emerge out of disorder and chaos. Managing at the edge of chaos implies learning in the here-and-now to be creative and innovative. The requisite cognitive and emotional skills of reflective practice (Argyris & Schon, 1996) and effective boundary management between people and between organizations are however rarely observed in practice (Diamond, Allcorn, & Stein, 2004). Managing at the edge requires adaptive feedback networks that function as evolving and emerging systems (Stacey, 1996). Organizations with ambiguous boundaries and fluid strategies and structures are becoming more typical when observed in the context of their task environments.

Companies, government agencies, and healthcare organizations are attempting to adapt to chaos and complexity. As they engage in bottom-up processes of strategic planning, they find that complex learning can be derived from tension and disorder. Members find they have to trust their unfamiliar experience of their emergent organization (Stacey, 1996). That is, evolving and changing strategies and structures are being transformed to better fit the growing complexity and chaos of the operating context. Organizational participants have to overcome their anxieties that are associated with unknowable outcomes. Leaders and managers have to move closer to the edge of chaos while creating an organization that is a good-enough holding environment positioned in a perpetual transitional space between order and chaos (Winnicott, 1971).

The Meaning of Organized Disorder

As a framework for thinking about twenty-first century organizations, organized disorder describes a perpetual, paradoxical state of affairs confronting businesses, government agencies, and healthcare systems. While organized disorder represents the objective reality of organized life, it also signifies psychological reality and human experience that become limiting factors in organizing strategies and developing the means to adapt to the changing task environment. If one embraces the disorder of organizational life and at the same time acknowledges and searches for organized patterns and emerging structures, then one can construct action strategies.

Organized disorder is located at the conceptual space between organizations and their complex and chaotic task environments. It is a psychological space that is transitional in nature and contains potential space (Winnicott, 1971) from which creativity and innovation can emerge. Organized disorder is characterized by nonlinear modes of interaction at multiple levels of analysis. These include dynamic relationships between an organization and its environment and across groups, roles, and interpersonal relationships. Organized disorder is fundamentally a function of boundary maintenance in the midst of chaos. As an action strategy, it differs from Stacey's (1996) concept of bounded instability, which is more narrowly a description of the state of affairs.

As an individual and organizational theory of action, organized disorder assumes integrated, strategic thinking that enables effective management of unstable and impermanent boundaries. And, despite the nature of what chaos and complexity theorists describe as evolving and emerging (organizational) structures of fitness to transmuting landscapes, organized disorder assumes goal-oriented and mission-driven practice. In other words, it is plausible to manage unpredictable task environments, markets, and hierarchies if the basic assumptions and practices of managers and leaders are transformed.

Envisioning the future must embrace and be balanced with a more reflective and insightful focus on the present and the here-and-now of theory and practice. Theoretical and practical adjustment to the dialectical nature of tensions between stability and disorder must occur. Ethical principles of honesty, openness, and candidness will have to become essential operating doctrines. Paying attention to psychological reality and the significance of organizational perceptions will become increasingly valued.

At a micro level and within institutions, organized disorder signifies a loosening of controls from the top-down. It minimizes hierarchies thereby minimizing psychological defensiveness that often leads to over-controlling of others and their work. Structure becomes less often an unwitting outcome of social defenses and more often a conscious strategy for adaptation to constantly changing environments. Organized disorder may be viewed as a form of play. It is a psychological space where reality, fantasy, culture, and imagination emerge. This playful regression stands in stark contrast to more typically destructive and counterproductive manifestations of regression at work. It reduces actions driven by unconscious fantasies, persecutory anxieties, and anxiety associated with relinquishing control over their roles, tasks, authority, and expertise in a manner that suggests that members can collaborate with each other regardless of status and position.

In sum, organized disorder is a productive alternative to destructive, defensive, and regressive actions often taken in response to hard to manage anxieties. It is a strategy not only for addressing moral violence in the workplace but also for managing tensions between order and chaos. Participants focus in the present and here-and-now of reflective practice and double-loop learning.

In his article, "Chaos, Complexity, and Psychoanalysis," Miller (1999) argues "that in complexity theory, the transitional chaotic phase is replaced with the idea that dynamic, living systems exist and maintain themselves at the edge of chaos, balancing themselves between predictable order and chaos. The many different elements that make up a complex system interact with one another and with their environments in such intricate ways that a stable yet constantly evolving order emerges" (p. 358). Butz (1997) describes dynamic systems as evolving through four states: (1) stability, (2) bifurcation, (3) chaos or complexity, and (4) a new and more complex adaptive order. As the instability of a system grows, it enters what appears to be a chaotic state. The system looks chaotic because on the local level you cannot predict the next state of the system. Yet, there is an underlying order that emerges that does not derive directly (linearly) from the previous state of the system. These perspectives are better understood by exploring the psychodynamic foundations of adaptive feedback networks located in the emergence of self and self-object relations. What are the psychological requisites of social character for nonlinear adaptive feedback networks and the ability to embrace organized disorder?

According to Ogden (1989), we begin life in a pre-verbal, pre-symbolic, and sensual state of attachment he calls autistic-contiguous. As we discussed in earlier chapters, it is a stable state of oneness and undifferentiated relations in which hard and soft shapes, smells, sounds, and feelings dominate the pre-subjective state of infancy, and no distinction exists between where self ends and the other begins. The paranoid-schizoid mode of experience follows and is characterized as one of bifurcation and polarization. Psychological splitting coincides with the *confusing* change in experience and interpersonal relations in the direction of differentiation and separation between self and other. Who am I? Who are you? What is our relationship? However, self and other are viewed in black and white and experienced as good or bad, rejecting or accepting, and loving or hating. It is a time in which the emerging child begins to experience omnipotent subjectivity and a perspective of the world evolving around oneself, what is called primary narcissism. The depressive mode of experience follows in which the child comes to acknowledge his or her lack of control of the other, the good and bad characteristics of the parental object. It is a time when the child begins to acknowledge the *chaos and complexity* of human relationships and the loss of innocence and the ideal of perfection.

Embracing organized disorder stresses the significance of the depressive position; however, that alone is insufficient. Acknowledgment of the state of constant change demands consciousness of the perpetuation and dialectical interplay of these three modes of experience throughout life. Managing at the edge of chaos requires psychological management of regression and the emotional forces of more primitive states of experience. Comfort is found in the disorder allowing for innovation and double-loop learning. The acknowledgment of the unknown, complexity, and chaos reinforces the value of paying attention to unconscious systemic forces as they impose their will on our best efforts at organizational change. A good enough holding environment for organizational change is a necessary step in facilitating participants' willingness to embrace organized disorder and better cope with an unpredictable future.

Conclusion

One might ask, have chaos and complexity theories added new knowledge to our understanding of organizations? These theories raise issues that have been addressed for many decades. Claims that organizations have radically changed are overstated and over-generalized. Although organizational membership may be challenged by the impact of new technologies, globalization, and continuous change, their actual cognitive, emotional, strategic, and structural barriers to transformation and adaptation have changed very little. Organizational participants still engage in defensive routines and psychologically regressive behaviors that protect the status quo. Therefore, the challenge for organizational members of the future is not terribly different than it has been for some time. In fact, the issue of adaptation to complexity and chaos may assume that all changes on behalf of adaptation are good organizational strategies because they ensure viability and survival. This very assumption might be questioned on a case-by-case basis.

Nevertheless, organizational participants and their leaders will continue to work at developing their adaptive capabilities. Consequently, their sense of organizational identity and its inherent meaning and integrity will become more significant rather than less so. Awareness of organizational identity is becoming increasingly under attack in a world of constant change in the form of policies, mergers and acquisitions, and downsizing and right-sizing. Organizational distinctiveness and uniqueness will become more important, strategically and socially.

In sum, organizational leaders will need to promote creativity and innovation among participants at a time when their unconscious proclivities encourage executives and management to become more controlling to regain predictability. If it is true that leaders and followers produce and perpetuate organizational cultures, then the maturity and quality of human relations and the facilitation of a good enough holding environment is crucial. Organizing the potential space for learning and reflectivity in the moment will produce nonlinear feedback systems that are humane, effective, and adaptive to chaos and complexity.

Chapter 8 continues the exploration of psychodynamically informed insights into aggression and violence in the workplace. In this chapter, the violence is more apparent, out in the open, and may leave behind a body count. Aggression and violence of this type may also be better understood from a psychodynamically informed perspective based on object relations theory. We begin the continued exploration of chaos and violence by asking: Why does it happen?

8

Shame, Oppression, and Persecution

> One of the earliest methods of defense against the dread of persecutors, whether conceived of as existing in the external world or the internalized, is that of scotomization, the denial of psychic reality; this may result in a considerable restriction of the mechanisms of introjection and projection and in the denial of external reality, and forms the basis of the most severe psychoses. Very soon, too, the ego tries to defend itself against internalized persecutors by the processes of expulsion and projection. At the same time, since the dread of internalized objects is by no means extinguished with their projection, the ego marshals against the persecutors inside the body the same forces as it employs against those in the outside world. These anxiety-contents and defense-mechanisms form the basis of paranoia.
>
> *Melanie Klein, "A Contribution to the Psychogenesis*
> *of Manic-Depressive States"*

The social and emotional paranoid-schizoid roots of aggression and violence in the self and within the workplace are a key to better understanding violence and aggression in groups and organizations. The intent in this chapter is to examine the psychological nature of the relationship between human nature and the origins of fear and aggression at work (Czander, 1993; Diamond, 1993; Kets de Vries & Miller, 1984; Levinson, 1972, 1981; Zaleznik & Kets de Vries, 1975). We suggest that oppressive organizational cultures and persecutory organizational experiences are toxic and contributing factors to violence and aggression at work.

Oppressive organizations are characterized by large scale unilateral managerial norms and practices. These practices are dismissive of workers' well-being, ideas, and complaints and do not acknowledge their need for recognition and respect. Typically, this means these workers feel unjustly victimized and taken advantage of by managers and executives. The absence of employee input into managerial decisions provokes feelings of powerlessness and hopelessness among workers. Over time, oppressive cultures are experienced by workers as persecutory. Employees become suspicious and paranoid of management. An organization experienced by workers as oppressive and controlling leads to persecutory identifications and to fighting back in defense of one's self integrity. As a consequence of feeling persecuted by managements' excessive control and disrespect, workers experience narcissistic injury, rage, shame, and anxiety. These are key ingredients to promoting violence and aggression in the workplace. Disregard and insensitivity for the emotional life of employees and their psychological attachment (transference) to the workplace is a fundamental omission of executive leaders and managers. Understanding this cannot be based solely on factual and observable data. A deeper understanding requires access to the inner psychological reality of workers' experiences as well (Diamond, 1984).

Overview of Violence in the Workplace

Beyond the statistics, most reports and studies of violence in the workplace provide little to no insight into the relationship between organizational cultures and the production of aggression and hostility between fellow workers and between management and employees. The psychological nature of worker attachments to each other, their leaders, and the organization is not taken into sufficient consideration. More important, the psychological roots of aggression and violence are not understood. And, finally, the examination of the corporate culture does not explore the deeper unconscious meaning of membership in oppressive and punishing cultures. The U.S. Postal Service is a case in point.

U.S. Government Accountability Office Report on the U.S. Postal Service

In September 1994, the U.S. Government Accountability Office (GAO) (1994a, 1994b) submitted a two-volume report on the U.S. Postal Service to Congress—the "U.S. Postal Service: Labor-Management Problems Persist on the Workroom Floor." This report responded to a congressional request for a comprehensive review of labor-management relations at the U.S. Postal Service and was prompted by the November 1991 shooting of postal employees in the Royal Oak Mail Service Center in Royal Oak, Michigan.

The GAO reported that in mail processing plants and post offices, many employees stated that they worked in an atmosphere of intimidation and tension that was too often characterized by the use of (1) formal disciplinary processes to correct employee problems, (2) grievance processing to obtain relief from disciplinary actions, and (3) arbitration to resolve the ensuing conflict. The GAO report concluded that "the 'us versus them' attitude and behavior of both management and unions must end if the Postal Service is to be successful in an increasingly competitive environment." (GAO, 1994a, p. 4)

In the second volume of the GAO (1994b) report, the authors go on to describe "an autocratic management style that promotes conflict on the workroom floor" and a non-participative, "corporate culture." One employee opinion survey dealing with performance dimensions showed that "many craft employees felt that managers and supervisors did not treat employees with respect and dignity and that the organization was insensitive to individual needs and concerns" (p. 42). Hence, "the postal workforce gives the postal service low marks" (p. 41). The report concludes that despite many accomplishments, the post office has not been able to change its corporate culture.

Researchers often describe the workplace as oppressive, however, they also often find it hard to explain why some oppressive cultures promote aggressive behavior and others do not. We assert that the key to understanding aggression and violence at work resides in the unconscious organizational terrain of intersubjective experience that lies beneath the oppressive organizational culture. Aggression and violence often erupt when a persecutory organizational experience is shared by a significant number of organizational members.

Toward an Object Relational Perspective of Violence and Aggression at Work

Many articles and studies on the subject of violence and aggression in public and private organizations have been reported (Driscoll, Worthington, & Hurrell, 1995; U.S. Government Accountability Office, 1994; Harvey & Cosier, 1995; Johnson & Indvik, 1994; Mossman, 1995; Nigro & Waugh, 1996; National Institute for Occupational Safety and Health (NIOSH), 1996; O'Leary-Kelly, Griffin, & Glew, 1996; Resnick & Kausch, 1995; Stone, 1995). These articles vary in analytic complexity, rigor, and insight into the problem. Yet, all agree that violence and aggression in the workplace is a serious issue (O'Leary-Kelly et al., 1996), and some suggest that employee-on-employee aggression may be a consequence of management practices and workplace culture (GAO, 1994). Nigro and Waugh (1996) conclude that management must "implement personnel policies and management processes that improve the organization's ability to identify and neutralize potentially violent employees, customers, and clients" (p. 330). In outlining a research agenda on occupational violent crime (OVC), Nigro & Waugh (1996) suggest that reliable intelligence from cooperating public agencies, the construction of a database that includes variables related to risk factors, an employer-level reporting system that "captures situational, organizational, and social-psychological information" (p. 330) and data on the primary motivations of offenders would be helpful. However, they admit that "strategies designed to prevent robberies, politically motivated terrorism, or other violent intrusions by outsiders may offer little or no protection against employee-on-employee assaults" (p. 331).

Much of the literature on workplace violence focuses on the need for additional security and training to better cope with disgruntled employees and angry customers. The heightened emphasis on security and training, although helpful, is a reaction to an inadequately understood problem. Nevertheless, social and behavioral scientists have proffered some insights into the roots of aggression and violence in organizations. For example, O'Leary-Kelly et al. (1996) look at "organization-motivated aggression" from a social-learning perspective. They propose that given the influence organizations have over employees, insider-perpetrated aggression is instigated by certain factors. They write, "Organizations that control the rewards and opportunities that insiders have available to them, as well as the policies under which they must operate, may at times take actions that are perceived as aversive by employees (aversive treatment)" (p. 240). The authors imply that aggressive acts on the part of employees are a reaction to the authorities who control and disperse rewards and other resources. These disbursements may be viewed by employees as unfair, what the authors call "aversive treatment." Hence, employees' perceptions of unfair treatment by employers and management may trigger hostilities.

According to Folger and Baron (1996) descriptions of the individuals who commit workplace violence often describe the violent-prone workers as "disgruntled" and as frequently mentioning resentment. In their article, "Violence and Hostility at Work: A Model of Reactions to Perceived Injustice," Folger & Baron (1996) offer evidence for a link between the findings of basic research on the causes and nature of human aggression and this sense of "injustice." O'Leary-Kelly et al. (1996), then, go on to say that "employers provide, through the socialization process, important information on the types of employee behaviors that are acceptable and will be rewarded (incentive inducements)" (p. 240). The authors also point to another contributing factor to organizationally motivated aggression, the method of controlling subordinate behavior by rewarding dominant and acceptable governing values, norms, and ideology. In some instances, cultures may be explicitly engineered by companies for these purposes (Kunda, 1992). Employees resent excessive infringement of their freedom and autonomy when management acts coercively or unilaterally. Some workers view incentive inducements as a method of indoctrination. In contrast, a number of employees accept excessive or extraordinary controls if they benefit by gaining job security and career opportunities. Should this psychological contract and expectation be broken by management, employees feel deceived and betrayed, and a few may react violently.

O'Leary-Kelly et al. (1996) continue to suggest that "during and after the socialization process, organizations provide important models that influence the types of behaviors that insiders' exhibit (modeling influences)" (p. 240). Although the authors do not argue the following point, their observation implies that workplace culture perpetuates the status quo through implicit requirements of role conformity. Organizational culture must in effect be incorporated by employees to join the team. From an object relational perspective, this phenomenon is powerful in its effect. Organizations promoting, consciously or unconsciously, "modeling influences" such as these promote inauthentic and defensive behavior among employees. In effect these employers are promoting what psychoanalysts call "as if performance," in which employees are coerced to operate with the mindset "I will be as you desire me" (Diamond, 1984). It is as if membership in these oppressive organizations requires self-denial and, for some workers, possibly death of self (Denhardt, 1987; Hummel, 1982). As we explained in Chapter 6 on moral violence, individual workers require greater authenticity and independence of mind if they are to feel sufficiently free and liberated to engage in creative and imaginative problem solving. Under the circumstances of oppressive and persecutory organizations, workers may become angry and hostile about the workplace limits placed on their self-expression and self-realization.

Finally, O'Leary-Kelly et al. (1996) write that "the organization provides the physical environment within which most employees work on a daily basis (physical environment)" (p. 240). Although an artifact of organizational culture, the significance of physical environment is often underestimated. Dating back to the Hawthorne Experiments at the Western Electric Company (Mayo, 1933/1960), the conditions and quality of facilities and office space or plant design have been known to affect workers' morale and satisfaction. This, in turn, influences the worker's sense of self-worth as communicated by the employer's attention and investment in the physical environment. In other words, physical is never merely physical and external; it is always partly symbolic and existential.

In sum, according to the social-learning approach, aggression is viewed as "prompted by external factors (situational cues and reinforcers), rather than internal factors such as instincts and drives" (O'Leary-Kelly et al., 1996, p. 230). No doubt, external factors such as these will affect employees.

However, not unlike many social and behavioral scientists, the authors who use the social learning approach minimize the theoretical possibilities in exploring the subject matter at hand. They regard the psychological nature of our lives as something unknowable. Positivists often divide self and other and subject and object in a manner that excludes the influence of subjectivity, intersubjectivity, and unconscious meanings and fantasies. It is as if workers, managers, and executives have no inner life, no experience of the workplace that they internalize that influences their experience of events and shapes their reactions to them (Czander, 1993; Diamond, 1993; Stein, 1994; Weick, 1995).

The Toxic Mix of Oppressive Cultures and Persecutory Experiences

Paranoid leaders foster excessively controlling and suspicious organizations with oppressive cultures. These organizations usually perpetuate an "us against them" mindset where ambiguity and diversity are hard to manage. In his book *Psychic Deadness*, Michael Eigen (1996) describes an absolutarian, paranoid, and schizoid mindset characterized by psychological splitting and relational distortions. Eigen reports, "The intellectual structure of discourse tended to be adversarial, me against you, one side against the other, whatever the sides might be at any given time. At any moment, there did not seem to be any room for multi-ocularity or ambiguity. Instead, aggressive one-sidedness was the rule. Implicit in this procedure was support for my side, attack against yours. There was not much intellectual cross-dressing" (p. 203).

Oppressive organizations are frequently patterned by superior-subordinate relationships that contain dominance and submission issues. Despite managements' espousing open-door policies, participation, collaboration, or workplace democracy, their theories-in-practice (Argyris, 1990) exhibit top-down, unilateral control as the governing value for managing subordinate behavior. These organizations are cynically thought of by workers as "talking the talk" but rarely "walking the walk." Managerial contradictions such as these can be costly and may result in depersonalization of the workers. As we noted in Chapter 6, in her book *The Bonds of Love*, Jessica Benjamin (1988) writes, "The more the other is subjugated, the less he is experienced as a human subject and the more distance or violence the self must deploy against him. The ensuing absence of recognition, indeed of an outside world, breeds more of the same" (p. 220).

Governing values that include dominance and submission are often disguised via an ideology of professionalism and rationalism that foster overdependency of workers on management. These organizational dynamics in combination with narcissistic and expansive leadership personalities are key ingredients in oppressive workplace cultures. Workers feel that they have no voice in policies and procedures that directly affect them and their work. Members assume a mistrustful and combative attitude toward management and not infrequently toward each other. Teamwork and collaboration are significantly diminished. Worker input comes with union representation and/or in the form of worker protests against management policies and practices.

Oppressive organizational cultures in the era of downsizing, reengineering, and reinventing are commonplace and quite often destructive. In our book *The Human Costs of a Management Failure* (1996), we chronicled the downsizing of a major metropolitan hospital. We reluctantly concluded that if one were to take this extensive case study as a specimen of the reengineering of other hospitals nationwide, the observer could not help but draw an analogy to a workplace version of a mass murder. The questionable (yet not uncommon) administrative practice in downsizing that requires employees to gather in an auditorium for the purpose of mass termination of their employment is one profound illustration of contemporary forms of oppressive management.

Workers, managers, and executives polarize into subgroups that view the other as "all bad" (evil and punishing) and themselves as "all good" (righteous and victimized). This is a (cognitive-emotional) phenomenon that we have referred to throughout this book as "psychological splitting." Sanctimonious attitudes emerge among group cultures that resist constructive and open-minded dialogue with the perceived opposition. Vamik Volkan (1988), referring to a similar phenomenon in international conflict and warfare, calls this phenomenon "the [human] need for enemies and allies." The infantile roots of adult relations, whether international or in an organizational context, stem from the primary processes of splitting and fragmentation, us against them or enemies and allies. Organizations frequently exhibit pathologies of power and politics mirrored in the host culture and the international arena.

These polarized and dangerously oppositional human relations between executive leaders and workers are supported by collective psychological splitting. This dynamic is typical of organizations riddled by conflict and excessive controls. Organizational participants project bad images and feelings onto others. Consequently, the projecting self under the influence of a paranoid shift comes to view the targeted and despised other as a dehumanized and depersonalized object, the enemy. Finally, and tragically, this enables the parties in opposition to engage in horrific verbal and sometimes physical attacks on one another.

The dynamic is illustrated as follows. An impatient executive ordered a new director to transform the culture of a public agency from control-oriented bureaucracy to one that was an entrepreneurial customer and service-oriented organization. The director felt the executive's time frame was unrealistic and assumed he could not say anything. Nothing was communicated. The director, who was then angry at the impatient executive, displaced his anger onto his employees by insisting they change immediately to a service orientation. His internalized aggression was expressed in the form of irrational, psychological splitting. He conveyed to his employees that they had been doing their work "all wrong" and that he knew how to do it "right." He, publicly, in meetings and conversations referred to his employees as "stupid." At the same time, the employees felt ignored, unacknowledged, shamed, and disrespected despite their past efforts at serving the public good and their commitment to the public service. Uncertainty, ambivalence, and ambiguity, as well as participant anxiety and psychological splitting and projection, increased. Workers could not manage their ambivalent feelings toward their boss. The effort to transform the culture failed as interpersonal and group combativeness and resistance to change predictably increased.

In sum, some workers who experience attacks in the form of disrespect and personal insult may lash out in some manner. Some aggrieved workers do not have the capacity to contain such aggression. Wishful thinking, and acting on grandiose fantasies, permits workers to believe that, by attacking or killing the other, they will eliminate shame and a deadened sense of self (Eigen, 1996; Gilligan, 1996). The workers' actions come to mirror the aggressive and denigrating actions of their superiors. In the above example, the director can blame his "incompetent" staff and avoid feeling responsible himself. Understanding persecutory workplace experience is, therefore, essential if violence and aggression are to be avoided.

Persecutory Organizational Experience

The persecutory experience felt by many workers arises from internalizing an oppressive workplace where they feel powerless and disrespected. They experience their relationship with the organization and its leadership in a manner that is passive. Things are done to them. They have little say in what happens and feel they have little recourse. This disrespect and lack of worker participation is also often combined with feelings of being persecuted by their leaders. As Briskin (1996) notes in his discussion of the "domination of souls" in the workplace: "No one can mature in a culture or organization without internalizing aspects of it. We are by nature dependent on family, community, social institutions, and our workplaces for our survival and to a large measure our sense of identity" (p. 65). People are becoming increasingly dependent on their vocations and careers for emotional rewards of enhanced self-confidence and competence. This is, however, problematic. When the workplace is heartless, there may be nowhere else for some workers to turn.

A sense of shame and narcissistic injury and resentment emerges when workers come to view their leaders as punitive and immoral feelings of being mistreated and discriminated against arise. "Leadership doesn't respect us," they say. "Management is out to get us," they add. "We are treated unfairly." Paranoia arises and psychological splitting and irrationality dominate. The psychological foundation is that the persecutory organizational experience is one that deadens the self and strips away self-esteem. These workers who feel abused are angry and hostile as well. Powerless workers who are subjected to multiple injustices become aggressive and, possibly, physically violent, fulfilling management's fantasy that employees are really out to get them (Folger & Baron, 1996).

In his book, *Violence: Our Deadly Epidemic and Its Causes*, James Gilligan (1996) writes that "understanding violence ultimately requires learning how to translate violent acts into words" (p. 62). Actions represent meaning and meaning resides within the intersubjective experience of organizational members. Examination of violent criminals offers insights for understanding the socio-psychodynamics of workplace aggression (VandenBos & Bulalao, 1996). Gilligan's studies suggest that individual perceptions of unjust treatment combined with the emotions of shame, humiliation, and an inevitable deadening of feelings produce violent acts. His analysis of more than one hundred violent criminals portrays men without emotional and often physical sensation. He describes murderers without remorse, an absence of self-esteem, and an underlying sense of shame but no guilt.

In sum, shame and persecution are motivating factors that drive workplace oppression and active and passive aggression. Violent acts are frequently the result of individuals feeling trapped and tortured. These feelings, when merged with deeply felt shame and rage, become the basis for aggressive acts inside and outside the workplace. According to Gilligan (1996), the perception of injustice is closely linked with one's estimate of self-worth and pride. The aggressor's view of being treated unfairly and unjustly provokes deeply felt shame and envy. The aggressor comes to view himself as persecuted and victimized and these feelings trigger violence and aggression. In contrast, self-esteem and pride are derivatives of a loving and nurturing facilitative environment. They are the necessary character ingredients for withstanding the assaults that exist within oppressive organizations.

Conclusion

Employee-on-employee/employer violence and aggression in the workplace are typically responses to real-world trauma such as firings, lay offs, and oppression. It is typically externally driven, such as the many cases of homicides and suicides preceded by layoffs. However, such acts do not always meet with violent reactions, and one must, therefore, understand why these events are interpreted and responded to differently. Understanding the worker's experience of shame and injustice makes an important contribution to understanding workplace violence and aggression. Oppressive organizational cultures promote persecutory workplaces and feelings of being abused, mistreated, and disrespected. If we are to reduce violence in the workplace, we need to understand the origins of violence in human nature, in organizational culture, and in the actions of leaders and managers.

How do we change violent and aggressive organizations into healthier and more productive workplaces? The key to transformation is intervention that restores self-confidence and mutual respect among organization members. This restoration occurs when employees feel that their experience of workplace injustices are heard and taken seriously by those who can make a difference.

We now turn to the question of what if anything may be done regarding this state of affairs. Organizational life is filled with many types of influences and dynamics that are not usually, if at all, covered by those writing management texts and self-help books. Part 1 provided a tripartite object relational model of how to understand taboo, difficult to discuss, and out of awareness aspects of the work lives of individuals and the unconscious dynamics of groups and organizations. Part 2 extended the discussion by inspecting the harmful and destructive side of organizational life, one filled with organizational violence that can destroy the spirit more so than the body, although this chapter pointed out that indeed the body may also be at risk. Repairing these problems from a psychodynamic perspective is at the heart of Part 3. What can we do?

Part 3

Intervention and Reparation

Organizational repair begins with understanding the underlying issues producing themes that may not be the same as the presenting problem communicated by the executives and organization members. This difference is revealed when the nature of the emotional ties and distortions and transference and countertransference themes between organization members and especially external consultants is explored. These relational dynamics lie at the heart of an object relational approach to understanding and changing organizations.

These relational phenomena are shaped by psychological defenses and regressive actions between and among organizational participants. In Chapter 9 we discuss how observing transference and countertransference dynamics between organizational actors; leaders and followers; and consultants and clients gives us valuable insight into the peculiar relational systems and their host organizational cultures. Next, in Chapter 10, "Perversions of Democracy," we explore the normative issue of workplace democracy and its prevalence and absence in contemporary organizations. Perversions of workplace democracy provide insights into what might ideally constitute an emotionally healthy, just, and virtuous place to work. This outcome depends on the degree to which organizational culture and structure can positively impact human relations at work. Part 3 concludes with Chapter 11 on "Immersion and Diagnosis" and a discussion of organizational intervention and change from the perspective of a consultation that also informs new executives and those that lead organizational change. The closing chapter returns to the silo metaphor and human nature in organizations. Here, we offer an illustrative vignette to summarize our relational psychoanalytic approach to organizational diagnosis and change.

9

Shared Emotions

Transference and Countertransference

All human experience, including transference-countertransference experience, can be thought of as the outcome of the dialectical interplay of three modes of creating and organizing psychological meaning. Each of these modes is associated with one of three fundamental psychological organizations—the depressive position, the paranoid-schizoid position, and the autistic-contiguous position. None of the three modes exists in isolation from others: each creates, preserves, and negates the others dialectically. Each mode generates an experiential state characterized by its own distinctive form of anxiety, types of defense, degree of subjectivity, form of object relatedness, type of internalization process, and so on.

Thomas Ogden, Subjects of Analysis

It is worth repeating that many social scientists find comfort in the assumption that what really matters in understanding and improving organizational performance is that which is visible and quantifiable. Buildings and offices; equipment and technology; systems and processes; policies and procedures; services or products; and organizational hierarchies and executives, managers, supervisors, and employees performing varied tasks are among other visible components (Jaques, 1995). It is regrettably the illusion of the concreteness of these organizational attributes that makes periodic reengineering and downsizing of organizations seem like a reasonable pursuit. Yet, as noted by many observers of the workplace, these draconian actions do not typically meet expectations and often have unintended human consequences (Allcorn, Baum, Diamond, & Stein, 1996; Kets de Vries, 2001). There is, of course, more to the workplace than meets the eye. Ultimately, emotional and unconscious organizational dynamics shape what happens in the workplace (Amado, 1995). Thus, the managerial pursuit of a "more efficient organizational structure" confronts the psychological reality of the workplace where techno-rationalism gives way to latent psychosocial dynamics that have so far defied reengineering.

We view organizations as processes of human behavior governed by unconscious dynamics, whereby "much thought and activity takes place outside of conscious awareness." This starting point leads us to discuss psychoanalytically informed organizational perspectives as a means of understanding how psychological reality and subjectivity shape organizational dynamics. In particular, psychoanalytically informed organizational diagnosis illuminates the crucial and complex role of transference and countertransference in the study of organizations (Stapley, 1996).

Interpreting data through the lens of transference and countertransference dynamics assists in unpacking organizational culture and its unconscious elements by relying upon an "experience-near" (Kohut, 1977) stance for examining the narratives of organizational life (Diamond, 1993; Kets de Vries & Miller, 1984; Levinson, 1972, 2002). This introspective and empathic stance makes transference and countertransference one of the core elements of an object relational approach to organizational diagnosis and intervention. It is also the case that it is this conceptualization of organizations that sets our approach apart from more traditional social and behavioral approaches to organizational research. The consultant's self-awareness becomes a means for interpreting transference and countertransference that occur between the organizational consultant and organization members and among organization members and groups. We conclude our exploration of the contributions of transference and countertransference for organizational analysis by offering some thoughts on how leaders, organizational members, and consultants can improve organizational performance by attending to the psychological reality and subjectivity of the workplace.

The Context for Organizational Study

As we discussed in Chapter 7 on chaos and complexity, organizations are buffeted by events that arise from their task environments. Political, economic, and marketplace events undeniably impact organizational behavior. Competitive markets, rapidly changing communications, information technologies, and globalization are dimensions of the environment from which organizations struggle for strategic advantage. Constant change requires frequent reexamination of the adaptive strategies of organizations to survive and ideally to succeed. This ability to manage and adapt directs our attention to the inner life of organizations where effective adaptation is unlikely without the successful integration of people and human nature, social and psychological structures.

At the surface of organizational culture, artifacts such as organization charts, rules and regulations, routine workflow, interior designs and architecture, dress, language and communications, distribution of benefits and rewards, company or agency policies, and many more manifest features of organizational culture, significantly influence organizational effectiveness and competitiveness. While political, economic, and marketplace variables are external factors that set the context for adaptive strategic decision making, the latter compilation of organizational and cultural artifacts, as well as the above-mentioned visible components, represent intra-organization phenomena that enhance or limit organizational performance.

These data, the external and internal organizational variables, must be incorporated into an organizational diagnosis, particularly one that is psychodynamic in nature (Baum, 1994; Czander, 1993; Diamond, 1993; Kets de Vries & Miller, 1987; Levinson, 1972; Stapley, 1996; Stein, 1994). However, in contrast to the quantitative and neo-positivistic empirical methodologies that are so frequently relied upon to study the above organizational attributes, a psychodynamic assessment focuses on the psychological nature of the ultimately not so concrete aspects of organizational culture—the subjective derivatives of reason, motivation, and meaning. Psychoanalytically informed action researchers and consultants indirectly ask questions such as the following: What are the underlying motives, desires, wishes, and fantasies that energize the thoughts, feelings, and actions of organization members? And, what is the personal experience of organizational reality, and what does it seem to mean to each and all organization members? How would I as a participant observer characterize the predominant patterns of relatedness throughout the organization?

Psychoanalytic anthropologist and organizational consultant, Howard Stein (1994) writes, "Political, economic, and structural 'reasons' are only part of an organization's story. Group [and organizational] life is complex, not neatly packaged. The surface picture presented to the consultant often is a symptom and symbol in which people invest because it protects them against pain . . . Client organizations often do not know what they, at some unrecognized level, already know too well. The consultant's role becomes that of mediating between the known and the unknown, the knowable and the unknowable" (pp. 8–9). Stein observes that many workplace phenomena most often exist outside of the immediate awareness of organizational participants and, therefore, are frequently ignored and taken for granted. Psychoanalytic organizational consultants, therefore, have among their tasks addressing this collective inattention to one's experience of work-life that so often includes hard individual, group, and organizational defenses.

In sum, the point that we wish to make at the outset is that, although psychoanalytic organizational consultants pay attention to the manifest elements of social structure, work groups, and task environment, they also view these data with appropriate suspicion. Their organizational diagnoses endeavor to elicit the unconscious meanings, assumptions, and collective anxieties of organizational participants. This endeavor then surfaces conflict, disappointment, and fantasies held by organizational participants, as well as thoughts and feelings concealed by suppression and other psychologically defensive actions that compromise reality testing. The psychological nature of the workplace may, therefore, be understood to reside in the participants' out of awareness experience of the workplace where structures of power and authority, strategies for adaptation and successful performance, and routine roles and relationships are defensive screens against unrecognized anxieties and fears rather than rational and intentional organizational designs. These considerations lead to the question, if unconscious processes are present within the workplace, how might they be made accessible for examination? Here, we focus on two related conceptual frameworks: organizational diagnosis and the interpretation of organizational text.

Organizational Diagnosis

Levinson (1972, 2002) offers a model for psychoanalytically informed organizational assessments that incorporates various levels of data collection and describes a psychodynamic process for engaging the organization and their leaders. These categories of data include genetic and historical data, structural and process data, and interpretive (or narrative) data. According to Levinson, "This was an adaptation of an open system biological model, which had been applied to individuals, for the study and analysis of organizations. It emphasized the need to understand organizations and their problems before trying to intervene. The diagnostic emphasis was a uniquely clinical contribution because so much of what had been done in organization development was essentially ad hoc application of established techniques without adequate diagnosis" (Correspondence 1985). Levinson's initial approach to organizational diagnosis integrated data from "objective reality" and "psychological reality," thereby illustrating the importance of analyzing the unconscious meaning behind supposedly concrete and rational organizational dynamics. In doing so, he introduced transference as an essential conceptual framework for organizational diagnosis.

The location and interpretation of transference and countertransference enable psychoanalytically informed organizational consultants to understand the subjective meaning of individual and collective actions and experiences within organizations. Psychoanalytically informed organizational diagnosis is thereby informed by the hermeneutic and "narrative" scholarly tradition (Ricoeur, 1970; Schafer, 1983; Spence, 1982) as much as it is shaped by the biological and medical models of diagnosis (Levinson, 1972). Thus, we turn briefly to the function of text and subtext of organizational narratives, which is supported by a process of locating and interpreting transference and countertransference.

Organizational Text

In their article, "Interpreting organizational texts," Kets de Vries and Miller (1987) propose four "rules of interpretation" that are consistent with Levinson's (1972) approach to organizational diagnosis and his attention to "patterning" and "integration." Following the collection of assorted data, the organizational narrative is constructed by assembling "the different observations into an interconnected, cohesive unit based on the first rule of thematic unity" (Kets de Vries & Miller, 1987, p. 245). The method of thematic unity becomes crucial to making sense out of the dense nature and sheer volume of historical, narrative, and observational data. The next step is to look "for a 'fit' between present day events and earlier incidents in the history of an individual or organization" based on the second rule of pattern matching. Pattern matching reveals repetition or what Kets de Vries and Miller (1987) call the tendency to become "entangled in 'displacements in time'" (p. 245). The relevance of these displacements (transferences) as a tool for introspection and the surfacing of pattern matching are discussed further below. The notion of pattern matching, however, like that of thematic unity, provides a theoretical context that guides organizational consultants in organizing seemingly disorganized quantities of narrative data into a coherent organizational story.

Next, and in contrast to a strict hermeneutic approach, the third principle rule of psychological urgency includes the assumption that somewhere in the text it is possible to identify the most pressing problems: "It is important, then, to pay attention to the persistence, enthusiasm, regularity, pervasiveness, and emotion surrounding decisions, interactions, and pronouncements" (Kets de Vries & Miller, 1987, p. 246). Members may repeatedly mention common or similar overriding barriers to organizational change and progress. They revisit the same organizational myths or stories in their narratives as a way of reenacting them to master painful organizational experiences. These narrative data, however, require interpretation, if the organizational researcher is to appreciate the associated unconscious dynamics. In other words, it is often the case that some of the more critical issues of the organization are disowned, disavowed, and displaced by members onto more superficial concerns.

Finally, Kets de Vries and Miller (1987) call attention to the fourth rule of multiple functions. They state, "Depending on the psychological urgency at hand, a part of the text can have more than one meaning and can be looked at from many different points of view" (p. 246). They continue, "It is thus necessary to seek out meaning at multiple levels, to determine the individual as well as the organizational roots and consequences of actions and decisions" (p. 246). The rule of multiple functions stresses seeking validation and confirmation of meaning with organizational participants.

In sum, understanding the workplace requires paying attention to the nuances of unconsciously shared thoughts, feelings, and experiences, and through interpretation, a deeper, multidimensional understanding of the organizational text can be gained. In his book *The Analytic Attitude*, Roy Schafer writes, "Its usefulness resides in its reminding us that psychoanalytic explanation depends on our knowing what an event, action, or object means to the subject; it is the specifically psychoanalytic alternative to descriptive classification by a behavioristic observer" (Schafer, 1983, p. 89). For psychoanalytic organizational researchers, understanding what organizational artifacts, critical events, and relational patterns and experiences mean to organizational members and how that meaning and experience shapes the quality of their work life is what matters most. Psychological reality frequently trumps objective reality in the diagnosis and assessment of organizations.

Organizational diagnosis, it may be concluded, presents a challenging milieu in which to function. Not only must commonplace organizational artifacts, events, and history be taken into consideration, but so must the subjective experience of organizational participants. These experiences are most often revealed by paying attention to the organizational story that unfolds as organizational data are collected. Making conscious the story and many of its fantastic qualities is enabled by paying attention to and interpreting transference and countertransference dynamics. In particular, the self becomes an instrument of observation and data collection, thereby revealing the subjective and intersubjective world of work. The use of transference and countertransference as a means of localizing the unconscious side of organizational life is examined next.

Transference and Countertransference in the Study of Organizations

Transference and countertransference are key conceptual tools for the psychoanalytic study of organizations (Baum, 1994; Czander, 1993; Diamond, 1988, 1993; Kets de Vries & Miller, 1984; Levinson, 1972; Schwartz, 1991; Stapley, 1996; Stein, 1994). According to Hunt (1989), psychoanalytic approaches to fieldwork take three assumptions into account. First, researchers assume unconscious processes exist in which "much thought and activity occurs outside of conscious awareness" (p. 25). Second, researchers assume that "unconscious meanings, which mediate everyday life, are linked to complex webs of significance, which can ultimately be traced to childhood experiences" (p. 25). That is, "the psychoanalytic perspective assumes that transferences, defined as the imposition of archaic (childhood) images onto present day objects, are a routine feature of most relationships" (p. 25). Hunt (1989) goes on to say that transference, whether positive or negative, "structures social relationships in particular ways" (p. 25). And, third, the researcher assumes "psychoanalysis is a theory of intrapsychic conflict" (p. 25).

Participants' conscious desires and wishes may contradict unconscious fears and anxieties stemming from childhood. These internal conflicts then affect workplace experience and performance and often shape the nuances of roles and relationships in organizations. Hence, organizations are understood, in part, by paying attention to the sometimes conflicted and contradictory ways in which the subjects (organizational members) engage each other, executives, managers, and consultants as well as our own responses to them. In particular, the interpretation of transference, whether in the nature of the attachment to the organization, super-ordinates, subordinates, or to the consultant, provides a deeper understanding of individual and organizational dynamics and greater insight into the meaning of organizational membership (Allcorn & Diamond, 1997; Baum, 1994).

In sum, psychoanalytically informed organizational diagnoses provide a means of knowing the psychological reality of the workplace. In particular, the inevitability of transference and countertransference in the workplace among organization members and relative to outsiders, such as consultants, provides context for knowing and understanding the workplace. Before proceeding to discuss transference and countertransference as ways of understanding the psychological reality of the workplace, it is essential to define these terms.

Transference and Countertransference Defined

Psychoanalytic terms are often used in idiosyncratic ways that may be thought of as placing a new spin on a term or that may be borrowed from a previous idiosyncratic application. There are also instances in which the terms are simply described differently. These considerations make it important from our perspective to provide a definition of these two concepts.

Transference

According to Moore and Fine (1990), transference is "the displacement of patterns of feelings, thoughts, and behavior, originally experienced in relation to significant figures during childhood, onto a person involved in a current interpersonal relationship" (p. 196). This process is largely unconscious and therefore outside the awareness of the subject. Transference occurs as a result of the nature of the here and now object- (self and other) relations that trigger familiar assumptions and archaic feelings rooted in previous attachments. It is the case within organizations that structural hierarchy and roles of power and authority frequently provide a context for transference and countertransference reminiscent of childhood and family experience. It is typically the case in organizational consultation that, despite our psychoanalytic orientation, we know little of the childhood experiences of those with whom we consult. Nonetheless, we can assume that organizational members bring to the workplace their internalized world of object relations and that this affects working relationships via transference and countertransference dynamics. There are then many opportunities to observe and experience repetitive patterns of object relationships that provide insight into the narrative of organizational diagnosis with insights into organizational culture and performance. In sum, the displacement of patterns of thinking, feeling, and action from the past onto the present in the workplace does occur and can be expected to be especially prevalent where issues of power and authority are present.

Countertransference

Countertransference is narrowly defined as a specific reaction to transference. Countertransference works much the same as transference. It arises out of a context in which the executive's, manager's, or consultant's feelings and attitudes are influenced by transference onto them, fuelling transference back onto the organization. Acknowledgement of countertransference dynamics leads to the next step, constructively utilizing countertransference data. It is also the case that some theorists include under the general concept of countertransference all of the consultant's emotional reactions to the client, conscious and unconscious. We designate this broader definition a counterreaction. The theoretical implications of using transference and countertransference to understand the psychological reality of the workplace are now explored.

Transference and Countertransference in Organizational Life

To begin, although we discuss each aspect of the concepts separately, it is important to appreciate that all of these potentialities coexist, thereby creating a hard to understand and even chaotic experience. It is this appreciation that leads us to a deep respect for the complexities that any endeavor to know the psychological reality of the workplace will encounter. There exists an exceptional challenge, that of locating the parts and the overarching organizational text from this "stew" of experience and unconscious organizational dynamics.

Organizational life is rich with a stockpile of transference dynamics between employees and executives, executives and employees, individuals and their organizations, and clients and consultants. Executives may evoke positive transference from some employees and negative transference from others depending upon the quality and vicissitudes of internalized authority relations and their childhood experiences. Employees may evoke positive or negative transference on the part of executives depending on how responsive they are to receiving direction. The perception of resistance may be unconsciously associated with a distant echo of a past relationship with a parent who stubbornly resisted the efforts of the child to affect the parent. It is also the case that groups and divisions within an organization most certainly end up transferring historical experience onto the groups and divisions that surround them within the organizational milieu. And last, these same processes of transference are frequently evoked by the presence of a consultant. In sum, the analysis of transference and countertransference dynamics supplies insight into the nature of consultant-client relations and the aims and fantasies of organizational members regarding their working affiliation with the organization and its leadership and members. The analysis inevitably reveals psychologically defensive responses to anxiety-ridden aspects of the workplace. These anxieties are often unconsciously and automatically responded to by familiar means worked out during childhood. These responses are referred to as psychological regression.

Transference and Countertransference as Shaped
by Psychological Regression at Work

Psychological regression (see Chapter 5) represents an unwitting endeavor of organization participants to manage their anxieties. Regression is defined here as a metaphoric return to earlier modes of object relations in which stage-appropriate conflicts reemerge in the present. To put it simply, adults come to rely on familiar, yet unconscious, childhood defenses to combat anxieties at work in the present. Regression is most often accompanied by the interplay of transference and countertransference dynamics.

Many have observed that group and organizational membership entails an intrapersonal compromise between individual demands for dependency and autonomy. These are dilemmas of human development rooted in the psychodynamics of separation and individuation. The mere presence of a group, Bion (1959) observed, presumes a defensive state of psychological regression among participants. Referencing Freud (1921), Bion wrote, "Substance is given to the phantasy that the group exists by the fact that the regression involves the individual in a loss of his 'individual distinctiveness' (p. 9) . . . It follows that if the observer judges a group to be in existence, the individuals composing it must have experienced this regression" (Bion, 1959, p. 142). For Freud and Bion, psychological regression coincides with group and institutional membership.

Workers with limited freedoms and a sense of powerlessness may engage in psychologically regressive behavior. Relations between divisions become contentious and riddled with conflict. Otherwise mature adults find themselves thinking in primitive and infantile categories of good or bad, all or nothing, and enemy or ally, characteristic of an active fantasy life fueled by psychological splitting and projective identification. And, finally, there is always the danger that bureaucratic, silo-like organizations might foster regression into more homogenized and conformist, authoritarian organizations (Diamond, Stein, & Allcorn, 2002). Shared individual anxieties of group and organizational membership generate a vicious cycle of regressive and defensive responses that reinforce a schizoid dilemma.

Kernberg (1998) recently explored several dimensions of psychological regression in organizations and organizational leaders as characterized by "paranoiagenesis in organizations." The term describes the paranoid-schizoid collapse of individuals in groups and organizations. According to Kernberg (1998), organizational paranoiagenesis stems from "a breakdown of the task systems of organizations when their primary tasks become irrelevant or overwhelming or are paralyzed by unforeseen, undiagnosed, or mishandled constraints; the activation of regressive group processes under conditions of institutional malfunctioning; and the latent predisposition to paranoid regression that is a universal characteristic of individual psychology" (pp. 125–126). Kernberg views dysfunctional group and organizational structures and their ineffective leaders as unwittingly fostering psychological regression with paranoid and schizoid features.

Therefore, if psychological regression is a tension in group-like organizations, the character of associated psychological defenses and coping mechanisms may then be observed in the patterns of transference relationships between consultant and organization, organization members and their organizations, and between organizational participants themselves. Participants' anxiety around forfeiture of individuality and relative autonomy is a central dilemma that evokes psychological regression and a schizoid compromise (Alford, 1994). In addition to the schizoid compromise and contrary to the wishes and illusions of many professionals, the workplace does not typically operate with linear precision. Losses of anticipated stability, predictability, and control are commonplace, provoking members' anxiety of the unknown and unmanageable (Allcorn & Diamond, 1997). Uncertainties and ambiguities of authority and task along with the problems of absentee leadership also tend to encourage psychological regression among organizational participants.

There are many forms of organizational malfunctioning and regression. Inordinate power at the top exaggerates the impact of personality deficits of leaders throughout the organization, negatively affecting organizational culture and climate. Organizational leaders may perpetuate paranoid-schizoid dynamics in an atmosphere of vicious competition, win-lose dynamics, mistrust, and secrecy. Defensive strategies, structures, and cultures may further produce oppressive policies and constraints that limit autonomy and suppress creativity and free-flowing ideas among workers—activating the schizoid dilemma and fostering psychological regression.

In sum, rather than effectively managing participant anxieties, the destructive pull of psychological regression in groups and organizations perpetuates members' anxieties. These anxieties provoke splitting and projective identification, which are experienced by consultants via transference and countertransference dynamics. The consultant must then *contain* (e.g., Bion) and *hold* (e.g., Winnicott) the toxic split-off and projected content. These dynamics, by promoting additional confusion (in the form of undigested emotions) and anxiety, deepen and reinforce psychological regression and fantasy to cope with the anxiety (Person, 1995). These psychodynamics tend to become self-sealing, repetitive, and compulsive processes embedded in people and their organizational systems if not contained. The underlying complexity associated with using transference and countertransference as a basis for organizational intervention is challenging to understand, contain, and manage for leaders and consultants.

Creating Change—Using Transference and Countertransference as the Basis for Organizational Interventions

Organizational life is filled with unconscious processes that are hard to locate and understand. Interpreting transference and countertransference dynamics between consultants and organizational participants represents a psychoanalytically unique frame of reference for in-depth exploration of organizational culture. It is within the context of (self-object) relationships that we can observe and experience underlying organizational dynamics peculiar to one or another organizational culture. Transference and countertransference transport members' anxieties and their concomitant defensive and regressive actions into workplace roles and relationships that shape the intersubjective structure and meaning of organizational experience. It is, therefore, essential in this context to retain a self-reflective stance in which subjective (and intersubjective) experience is accessible for examination and reflection. The capacity to contain anxiety-filled workplace experience on the part of the consultant enables organizational clients to engage in reflective learning for change.

Conclusion

This chapter has emphasized that organizational experience is in large part a derivative of unconscious and very often psychologically defensive individual and group processes. This appreciation leads to the conclusion that knowing an organization necessitates a complex, lengthy, and, at times, problematic journey into the psychodynamics of individual and group behavior in the workplace. This journey, we have emphasized, leads to the discovery of the psychological reality of work that is most eloquently revealed by careful collection and interpretation of "objective" organizational data.

Identifying the psychological reality of organizations requires that researchers and consultants develop a capacity for self-observation and an ability to pay attention to transference and countertransference dynamics between them, organizational participants, and within organizational cultures. Awareness and processing of these transference and countertransference dynamics often reveals valuable insights into organizational regression and dysfunction.

Chapter 10 continues to explore organizational diagnosis and intervention by considering the concept of workplace democracy. In so doing, we suggest that the failure to realize this ideal may be discovered by an exploration of perversions of workplace democracy and a failure to surrender to the natural tensions, conflicts, paradoxes, and contradictions of organizational life. These instances of perversions are rooted in the infantile origins of the three modes of organized experience developed in Part 1.

10

Perversions of Democracy

Conflict, as a form of communication, need not be debilitating; it may potentially be creative, supporting the ends of tolerance, as long as the public or political realm understands that conflict (and occasionally ugly emotions) motivates human action and identification, that this "uncanny other" in the self cannot be healed "out," and that the place where these nasty emotions are contained is in the public/political realm. Containment of the uncanny other becomes, simultaneously, the purposive and creative end of democratic institutions.

Glass, Psychosis and Power

The workplace is a complex and puzzling milieu to try to understand. Logic and common sense do not always apply. Organizations may possess a culture where work groups and subcultures act in ways that promote communication and effective organizational performance. This may happen by management and workers acknowledging and working with, rather than suppressing and denying, internal differences, new ideas, challenges to the status quo, and conflicts. Within such organizations, plurality, diversity, conflict, and complexity are driven by democratic processes. These processes are supported by a culture that emphasizes cooperation and embraces chaotic properties of emergent direction, institutions, and relationships capable of containing paradox and the uncanny emotions associated with it.

At the other end of this cultural continuum, organizational regression turns work groups and divisions into defensive silos (see Chapter 3) that shut down knowledge sharing and communication and leave participants puzzled and bewildered at their ineffectiveness. These closed, totalitarian-like dynamics emphasize control and loyalty where submission and domination reinforce ideological and epistemological homogeneity, uniformity, and simplicity. These institutions have limited ability to contain differences and the conflicts associated with them. Developing and maintaining a culture of democracy may, therefore, be understood to require surfacing what we call "perversions of democracy" in the form of defective containment and, by attending to the psychologically regressive, pull toward more closed and oppressive human systems and away from more open and resilient ones.

In *Creativity and Perversion*, Chasseguet-Smirgel (1984), writing on narcissism and group psychology, states, " . . . the propensity to lose ego boundaries renders the individual particularly liable to identifying himself, not only with each member of the group, but with the gathering as a body. Thus, his megalomania is satisfied, each individual's ego embracing the whole group. The members of the group lose their individualities and start resembling ants or termites; this loss of individual characteristics is all the more necessary as it contributes to homogenizing the whole group. Thus, each member need not feel like an indistinguishable particle in a huge gathering, but on the contrary, can identify with the aggregate" (p. 63). It is this regressive collapse and fragmentation of object relational (ego) boundaries in groups that we find occurs as well within simple and more complex organizational arrangements. Thus, we suggest that the psychodynamics of large groups and organizational regression foster homogeneity and a perversion of democracy in the workplace.

A review of the literature over the last ten years leads us to conclude that the discussion of democracy in organizations is but a faint whisper among contemporary scholars in the social and management sciences. It is as if the subject of democratic processes at work were a thing of the past and no longer relevant to our technologically advanced globally networked organizations. We disagree. All of us routinely encounter complaints about how the workplace functions. Frequent complaints include insufficient participation in decision making, inequities and injustice in treatment of employees, and disregard for the value of psychological contracts between participants (workers) and their organizations (executives). These are common themes of discontent among workers in the twenty-first century across multiple sectors and indeed historically. They point to the problematic presence of democracy in the workplace. Democracy at work implies maximizing participation, delegation of authority to match responsibility, and employee input. It does not refer to political democracy such as "one man, one vote," or the notion of free markets, individualism, and equality of opportunity, as in the ideology of liberal democracy.

Perversions of Democracy in the Workplace

Exploring the psychodynamics of democracy in the workplace with a particular focus on unconscious and collusive forms of perverting democratic processes at work is essential. At the outset, we suggest that there is a psychoanalytic rationale, if not a moral imperative, for supporting democratic processes in organizations. We start by defining democratic workplaces as organizational cultures that actively promote the following features and values: (1) employee inclusion and participation in organizational operations; (2) a fluid mix of organizational centralization and decentralization; (3) development of resilient organizational structures based on shared strategies informed by individual and group reflection and the ability to learn from experience; (4) a capacity for conflict resolution between individual and group interests; (5) voluntary and unobstructed cooperation on tasks across horizontal and vertical organizational boundaries; and (6) mutual trust and respect.

Democratic organizational cultures are enabled by the following organizational attributes: (1) an appreciation of the tensions between leadership styles (authoritarian, participative, charismatic, and consensus are examples) and their effect on shared expectations held of leaders; (2) clarity of roles, authority, responsibility, and accountability; (3) acknowledgement of interpersonal and intergroup tensions and conflicts arising from pluralism (competing group interests); and (4) the capacity of participants to share a collective vision for the organization. These cultural and enabling qualities, while not all-inclusive, nonetheless set high standards and ideals for organizations and their leaders. Indeed in our experience, these qualities, while frequently aspired to by organizational participants, are typically absent, or only partially present.

We begin our discussion by considering recent writing on democracy for the twenty-first century organization. We return to the tripartite model presented in Part 1. We then explain how interpersonally and collectively the dialectical interplay between these three modes of experience affect workplace stress, anxiety, and psychological defenses that inhibit democratic processes in the workplace.

Workplace Democracy

During the 1960s through the 1970s, democracy in the workplace was seen as a social and political inclination on the ideological left in American society. Academics and writers focused on labor-management conflicts, employee-ownership and management, and citizen participation in public sector agencies. Employee satisfaction, performance, and motivation were frequently central to the authors' concerns. Marxism in sociology and political science, humanism in psychology and management, and the trend of New Public Administration were influential in shaping theoretical and ideological direction. More recently (1980s through 2005), downsizing, right-sizing, reengineering, globalization, corporate scandals, government restructuring, and coping with the technology-driven virtual organization have shunted aside discussion of democracy in the workplace.

In the last five to ten years, what little has been written on workplace democracy is varied and absent of any thematic pattern or central argument. In fact, there is some controversy over whether or not the concept (at least as it is applied to the corporate world) has legitimacy at all given the view of some that private sector employment is the result of voluntary association and free choice. Mayer (2001) argues that employers are not accountable to employees. Once citizens are employed by private sector organizations, they forfeit their rights to democratic processes and expectations of equity, fairness, and justice, at least in the workplace (Mayer, 2001).

In contrast, Cloke and Goldsmith (2002) argue that democratic features are perpetuated by organization theorists in their work on organizational culture, total quality management, gain sharing, and other systems of management that encourage decentralization. Also, according to these authors, ethics scholars focused on societal accountability of organizations also make their contribution. Are ethical concerns gaining momentum in the wake of corporate misconduct (Enron and WorldCom)? There exists little evidence to suggest this is occurring. One might be skeptical of such claims of inevitable shifts toward more democratic processes, particularly if these efforts by "organizational theorists working on organizational culture" ignore the unconscious dimensions of divided and conflicted groups and organizations. Suppression of conflict or conflict resolution as an instrument to rid organizational members of discord and division is misleading and often an unconscious fantasy. It is an assumption certainly contrary to a contemporary psychoanalytic object relational view of human nature.

DeLeon and DeLeon (2002) write, "one of the few issues on which public management scholars agree in theory is the centrality of the democratic ethos" (p. 229). Many scholars would argue with the authors' premise. Nevertheless, the democratic ethos to which they refer is that of citizen participation rather than the parallel internal management processes of administration and leadership and their effects on the culture of public bureaucracies. And, while the emphasis on citizen participation may be commendable, one has to wonder why the equivalent value is not placed on the actual management of those civil servants?

Critiquing the fields of organization and management theory, Collins (1997) pointed out the anti-democratic trend in organization theory. He wrote, "Persons who experience significant benefits as a result of the central position of 'liberty' in the social philosophical assumptions of democracy and capitalism tend to design organizational systems that significantly restrict the liberty of employees" (p. 489). And, in the same article, Collins (1997) quotes the philosopher and management scientist C. West Churchman (1994, p. 99) as concluding,

> As the first editor-in-chief of Management Science, I expressed my ambition for the society (TIMS) and its journal. My notion was that a society and journal in the subject of a science of management would investigate how humans can manage their affairs well. For me, "well" means "ethically," or in the best interest of humanity in a world of filthy oppression and murder. (I'm a philosopher and therefore have a philosophical bias, the same bias Plato had when he wrote The Republic.) I find that 40 years later management scientists have been inventing all kinds of mathematical models and novelties (management by objectives, game theory, artificial intelligence, expert systems, TQM, chaos theory), and none of these has contributed much to the ethical benefit of human beings. Hence, in 1993, we are still waiting for a science of management to emerge, although there are some lights at the end of the tunnel. (p. 439)

Collins (1997) goes on to argue for "uniting the social philosophical assumptions of organization theory with those of political and economic theory" (p. 490), ignoring the fact that these theories and their associated philosophical principles and assumptions are dissimilar, not to mention varied among individual theorists and philosophers.

In an article entitled "Organizational Democracy," Butcher and Clarke (2002) claim that the "effective organization demands that significant decisions be made lower in the hierarchy, and that leaders at all levels shape both strategy and front-line innovation." However, the authors are led to conclude that "there is substantial evidence that employees do not see themselves as beneficiaries of these changes. Surveys and reports consistently highlight unacceptable levels of cynicism, disillusionment and alienation at lower organizational levels. True organization democratization, it seems, continues to remain elusive, as does the reason for this." They conclude arguing that "the acceptability of organizational democracy depends on the legitimization of organizational politics" (pp. 35–36).

Absent among these mainstream organization, theorists' writings on democracy in organizations is an acknowledgement that is at the heart of this book of the interaction of psychological structures with organizational structures where human nature collides with hierarchies, bureaucracies, formal and informal groups, and divisions. Social structure can be understood to be an externalization of internalized psychological worlds (Diamond, 1984). In contrast, for the mainstream organization theorists, it is as if these organizations and their inhabitants have no inner life, no sense of self or identity that resides beneath the surface of formal roles and relationships. These theorists, rather than acknowledging the dialectical confrontation between person and organization, which psychoanalysis in its interrogation of reality does, take a Foucaultian-like perspective that in effect, organization defines self.

Limitations to the Foucaultian View

From reading Foucault's (1977, 1994) writings, one comes away with the perspective that organizational structure demarcates the person. Certainly one gets this idea from his *Discipline and Punish: the Birth of the Prison* (1977) and in particular his discussion of the powerfully penetrating gaze known as "panopticism." The term refers to "panopticon," which is the central observing tower inside modern prisons, where authorities observe prisoners and where prisoners cannot see that they are being observed. According to Foucault (1977), the "constant gaze" controls the prisoners, affecting not only what they do but how they see themselves. Identity and self-perception are imposed from the outside. For Foucault, this image served as a metaphor for the power of "governmentality" in the modern state.

It is as if the self is void of a private self, an internal world of lived and imagined experiences and perceptions, differentiated from one's host institution. Social structure and institutions dictate human emotions and perceptions beyond simply defining roles and human interactions. In a Foucaultian world, much like mainstream organization theory, transformation would come about with structural change and redesign. The self is treated as an empty vessel awaiting the injection of content, substance, shape, and form, from the external object (institution or organization). Such notions from our observations in the field as action researchers and participant-observers are naive and ignore or simply reject the internal and unconscious dynamics of organizational participants and their capacity to negotiate with the external world and for resistance to change. However, we are not suggesting that an imposing structure such as the panopticon does not affect prisoners or guards. We are saying Foucault's view is limited by its insufficiently dialectical view of human engagement with social reality. It is as if the human subject is in fact a tabula rasa.

In contrast, we find that organizational cultures become the context within which participants, leaders, and followers engage one another. These organizational cultures and social structures contain a paradox of will and unconscious intentions as workers join and associate with their individual, conscious, and unconscious needs, desires, and expectations. In our view, organizational structure collides with personality structure and human nature. Organizational politics and pathology signified by unconscious, repetitive patterns of dominance and submission and sadism and masochism are the outcome of this collision of internal and external structures (Benjamin, 1988; Diamond & Allcorn, 2004).

We find psychoanalytic object relational theories, such as Ogden's "Dialectical Modes of Experience" (1989, 1994) and Benjamin's "Paradox of Recognition between Self and Object" and the "Problem of Domination" (1988), more representative of actual self-other and self-object relations in organizations than Foucault's (sociological) structuralism. This seems particularly true in conceptualizing the nuances of change, resistances, and perversions of democratic processes within complex organizations. These institutions do not simply define their inhabitants. Organizational participants place demands on these institutions and their leaders. These expectations include conscious and unconscious needs for containment of members' anxieties of uncertainty, division, and conflict.

These anxieties and concomitant social defenses accelerate when contemporary organizations provide increasingly less job security. Consequently, the looming threat of job loss due to downsizing, reengineering, and outsourcing leaves workers with a precarious, insecure, and frequently hostile relationship with their employers. Employers also focus on socialization and indoctrination (training) to maintain control over subordinate behavior. These aspects of the workplace alienate workers and encourage them to feel as though they are powerless and disposable human resources. Participants respond and react to these conditions in various ways unintended by management and organizational design.

Dependency and powerlessness lead to self-experience that becomes the basis for psychological regression and primitive and unconscious relational processes. These processes include cognitive and emotional splitting of the self and object world into good or bad and accepting or rejecting. Splitting is supported by projection of rejected introjects outward onto others and by projective identification from which others take on the projected parts of self and object.

Theoretical Orientation: Psychoanalysis, Object Relations, and Organizational Politics

The emergence of Kleinian and post-Kleinian object-relations theory (Fairbairn, 1952; Winnicott, 1965, 1971; Greenberg & Mitchell, 1983; Ogden, 1989, 1994), infancy research (Mahler, Pine, & Bergman, 1975; Stern, 1985; Fonagy, 2001), and self-psychology (Kohut, 1977; Atwood & Stolorow, 1984) have created a paradigm shift in psychoanalysis from Oedipal to pre-Oedipal theory and from drive and instinct to relational models of human nature. Psychoanalysis, as Modell (1984) indicates, has evolved from a one-person to a two-person psychology. The battle for insight and change has moved from individual drives and instincts to the intra- and interpersonal (intersubjective) dimensions of self and other relations (Gedo, 1999; Mitchell & Aron, 1999; Fairfield, Layton, & Stack, 2002).

The linking of repression with more primitive, pre-Oedipal, defensive acts of psychological splitting came to the fore with the work of Melanie Klein and the British school of object relations (Fairbairn, 1952; Bion, 1959; Winnicott, 1965, 1971) when the influence of the mother took over from that of the father. Object-relations theorists describe an internal, infantile world of relations ("me and not me") as one of fragments; awareness of good and bad, loving and hating, accepting and rejecting, and satisfying and depriving; and experiences of self and other via projection. These modes of experience in the moment are largely unconscious arising from transference of forgotten parts of one's past onto the present. These perspectives provide insight into the workplace. The application of psychoanalytic object relations to formal groups and organizations addresses horizontal and vertical divisions and fragmentations between functional specializations, subsystems, subcultures, and professions that may well contain denial, splitting, and projection (Diamond & Allcorn, 2003; Diamond, Allcorn, & Stein, 2004).

The Dynamics of Workplace Democracy

Dysfunction and conflict within organizations are frequently manifested in defensive splits and black and white categorizations, creating polarizations between groups and their members. Typical oppositional groups and splits are younger versus older generations of employees, racial and ethnic tensions, one profession (such as engineers) versus another profession (such as architects), men versus women, workers versus management, and one office (division) versus another. It is not unusual to find one health-care specialization aggressively competing with another and consequently becoming polarized and fragmented in their broken relations and ability to coordinate tasks, to the detriment of a shared patient.

Healing these splits requires intervention directed at reparation and reintegration of organizational parts via an ongoing psychodynamically informed process of reflective learning, mutual recognition, and change. This approach to organizational change embraces the inevitability of the presence of intergroup and interpersonal conflicts and rivalries. Perversions of democracy in the workplace, therefore, require understanding the psychological nature of horizontal and vertical organizational splits and boundaries. In particular, boundaries are points of contact between groups and individuals (see Chapter 2). They create comforting differentiation between self and other and one work group and another. However, boundaries are also troublesome for participants when they seem to become insurmountable organizational silos that fragment working relationships (see Chapter 3) (Diamond et al., 2004). In the complex world of organizations, relational dynamics matter. Horizontal and vertical administrative relations are typically filled with conflict and tension between forces of oppression and forces of freedom. It is not surprising to find individual and collective desires for change resisted by those in favor of the status quo. These dynamics, shaped by unconscious processes, influence the subsystems and units that comprise the organization and its culture. They are the focal point of our attention.

Just as political scientist and co-founder of political psychology Harold Lasswell (1930, 1948) thought, we assume psychoanalytic theory provides insight into these political and psychological dynamics. He understood that the connection between public actions and private motives is frequently unconscious, where private motives become displaced onto public causes and rationalized in the public interest (Lasswell, 1930). Lasswell underscored that the value of psychoanalytic theory is not limited to individualistic and intrapsychic processes. It is aimed at the social and collective as well as intrapersonal dimensions. As Freud (1921) wrote in *Group Psychology and the Analysis of the Ego*, "individual psychology . . . is at the same time social psychology as well" (p. 1)—a claim that preceded object-relations theory and relational psychoanalysis.

The application of psychoanalytic theory to social and political issues takes into account an imperfect and conflicted human nature; one that, despite itself, has a capacity to support democratic processes within groups and organizations. Consistent with Winnicott's "good enough mothering" and his notion of the "good enough facilitative holding environment," we evaluate the quality of human relationships at work according to whether or not they promote healthy attachments that develop along a continuum from total dependence to relative independence. We assume that leader-follower, interpersonal, and group dynamics exist along a range from "good enough" to "not good enough" in their promotion, facilitation, and support for democratic workplace processes. "Good enough" leader-follower psychodynamics, social structures, and processes promote a group and organizational culture with "transitional and potential space" for creativity, diversity, learning, and change (Winnicott, 1971). This space creates requisite containment of emotional and intellectual tensions, individual and group differences, and divisions and conflicts between participants to foster productive organizational dynamics (Bion, 1959). These unavoidable tensions, when contained, become the emotional and psychological sustenance of democratic tendencies in the workplace. The value of a dialectical interplay between dimensions of self-experience and object relationships and the importance of "good enough" holding environments has been stressed throughout this book. Political theorist James Glass understands these paradoxical dimensions of human nature.

In *Psychosis and Power*, Glass (1995) writes,

> There is a difference between celebration of fragmentation and celebration of division. Acknowledgement of division is acknowledgement that the unconscious is not going to go away, that conflict cannot be purged out of human experience but is essential to what it means to be human and to live within the universe of will, desire, and need. Conflict sustains division. Fragmentation, however, is the destruction by conflict of its containing framework; fragmentation shatters experience, destroys recognition and tolerance, immobilizes the ego, and annihilates identity. Division implies the acceptance and recognition of boundaries and culturally defined spaces that require both acceptance and representation. Division enhances identity by pushing awareness to grasp the divided, yet communicable parts of the self. (p. 202)

Perversions of Democracy

Perversions of democratic processes in the workplace are manifested in unilateral, defensive, sadistic, and, at times, draconian executive actions (Diamond & Allcorn, 2004). These human actions typically insult and traumatize the emotional and intellectual integrity of workers. These actions are perversions of democratic processes as they represent arbitrary abuse of power and authority. These abuses often contain primitive psychological processes of splitting and fragmenting self and other into good or bad and lovable or despicable part-objects. Democratic practices at work require a democratic capacity of self in relation to self and others. This is manifested in more than simple tolerance for diversity among individuals. It is reflected in the treatment of others as subjects in their own right. Such practices have their psychological origins in a "good-enough" facilitating environment from infancy through adolescence and into adulthood. This maturational environment originates with the internalization of "good-enough mothering" and the containment of paradoxical and contradictory feelings and thoughts about self and other as highlighted by the depressive mode of experience (Winnicott 1965, 1971; Ogden, 1989).

Nevertheless, the rendering of these perversions as conscious-unconscious aspects does not result in the elimination or magical disappearance of the "uncanny other" (Glass, 1995)—the darker side of self and private selves within organizations. These shadows of humanity evoke the need for acknowledgment and containment of the other as self-object created by acts of psychological splitting and projections. These negative and aggressive projections and associated psychological splitting inevitably occur between organizational participants, particularly during stressful times (Allcorn & Diamond, 1997). Democratic institutions, we argue, are only as "good" or as democratic as their leaders' and followers' capacity to contain and attend to their own undemocratic and tyrannical proclivities. Group culture that respects members' paradoxical needs for identity through affiliation and differentiation and autonomy requires a safety net in the psychological form of an emotional floor.

The tripartite model informs our understanding of human relations in organizations. We briefly revisit its three modes of experience.

The Depressive Mode of Experience

The depressive mode of experience serves to contain experience. A self-interpreting subject is able to generate interpretive space between the symbol and that which it represents. One's self is experienced as a person who thinks one's own thoughts and feels and assumes responsibility for them. This permits experiencing oneself as a subject and other people as subjects rather than objects. Others are seen as capable of their own thoughts, feelings, and actions. They are seen as remaining the same people over time despite shifts in affection one may feel toward them. Along with the separateness of whole object relations, this continuity of experience of self and other reflects the capacity to have experience situated in time (historicity). This subjectivity is also the source of the primary anxiety of this mode. One fears the loss of the loved object that may act independently. A defensive stance characterized by denial of one's need for and attachment to others secures one against this anxiety.

The Paranoid-Schizoid Mode of Experience

The paranoid-schizoid mode is characterized by efforts to manage and evacuate psychic pain. Part-object relations characterize this mode. Others are experienced as fragmented mental objects that possess different qualities at different times. The primary dilemma is managing the intolerable anxiety related to loving and hating the same object. The resulting primary anxiety is managed through splitting, where one separates the loving and hating aspects of oneself from the loving and hating aspects of the loved object in order to prevent the bad and the endangering from destroying the good (the endangered).

In the paranoid-schizoid mode, immediate experience eclipses both past history and the future, thereby creating an eternal, ahistorical present. There is no interpretive space between subject and object to allow differentiation of the symbol from that which is symbolized. Consequently, the experience is two-dimensional. The world is concrete. Everything is and can only be the single thing that it is.

The Autistic-Contiguous Mode of Experience

In addition to recognizing the depressive and paranoid-schizoid positions described by Klein, Ogden posits a third mode of organization, which he refers to as the "autistic-contiguous." Ogden suggests that it is in the autistic-contiguous mode that the most elemental forms of human experience are generated. It is a pre-symbolic, sensory mode in which sensations of rhythm and "surface contiguity" (Ogden, 1989, p. 32) form the core of a person's first relationships with the external object world. In other words, experience of human contact is generated by the sensation of two surfaces coming together. Ogden emphasizes that there is a fundamental difference between this form of relatedness compared to the subject-to-subject relatedness of the depressive and the object-to-object relatedness of the paranoid-schizoid. What is important in this mode of experience is the sense of "pattern, boundedness, shape, rhythm, texture, hardness, softness, warmth, coldness, and so on" (Ogden, 1989, p. 33). The primary anxiety of this mode resides in the terror generated by the disruption of the continuity of sensory experience. Ogden refers to this as "formless dread." Defensive efforts are directed toward reestablishing a feeling of continuity and integrity of one's surface. This mode of experience has an important place in psychoanalytic organizational work.

Upon initial consideration, it may appear that the depressive and autistic-contiguous modes of experiencing are most different in terms of degree of psychological sophistication and achievement. Ogden points out, however, that they are similar insofar that in both modes, the primary anxiety depends upon integrative and containing processes. In the case of the autistic-contiguous, continuity is sensation based while in the depressive mode containment is accomplished through the distance afforded by language and interpretation. Discrimination, disintegration, and fragmentation, on the other hand, predominantly characterize the paranoid-schizoid mode. It is also the case that both disintegrative and integrative processes are required to maintain the dialectic among the positions. Cases of perversion of democratic processes are frequently characterized by organizations in which human relations collapse into the paranoid-schizoid mode, presenting multiple splits and fragments of a broken dialectic within an "us against them" social structure.

Modes of Experiencing and the Critical Dimension of Dialectical Interplay

The notion of dialectical interplay is central to our conceptualization of organization democracy. Democratic processes require a "good enough" psychological space for communication between people. This space is safe and valued, permitting the engagement of differences of opinions and conflicts. It is often a virtual space in which people play with ideas and feelings as well as invent possible solutions to difficult problems. Democratic practices are inherently creative including the uncertainty that creativity introduces.

We believe that creativity and imagination emerge out of the ongoing interplay between disintegrative and integrative relational processes, which occur in Winnicott's notion of potential and transitional space. These imaginative dynamics are not, however, exclusive of the depressive mode. Rather, democratic practices and creativity emerge in this potential space generated by the dialectical interplay between these three modes of experience. It is also the case that collapse of the dialectic, in the direction of one of the three modes of experiencing, arrests the capacity for creativity and perverts democratic processes. The collapse and its disintegrative processes break interpersonal and organizational boundaries into fragments disrupting surface containment and evoking primitive defenses such as splitting, projection, and projective identification. Psychological regression in the individual, group, and organization ought to be viewed as a danger signal for perversion of democratic processes at work.

Organizations and the Depressive Mode: Containment versus Control

In the context of a sustained dialectical interplay among the three modes of organizational experience, generative influences of the depressive mode may be evidenced in a number of ways. The depressive mode influences the organization to maintain a competitive edge by enabling acknowledgment of loss across the multiple domains in which it occurs, including unfavorable financial outcomes and market shifts, cultural changes, and interpersonal loss. History is acknowledged but is neither considered a future determinant nor deterrent. A sense of efficacy and competence in units and individuals exists in the context of interdependent relationships that contribute to coherence in organizational identity and functioning. There is a balanced attention to brainstorming ideas and operating pragmatics. Conflicting ideas can exist without the threat of compromising relationships. Strong feelings are talked through rather than acted out. People take responsibility for their actions.

Collapse in the direction of the depressive mode is evidenced by characteristics that Stacey (1992) refers to as organizational "ossification." Coherence gives way to rigidity. Communication structures become formalized. The cultural ambience becomes one of stagnation and deadness. Power is concentrated at the top. Access to those in power is tightly controlled. Those who have responsibility may not be delegated appropriate and adequate authority. Cultural norms and values are enforced, stifling emergent creative change. Efforts at containment become mandates for control. Adaptation and competition are replaced by defensive control. A gap between the realities that are internal and external to the organization develops. Morale, creativity, and effectiveness are compromised.

Organizations and the Paranoid-Schizoid Mode: Division versus Fragmentation

The influences of the paranoid-schizoid contribute to efficiency and productivity through differentiation and decentralization of tasks and functions such as splitting up work and control. Diversification and innovation are promoted by questioning tradition and by productive internal rivalries. The time between idea conception and product production is short, facilitated by energized informal lines of communication. Energy, intensity, spontaneity, and a sense of competing at the cutting edge characterize the ambience.

When an organization collapses in the direction of the paranoid-schizoid, idealization (often of the leader), envy, and competition characterize relationships. Open conflict and confrontation are, however, typically avoided in favor of scapegoating and blaming others usually outside the group. Issues that arise engender difficulty in articulation and working through polarized disagreement. Efficiency is poor. Individuals avoid personal accountability to avoid blame. Mistakes are concealed, making it hard for individuals and the organization to learn from experience. The resulting climate is one of mistrust, suspicion, and polarization.

Organizations and the Autistic-Contiguous Mode: Integration versus Isolation

The primary contribution of the autistic-contiguous mode of experience to organizational functioning is maintenance of a sense of stability, emotional integrity, and grounding in the face of problems and change. Intuition is valued. A strong sense of cultural identity is maintained. High standards for selection of organizational members promote organizational success. Everyone shares a valued sense of direction, creating purpose for his or her work.

Collapse into the autistic-contiguous engenders the most varied manifestations that are driven by a loss of cohesion and self and organizational integration. It may be easy to miss the multiple telltale clues that an effort is being made to generate a palpable organization surface that is reliable in its ability to ensure comfort and protection. For example, organizations may become closed systems, generating an ambience of being disconnected, vacillating between different states, out of touch with time and events, and developing a sense of elitist isolation. Processes, policies, and procedures become bureaucratized to the degree that they are ends in themselves to achieve machine-like perfection and predictability to contain anxiety. An organization collapsed toward the autistic-contiguous pole may use mimicry to make use of the surface (identity) of another object in place of its own identity. Mergers, the ultimate violation of the boundary with the external world, may be resisted at all costs. The organization may selectively maintain pressure to continually meet deadlines in the service of producing a self-defining surface to experience. These organizations may compulsively operate in constant crisis mode in order to create some sense of organizational identity.

In sum, the three modes of experience of the tripartite model encourage a close inspection of workplace dysfunction and perversions of democratic processes. These modes of dialectical experience produce an individual, interpersonal, group, and organizational context that contains potential space, where accurate reality testing, creativity, play, trust, respect, and fair play are the cultural ideals. Breakdown of the dialectical tension, in the form of polarized and fragmented object relations, perverts democratic values and practices. Retreat from the dialectical tension in the direction of any of the three modes of experience and the accompanying identifiable outcomes may be responded to in order to restore the interplay. These responses invariably require leaders to contain participants' anxiety in order that psychological regression is minimized. This set of events leads to losses of self-efficacy and integrity that collectively compromise organizational performance just when outstanding performance is the key to minimizing anxiety and restoring the dialectical tension.

Conclusion

Democratic organizational features and values, particularly the capacity to publicly acknowledge and process conflicts and divisions, are crucial. This organizational leadership and cultural capacity enables containment of human aggression that so often yields tyrannical and out-of-control organizational outcomes. Collective preoccupation with personal survival in the absence of inclusion, participation, fair play, trust, and respect displaces productive rewarding work. Object relational theory and its emphasis on differentiation and individuation over psychological splitting and fragmentation; subject-to-subject relations over object-to-object; and equity, fairness, and mutual recognition over dominance and submission; offers many insights into how democratic practices at work are fostered and sustained. Just as important, it provides a lens for understanding unconscious organizational and interpersonal trends that compromise one's experience of the organization as possessing democratic qualities.

In Chapter 11, we discuss the processes of intervention and change from a psychodynamic perspective. If organizations and their leaders are serious about democracy and participation in the workplace, then they will need to open their systems to interventions that can assist them in containing conflict and division in a productive manner and thereby in changing the foundations and assumptions underlying their relational systems, cultures, and identities.

11

Immersion and Diagnosis

It appalls me to think how much deep change I have prevented or delayed in patients in a certain classification category by my personal need to interpret. If only we can wait, the patient arrives at understanding creatively and with immense joy, and I now enjoy this joy more than I used to enjoy the sense of having been clever. I think I interpret mainly to let the patient know the limits of my understanding. The principle is that it is the patient and only the patient who has the answers. We may or may not enable him or her to encompass what is known or become aware of it with acceptance.

Winnicott, "The Use of an Object and Relating through Identification"

Organizational change is difficult whether you are a CEO, executive, manager, supervisor, or consultant. There are no simple answers, no stepwise quick fix that does justice to the complexities of organizational life. There are also no easy ways to avoid the inevitable costs that are associated with organizational change (emotional, financial, time and effort, and unintended consequences). What does make a difference is the approach described in this chapter and throughout the book. Our theory and method are a mix of change elements from more traditional approaches (Argyris, 1970; Burke, 1982; Harrison & Shirom, 1999; Harrison, 2005) that are combined with a psychodynamic model for organizational diagnosis and change. Genuine organizational change requires patience, deep listening, a sense of timing about participants' readiness for change, and sensitivity to the timing and rhythm of change.

Change, in this sense, cannot be forced or coerced. It has to be facilitated with patience and empathy with the participants. Enabling change to emerge and evolve over time is a process rooted in reflectivity and learning from experience. Providing organizational participants with an organizational diagnosis confirmed by them is crucial. Without this deeper, shared resonance and confirmation, change cannot take hold.

Psychologist Harry Levinson stresses organizational immersion as essential to comprehensive and meaningful organizational diagnosis (Levinson, 2002; Diamond, 2003). Levinson, an early pioneer of organizational diagnosis, insists that one cannot know an organization nor analyze its core problems without studying it from the inside-out. He has described his model of organizational assessment as a method of psychological anthropology (Diamond, 2003). Action researchers and consultants who facilitate change apply the methods and techniques of participant observation, ethnography, and analysis of transference and countertransference between organizational members and relative to anyone leading change. Factual, historical, generic, and interpretive (narrative) data are collected to answer the question: "What is it like to be a member of this organization?"

The psychodynamic processes and the method of organizational analysis and change presented here imply the consultant's (or social scientist's) use of the self as an instrument of reflective observation. Use of self is at the core of psychoanalytically informed organizational diagnosis and change. For instance, those using this approach to organizational change start by attending to the autistic shape (see Chapter 1) of organizational experience as they move across the surface of organizational boundaries. What does the organization feel like? Does it feel cold or warm? Is that experience shared by organizational participants? And what does it mean to them? What is the rhythm of the workplace? Is it fast paced or slow? Who talks to whom and how frequently? Who reports to whom and how effectively? Is it cumbersome or seamless when trying to gain access to one individual or another in the organization?

It is also the case that using oneself as an experiential instrument of data collection and sense making introduces the hazard of potentially over-identifying with participants and groups. This results in losing self-other boundaries and in getting pulled out of one's role as participant-observer. As indicated in Chapter 4, developing the analytic third and moving into the triangular (or potential) space permits articulating subjective and objective data in the organization. In contrast, merger and over-identification with clients and their organizations and the loss of self-other boundaries is troubling and problematic. It leads to alienating participants and losing their trust and confidence. It also produces mixed messages and inappropriate expectations leading to disappointments and anger at the consultants. Awareness of oneself is critical to managing these boundaries and taking up the position of the analytic third with organizational participants. After all, they are the source of meaning and information relevant to better understanding that informs change. This self-integrity and emotional capacity enable containment of uncanny participant emotions in organizations. Our use of containment here is derived from Bion's (1967) notion of interaction between "container" and "contained," the former referring to the baby with toxic or uncanny emotions such as aggression and the latter referring to the mother as recipient of these intolerable emotions. Successful containment, whether between mother and child or consultant and participant, produces a "good-enough" holding environment and is the basis of organizational repair and change. These change dynamics are the subject of the balance of this chapter.

Applying Transference and Countertransference to the Workplace: A Case Example

In object relations theory and practice, the self and awareness of transference and countertransference contribute to empathy, introspection, and understanding intersubjectivity and unconscious communications. They help us shape questions and interpretations that give better insight into the individual leaders, members, and their organizational cultures and identities. In this regard, the application of knowledge about transference and countertransference to organizations is a worthwhile challenge.

For our purposes here, we discuss the role of the psychoanalytically informed change agent, in particular the external consultant, in observing and intervening in organizational dynamics. We, however, also want to make clear that this discussion informs new executives who very often serve as change agents as well as those recently promoted or transferred and those in place for a considerable period of time. Every consultant, executive, and manager is faced with the need to adapt to changes in the external reality of the economy and body politic as well as the internal world of the organization. These roles and the individuals within them introduce transference and countertransference to and from organization members. We begin with an illustrative consultation divided into four discreet parts: (1) contracting, (2) organizational diagnosis, (3) intervention, and (4) follow-up. A case example is also provided to further ground the consulting stages within workplace interventions and change.

The Consultation Contracting Phase

The contract phase is a critically important aspect of an external intervention and in many ways also informs internal change agents as well. A number of precepts apply to this phase.

1. The executive in charge of the organization as well as the executive in charge of the area under study, if the consultation is limited to a division,

must provide a clear commitment to the intervention process and change.

2. The leaders must understand the methods to be used will include individual and group interviewing, participant observation and immersion, and surveys and collection of data pertaining to key performance indicators.
3. Interim progress reports and discussion of problems with the CEO and executives in charge of areas under examination will be provided, including findings of unethical or illegal behavior.
4. Expectation setting as to what can likely be accomplished by the consultants and what the CEO and executives in charge will be obliged to handle has to occur at the start.
5. The proposed time line and associated costs are discussed and agreed to.
6. The resulting contract should be clear, concise, and establish when payments for services will be made.

Case Example

The dean of a law school (Thomas) in a large public university requested assistance in helping him and his associate deans resolve a dispute between a majority of the faculty and their chairman in one of the school's highest profile and most successful departments. A faculty spokesperson (Richard) had presented the dean with a petition signed by a majority of the department's faculty demanding the removal of their chairman (Harold). Our discussions with the dean, Thomas, and the nature of the petition encouraged us to not contract to provide recommendations regarding personnel assignments and retention in order to avoid being seen from the outset as having Harold's removal as our task. We also requested that a task group be formed that included the dean, the associate deans, Richard, and a few faculty representatives from the department. The task group was convened to review the contractual scope and parameters of our work. In particular, it was made clear that we would provide no personnel recommendations. We also used this opportunity to review our methodology and our time line for accomplishing the work. We commenced our work with a clear scope that explicitly excluded being seen as on a mission to "take out" the chairman.

The Diagnostic Phase

We commenced our diagnostic work by conducting interviews with faculty and staff within the department in question. We also interviewed within the dean's office as well as department chairs whose primary tasks were linked with the client department. Our findings confirmed many of the problems we had learned about in our initial contracting interviews.

It was generally felt that the chair, Harold, was interpersonally "clumsy and had lost the respect of faculty." The chairman's relationship with the dean was also ambiguous. This further accentuated the problematic nature of his leadership role. The responsibility for the ambiguity belonged to the dean. He had failed to make clear his performance expectations for Harold and for the department as a whole. This included not clarifying how the departmental budget was to be managed. We also discovered that a respected and influential semi-retired faculty member was playing a significant role. He was using his considerable influence to promote the view that Harold was an ineffective leader and administrator. The department had received a major grant. But, it was unclear whether the department would be able to keep the grant. The dean was maneuvering to take a substantial portion of the grant for the school in order to benefit other departments that threatened its loss.

In sum, the new department chairman was under pressure from all sides. He was not effectively responding to his leadership opportunity. He appeared weak, divisive, and indecisive. It became clear from interviews and observations of him interacting with faculty that he lacked authority as well as communication and interpersonal skills. Harold had failed to take charge of the department and had succeeded in alienating many of his colleagues.

Our diagnostic work revealed that there were other less apparent elements contributing to this outcome. We found a long history of ineffective and unsupportive leadership from the dean's office that served to undermine the effectiveness of the department chairs throughout the law school. In particular, there existed an inordinate degree of centralized power and authority within the dean's office accompanied by insufficient delegation of authority and empowerment to the departments and academic programs. This highly centralized power combined with limitations and deficiencies within the dean's office was consequential. There existed ambiguity that led to departmental confusion, ineffectiveness, and weak representational leadership at the departmental level. It was reasonable to conclude that a portion of Harold's and each chair's poor performance was attributable to the dean, his immediate staff, and the character of organizational culture embedded within the law school.

It was also the case that Richard's role as the spokesperson for the dissenting faculty contained elements not readily apparent at the outset of the engagement. Richard had served as the interim chair during the recruitment and selection process for the new chairman eighteen months prior to his presentation of the faculty petition. It was also public knowledge that Richard was disappointed that he had not been selected by the dean to serve as the permanent chairman. Richard, although highly respected by his colleagues for his scholarly achievements, had a lengthy history of feeling that his many accomplishments were insufficiently recognized and compensated by the dean. His not being selected chairman underscored this lack of acknowledgement and approval. This made him an invaluable "container" of faculty disappointment and disenchantment. Thus, Richard had become identified by the faculty as someone who could represent their sentiments about their chairman's failures and deficiencies and who could be depended upon to be angry enough to "take him on."

In sum, the diagnostic work revealed that the initial presenting problem was only part of the story. It was now time to reflect back to those in the leadership group, our findings that had to include a note of caution in responding to Harold's performance problems, and the faculty's wish to be rid of him. We had also kept Thomas, the dean (our client), informed of our progress and some of our findings. It was apparent that Thomas was aware of much of what we learned and was contemplating changes in how he supervised his department chairs.

The Intervention

Our findings from the organizational diagnosis were organized for a feedback session with the task group (dean, associate deans, the selected departmental faculty, and Richard). As the feedback session commenced, several participants offered flattering compliments on our diagnostic work. It was also clear from other comments that were made that they spoke for the majority of those in the meeting. Everyone reported feeling "listened to" and that the consultant's depiction of the findings, although critical of their department and school, was "fair and balanced." In particular, Richard and the faculty members felt that what they heard communicated in the organizational story represented their shared "perceptions, views, and ideas" that were critical for the dean to hear.

This unexpected wave of approval, although sincere and heartfelt, signaled for us as the consultants a desire on the part of those present to ally themselves with us in our role as outside "authorities." We typically expect more dialogue and more back and forth with some suggested revisions and clarifications. However, this did not occur. While confirming responses such as these are welcome, they may signify splitting, projection, and transference dynamics at work creating an idealized object—the consultants. In particular, it is not uncommon for consultants (powerful, mysterious, authority figures) to be unconsciously associated with childhood experiences with parental figures. We were alerted to the presence of these out of awareness psychodynamics that would have to be "watched" for as adverse affects upon the group's ability to accomplish work.

The presentation of our findings continued to be well received right up to the end when it became clear to Richard and his departmental colleagues that the consultants were, true to the contract, not advocating or in any way tacitly supporting the removal of their chairman. This realization lead to a reasonably well modulated but hostile response from Richard who held up the signed petition for Harold's removal. In effect, how could the consultants or anyone else in the room not believe that this was essential? Efforts to assuage Richard failed as the intensity of his comments escalated. We intervened by recommending a separate meeting be held with Richard, the faculty, and the dean. Richard immediately embraced the proposal as a face-saving way out of what had gradually become an over-wrought response on his part.

Follow-Up

The meeting was immediately scheduled for our next visit to campus. It was clear that Richard and his colleagues were severely disappointed. Predictably, when the meeting was convened, Richard expressed outrage at the betrayal of his and the faculty's now disillusioned fantasy that the outcome of our work would lead to Harold's termination as chairman. Richard was convinced beyond any reasonable doubt that a conspiracy existed against him and the faculty, a conspiracy planned from the very beginning. The consultants, he asserted with increasing paranoia, had colluded with the dean from the start to retain Harold. Paradoxically, this view was held despite the fact that Richard was initially one of the most outspoken proponents of the content and integrity of the organizational diagnosis, which he described as "fair and balanced" and as having given him and others "a voice they had previously lacked." Moreover, his outrage was contradicted by other aspects of the organizational diagnosis that pointed to disarray in how the dean's office managed the school and related to the departments and their chairs. Finally, he was also fully aware that the scope of work contracted for explicitly excluded recommendations consistent with his desires. It was, therefore, important on the part of the consultants to appreciate that a shared fantasy had been shattered with concomitant psychological regression, splitting, and projection, transforming the consultants from idealized, good objects to despised, bad ones.

Reflections

As Richard proceeded with his accusations, we came to understand that his antagonism was a reflection of his lack of influence and power over the dean's decision making and his historical absence of recognition by the dean as underscored by him not being selected as chairman. It was reasonable to assume that his aggression could not be safely acted out relative to the dean. Prior to our arrival, Richard found the chair to be a safe depository of projected aggression. Subsequently, Richard's hostility was displaced onto the consultants who, after becoming all bad persecutory objects who support the dean, were not only safe to attack but merited attack. Once idealized by Richard, we were now despised and expendable intruders. After all we (consultants) would be leaving and, as Richard fantasized, we would be taking these bad, angry, hostile feelings and part-objects with us.

One might speculate in this case that the outcome could be associated with childhood experiences of parental withholding of affection and appropriate adoration, inflicting narcissistic injury on Richard. Acting upon these feelings required locating a safer target for the child's rage or perhaps a retreat into fantasy where unlimited aggression could be directed against parental figures without harming them. We remind the reader that this is merely speculation.

However, we were aware of our own countertransference evoked by Richard's intensely hostile and persecutory statements. If these countertransference experiences went undigested and unarticulated, we could be faced with the potential of a failed consultation. At first, we felt helpless, defenseless, and angry. While "sitting with" these aggressive attacks, we had to sort through our own thoughts and feelings to avoid countertransference fueled defensive reaction to Richard's accusations and condemnations. In so doing, we came to experience Richard's frustrated desires to successfully lead a coup and his fear of the possibility of directing his anger at the dean who had so consistently disappointed him but from whom he continued to seek approval. We, who had initially provided him voice in much the same way that he had given voice to the faculty's concerns, were now summarily judged to have failed to fulfill his fantasy of annihilating his boss. This fantasy he had carried on behalf of the faculty, and he had failed to deliver on it. Our ability to locate the projected content and our countertransference experience permitted us to respond to Richard and the larger context of the meeting in a candid and empathic way.

We responded by acknowledging Richard's disappointment as legitimate. We also validated his feelings of anger and paranoia by stating sincerely that if we were in his position, we might feel much the same way. At the same time, we also wanted to engage him in a reflective process that drew into question the role he had assumed on behalf of the faculty to achieve Harold's termination by using the consultants to accomplish the task. A process such as this validates the individual's thoughts and feelings while not judging his experience and perceptions. It also restores reflectivity and a more mature (non-regressive) handling of the disappointment. Moving between paranoid-schizoid and depressive modes of experience, this approach provides the client with a firm relational surface in the autistic-contiguous experience against which he could engage in reality testing by acknowledging the fantasy moving his actions and reactions.

Thus, we had attempted to unload Richard's projections onto us and to support him in a process of reintegration. In particular, we indicated that we were neither perfect in our work nor perfectly imperfect. We had done our work to the best of our ability and had stuck with the scope of the contract, despite the regressive pull of wanting his approval, which we acknowledged included recommending Harold be removed as chair. Richard was receptive to our feedback so we ventured one additional step. We pointed out that we felt that we had been made the focus of displaced aggression that he held for the dean but felt safer in acting out toward us. We conjectured that this possibly mirrored his relationship to the chair. We encouraged him and the dean to meet to discuss their history and how they might better work together in the future.

Although not entirely accepting the outcome, Richard and the faculty group for whom he spoke acknowledged the validity of the consultation process. We also want to point out here that by our using a clearly defined organizational change methodology and scope of work that stipulated phases (contractual agreement, organizational diagnosis, intervention, and follow-up), we created for ourselves and the clients an important procedural and psychological anchor from which to proceed. This anchoring effect is especially critical when unconscious and irrational forces work against a successful organizational change process.

The Case in Sum

This case example illustrates much of the organizational terrain that exists within the psychologically defensive workplace (Allcorn & Diamond, 1997). Several fantasies existed. The first was that this group and its leader could dispose of their chairman. The second was that the consultants possessed sufficient authority and power so as to fulfill this fantasy and would act contrary to the contractual agreement. The consultants failing to do so provoked a dramatic collapse of the fantasy and accompanying positive transference and the rapid emergence of bitter disappointment, helpless rage, polarized black and white experience, and a highly energized transference-fed attack on the now disposable consultants. The individual most mobilized by this outcome was Richard, who carried for the faculty the wish to be rid of their chairman.

Richard's hostile reaction to his inability to manipulate us as the consultants or to control the dean points toward psychodynamics that are mutually interactive and reinforcing. As mentioned in the case, psychological splitting and projection creates all-bad objects that deserve annihilation. Confrontation with this individual's (and group's) helplessness to affect the wished for change relative to the bad object appeared to lead to a revisiting of childhood experiences in which the child's fantastic wishes were not attended to by parental figures. In this case, the coping response on the part of the child appears to have been feelings of narcissistic rage that were displaced onto safer objects or acted out in fantasy in order to avoid destroying the necessary parental figures.

In conclusion, this case illustrates how psychological regression, splitting, and projection of aggression via transference combined to create a challenging multidimensional and psychologically defensive workplace for the consultants. It is also equally clear that countertransference dynamics and psychologically defensive splitting and projection, if recognized and sensitively interpreted, can inform interventions. We now turn to a discussion of several important perspectives implicit in psychoanalytically informed consultation not thus far discussed.

Additional Perspectives

During the course of consultation, we suggest that positive transference dynamics that we were aware of (despite their regressive nature) enabled us to establish therapeutic alliances with organization members. An essential component of this alliance is the capacity for "containment" and "holding" where as consultants, we stand at the interpersonal and organizational boundary with one foot inside and one foot outside the organization. Trust is an essential component of this relationship. And, although we may inevitably develop a unique working relationship with the executive who authorizes the organizational diagnosis, the integrity of the work and thereby the establishment of trust ultimately comes about as a result of fair and unbiased listening and observing on the part of the consultants in the collection of data.

Action researchers and consultants producing organizational diagnoses cannot recommend personnel changes as a part of their contractual agreement, otherwise they may find themselves in the position of promoting, rather than observing and interpreting, psychological splitting and regression in the form of blaming and "scapegoating." Consequently, they may become participants in, rather than consultants to, organizational dysfunction. Consultant commitment to listening to all participants while withholding judgment and asking for clarification of communications of affect, experience, and perceptions of organizational members is viewed positively by the large majority of participants (Stein, 1994). In particular, interviewees are protected by confidentiality and anonymity, which encourages openness and the establishment of trusting relationships with the outsiders. Organizational participants often scrutinize processes of consultant data gathering and communicating findings with clients for potential bias, prejudice, and untested assumptions. Fair, inclusive, objective data collection and openness reinforces the willingness of many organizational participants to share openly and candidly their experiences, observations, and desires with consultants. Nevertheless, as illustrated in the case example, these measures will not suppress nor are they intended to suppress the proclivity of participants to engage in psychologically regressive processes such as splitting, projection, fantasies, and transference processes, which then become valuable data in the psychoanalytic organizational study.

Organizational Reparation

We now turn to the unique nature of organizational reparation, repair, and restoration, which is at the heart of a psychoanalytically informed approach to organizational change.

Reparation requires a four-step process that includes the following steps:

1. Confrontation and Interpretation. Confronting the problem of workplace aggression and hostility requires understanding, interpreting, and validating the roots of violence and aggression in the organization. This step includes collecting interpretive data from confidential one-on-one interviews; collecting survey data on stress and morale; and collecting documents, artifacts, and on-site observations. Trust between analyst/ consultant and organization members at every level is essential and requires deep listening and empathy (Stein, 1994; Kets de Vries, 2001).
2. Problem setting: Sharing feedback and rendering public. Problem setting requires that organizational members agree on what the problems are in addition to their origins in the system. Shapiro and Carr (1991) would call this a negotiated interpretation. This step follows the first step of analysis and diagnosis and requires reporting the findings to the organizational members for confirmation or rejection. Often, these data are collected through confidential interviews and anonymous surveys so that employees feel protected from intimidation or retribution. In cases of violence and aggressive acts at work, confidentiality and anonymity become exceedingly important.

3. Problem solving: Working through grieving and reparation. Creating a safe physical and emotional haven and transitional space for employees to work through feelings of anger and rage enables them to feel loss and begin the process of letting go and healing their wounded spirits. Then, engaging in solving problems and resolving conflicts empowers the organizational participants. Problem solving is a collective action that heals through the process of collaboration and mutual respect, rendering people who have experienced injustices passively to feel proactive through effective, concrete improvements in the workplace. In other words, once the precise problems are agreed upon, members can take charge again and potentially heal themselves and their organization. This third phase of intervention is atypical of most interventions and is central to a psychoanalytic organizational change methodology.

4. Reorganization: Taking action and changing culture and identity. Reorganization is the period following mourning and grief that any culture must undertake in order to change itself and to forgive the injustices of the past. Surfacing internalized images of self, other, and organization are critical here. Sharing of individual and collective experiences of organizational participants enables cognitive unlearning of old ways and assumptions as well as emotional release of privately held images and experiences that governed behavior. Reorganization implies a new framework for accomplishing work through cooperation; it means that employees participate in the social construction of a new organizational identity.

In Sum

Psychoanalytically informed consultation attends to unconscious dynamics. It does so by having a theoretical framework for understanding complex human relations in organizations. It also accomplishes this by applying a method for analyzing and articulating the effect of human relations, as contained by the consultants, on the capacity to coordinate work, decision making, planning, authority, and responsibility. Clarifying the intervention process and method at the outset is crucial. The interpersonal security and safety provided by this up-front agreement and roadmap for consultation are significant in managing, but certainly not eliminating, projection and projective identification and transference and countertransference, where the processing and analyzing of feelings of anxiety are essential to promoting reflectivity and resilience in organizations.

Conclusion

Human Nature and Organizational Silos

As a mode of cognition, metaphor is doubly embodied, first, as an unconscious neural process and, second, in that metaphors are generated from bodily feelings, so that it is possible to speak of a corporeal imagination.

Arnold H. Modell, Imagination and the Meaningful Brain

The purpose of this book was to explore the psychological and social complexities of organizations from an object relational, psychoanalytic perspective. The construction of organization theory was derived from action research, fieldwork, consultation, and what we learned from observing and interpreting thematic patterns and common characteristics of actual organizations. The idea for this book evolved out of nearly three decades of organizational research and consultation, and the desire to reflect on that experience with organizations. One critical lesson we learned over the years, which we discussed in the previous chapter and tried to convey throughout this book, was the value of organizational diagnosis and assessment as a reflective process for organizational change.

Workers want to be heard and understood. Organizational stories make a difference to them. These narrative depictions of organizational culture and circumstances, if done well, resonate with participants' experiences, relationships, and perceptions. And, when participants confirm the narrative truth of their organizational stories, they are claiming ownership of their actions and personal responsibility for their organizations and predicaments, minimizing scapegoating and fragmentation. If consultants and action researchers can adequately capture workers experiences in thematic patterns, stories, and metaphor, then change through processes of group identification and reparation becomes possible.

In the process of listening to and repeating organizational stories, one particular theme had persistently stood out as meaningful to organizational members, the experience of silos. The silo metaphor (see Chapter 3) explained something conceptually and emotionally rich and valuable about individuals, working relationships, and organizational structures. Silos emerged as one of the predominant themes in the study and consultation to over fifty organizations in government, business, healthcare, and higher education. For us, the metaphor signified the participants' defensive preoccupation, conscious and unconscious, with their anxiety about facing conflict and restoring cooperation between diverse groups and individuals. Of course, this is precisely what has to be publicly addressed in a change effort, if deep change is possible. If, as we stated at the beginning of this book, organizations are the context of a collision between psychological and social structure, then our approach to organizational change ought to reflect and promote that awareness.

Vignette

One of our earliest experiences with the silo phenomenon appeared in a large public works agency. Responsible for statewide public works projects, this bureaucracy was haunted by a poor record of timely project completions. It was threatened by competition from the private sector and threats of elimination by the legislature. Administrators, lawyers, architects, engineers, and construction managers were located in their respective technical-functional and disciplinary divisions. Workers frequently referred to these divisions as silos. And, while the use of the metaphor was aptly descriptive of social structure and the location of various professions within their own jurisdictional areas, we felt from interviews and observations that the metaphor signified workers' experience, sense of self, and group identity in the context of the public agency. It was a subjective as well as an objective phenomenon.

Silos were not only descriptive of organizational structure but also reflected a defensive frame of mind, a social defense. By way of metaphor, workers had accurately and unwittingly described the collision of social and psychological structure. Silos were proffered by managers as a rationalization for dysfunction and resistance to change. Professional workers claimed they did not know what other professionals knew. They could not see, and should not look, into the other's silo. Professional knowledge was secretive and information withheld. The social structure of us against them was treated by members as routine and unavoidable. It was also not discussable during the course of everyday work routines. There was little insight among workers around personal responsibility for their actions, which perpetuated silos and a silo mentality. Projects exceeded budgets and deadlines for completion. Construction crews stood by unused equipment, idly waiting for change orders that required multiple signatures for approval. The poor quality of work was frequently criticized by legislators and administrators of other public agencies. Consequently, architects would blame engineers. Engineers would blame construction managers. Administrators would blame project managers and so on. Mistrust, paranoia, and scapegoating evolved over time. Psychological splitting of self and others into good and bad and accepting and rejecting reinforced us against them social and psychological structure.

Applied Object Relations and Organizational Change

The object relational (tripartite) model (see Chapter 1) made it possible to see the collective psychological regression in the form of a paranoid-schizoid collapse among organizational members who were retreating to their objective (external) and subjective (internal) divisional silos. From a rational organizational framework, we knew the hierarchical bureaucratic design was part of the problem. Social structure matters and in our framework it is an important piece of the puzzle. A flatter, cross-functional organizational design based on regional project teams seemed more rational and made sense to everyone. Structural change was necessary, but it was not sufficient. We knew that certain psychodynamics were driving the perpetuation of defensive routines and horizontal fragmentation reflected in the silo metaphor. These organizational psychodynamics would have to change. Psychological structure matters and is often overlooked in organizational change.

A dynamic process for planned change enabling participants to reflect on their dysfunctional and regressive relational patterns was necessary (see Chapter 11). This process for change had to enable competent professionals to feel safe and secure with experimentation and innovation. We needed to produce a holding environment in which participants could explore how their mindsets and practices reinforced dysfunction and limited effectiveness. They had to feel safe enough to talk about that which they were unable to discuss previously.

Psychoanalytically informed, organizational diagnosis and change take seriously the psychological reality of the workplace (see Chapter 9). Experiences and perceptions matter a great deal despite what many managers, executives, and social scientists are taught to assume about human nature reduced to goal-seeking economic beings. This intersubjective, psychological structure of organizations is comprised of transference and countertransference and projections and projective identifications (see Chapter 4). People are tied together emotionally and cognitively. They are frequently unaware of the nature of their relationships and consequently cannot explain their own actions or the actions of others. The intersubjective structure of organization is the context where the meaning of work and affiliation to leadership and organization is located. It is where the rationale for irrational acts is found. Analysis of transference and countertransference dynamics between and among organizational participants and with consultants and action researchers facilitates crafting the organizational story.

These stories are comprised of relational dynamics over time in which meaningful thematic patterns and repetitions are discovered by immersion in the workplace and trying to make sense out of the experiences. The capacity for empathy, identification without over-identification, and containment is crucial for the collection of meaningful data about organizational life. Organizational diagnosis is then a product of immersion and participant observation. Organizational change based on effective intervention relies on the establishment of trust and mutual respect through empathy and understanding of organizational participants. Psychoanalytically oriented diagnosis and intervention are intended to facilitate the production of a liberating potential and holding space for participants' thinking, feeling, experiencing, learning, and changing.

Rooted in the safety of Winnicott's idea of a *holding environment* and *potential and transitional space*, participants consensually validate *their* organizational story, weaving threads of connection and mutuality that were absent among seemingly disparate groups such as the professionals in the public works agency. We find organizational participants develop greater self-awareness and the capacity for reflectivity with good enough holding by leaders and consultants. Potential space for creativity and experimentation with feelings and ideas is a critical component of effective change processes. By moving beneath the surface of organizational strategy and structure to meanings and motives, participants find they can move forward and change.

Finally, genuine and comprehensive organizational change cannot happen without the support, endorsement, and participation of organizational leadership. Not all organizational diagnoses and interventions end happily. In some instances, leaders' anxieties and defenses get the best of them. Leaders may find that they do not have the emotional capacity for holding and containing tensions and conflicts among followers. Their resistances are such that leaders cannot transition, emotionally and cognitively, with the organizational participants.

We are struck by how often leaders get "cold feet" and panic, and despite all the espoused commitments and statements of "readiness for change" and support for opening-up the organization and themselves, they resist change. They may call for more consultation but to no avail. Or, they may indicate that they are going to implement changes and evidently have no intention of doing so. Consequently, these leaders deeply disappoint and anger their employees for years to come. From our research and consultation experience, we have found that many leaders who fail to implement positive change remain unconscious of their private selves and unaware of their personal impact on workers, human relations, and organizational culture.

Having gone through the reflective processes of organizational diagnosis and intervention, participants themselves may be changed despite their leaders and executives frequent defensive resistances to altering the status quo. We do not claim here that personality change is an outcome of these processes, although some may make that claim. However, we do think that organizational participants experience an expansion of self-consciousness and organizational awareness by reducing defensive routines. They may develop a better idea of how things might change and how divisional silos and moral violence in their organizations might be remedied. They are frequently less defensive with their colleagues as a result of consultation because they have come to see the value of minimally defensive and candid dialogue that confronts rather than conceals problems in the workplace. They may also develop a better idea about the role and function of leaders and the need to recruit executives with self awareness and the capacity for empathy and reflectivity. And, they typically develop a greater appreciation for genuine democracy and participation in the workplace. They understand the dysfunctional and destructive impact of dominant-submissive relationships inside and outside of organizational hierarchies. Finally, if workers do change personally, then it has to do with understanding themselves better in the context of organizational psychodynamics. As human beings, we construct our institutions and in turn are affected by them.

We hope in reading this book, that organizational researchers and consultants develop a deeper, more nuanced, and richer idea about the links between our private selves and *public* organizations. We hope that in your studies of organizations you come to value the subjective and objective dimensions of the workplace. We also hope that readers gain a healthy dose of skepticism about superficial approaches to organizational change that deny psychological structure and overestimate social structure.

References

Abram, J. (1997). *The language of Winnicott*. Northvale, NJ: Jason Aronson.

Adams, G., & Balfour, D. (1998). *Unmasking administrative evil*. Thousand Oaks, CA: Sage Publications.

Alford, C. F. (1994). *Group psychology and political theory*. New Haven, CT: Yale University Press.

Allcorn, S. (1992). *Codependency in the workplace*. Westport, CT: Quorum Books, Greenwood Publishing Group.

Allcorn, S. (1994). *Anger in the workplace*. Westport, CT: Quorum Books, Greenwood Publishing Group.

Allcorn. S. (1995). Understanding organizational culture as the quality of workplace subjectivity. *Human Relations, 48*(1), 73–96.

Allcorn, S. (2002). *Death of the spirit in the workplace*. Westport, CT: Quorum Books, Greenwood Publishing Group.

Allcorn, S., & Diamond, M. A. (1997). *Managing people during stressful times: The psychologically defensive workplace*. Westport, CT: Quorum Books, Greenwood Publishing Group.

Allcorn, S., Baum, H. S., Diamond, M. A., & Stein, H. F. (1996). *The human costs of a management failure: Downsizing at general hospital*. Westport, CT: Quorum Books, Greenwood Publishing Group.

Amado, G. (1995). Why psychoanalytical knowledge helps us understand organizations: A discussion with Elliott Jaques. *Human Relations, 48*(4), 351–357.

Argyris, C. (1970). *Intervention theory and method: A behavioral science view*. Reading, MA: Addison-Wesley Publishing Company.

Argyris, C. (1985). *Strategy, change, and defensive routines*. New York: Putnam.

Argyris, C. (1990). *Overcoming organizational defenses*. Boston: Allyn and Bacon.

Argyris C., & Schon, D. (1996). *Organizational learning*. Reading, MA: Addison Wesley Publishers. (Original work published 1978).

Argyris, C., & Schon, D. (1996). *Organizational learning II: Theory, method, and practice*. Reading, MA: Addison-Wesley Publishing Company.

Aron, L., & Summer. F. (Eds.) (2000). *Relational perspectives on the body*. Anderson, NJ: Analytic Press.

Atwood, G. E., & Stolorow, R. D. (1984). *Structures of subjectivity*. Anderson, NJ: Analytic Press.

Barnard, C. I. (1938). *The functions of the executive*. Cambridge, MA: Harvard University Press.

Baum, H. S. (1987). *The invisible bureaucracy*. London: Oxford University Press.

Baum, H. S. (1994). Transference in organizational research. *Administration & Society*, 26(2), 135–157.

Benjamin, J. (1988). *The bonds of love: Psychoanalysis, feminism, and the problem of domination*. New York: Pantheon Books.

Benjamin, J. (1995). *Like subjects, love objects*. New Haven, CT: Yale University Press.

Benjamin, J. (2004). Beyond doer and done to: An intersubjective view of thirdness. *The Psychoanalytic Quarterly*, LXXIII(1), 5–46.

Bick, E. (1968). The experience of the skin in early object relations. *International Journal of Psycho-Analysis*, 49, 484–486.

Bick, E. (1986). Further considerations on the function of the skin in early object relations. *British Journal of Psychotherapy*, 2, 292–299.

Bion, W. R. (1959). *Experiences in groups*. New York: Basic Books.

Bion, W. R. (1962). *Learning from experience*. London: Karnac.

Bion, W. R. (1965). *Transformations*. London: Tavistock.

Bion, W. R. (1967). *Second thoughts*. London: Karnac. (Reprinted 2003).

Bion, W. R. (1970). *Attention and interpretation*. London: Tavistock.

Blau, P. (1956). *Bureaucracy in modern society*. New York: Random House.

Bollas, C. (1987). *In the shadow of the object: Psychoanalysis of the unthought known*. New York: Columbia University Press.

Bollas, C. (1992). *Being a character*. New York: Hill & Wang.

Bowlby, J. (1969). *Attachment, Vol. 1*. New York: Basic Books.

Bowlby, J. (1973). *Separation, Vol. 2*. New York: Basic Books.

Bowlby, J. (1980). *Loss, Vol. 3*. New York: Basic Books.

Brainard, J. (1999, November 19). Researchers are urged to work toward new treatments with health-care providers. *The Chronicle of Higher Education*.

Braverman, M. (1999). *Preventing workplace violence*. London: Sage Publications.

Briskin, A. (1996). *The stirring of soul in the workplace*. San Francisco: Jossey-Bass.

Britton, R. (2004). Subjectivity, objectivity, and triangular space. *The Psychoanalytic Quarterly*, LXXIII(1), 47–62.

Burge, F. J. (1993). Silo commanders and the enterprise-wide vision. *Electronic Business Buyer*, 19(10), 188.

Burke, W. W. (1982). *Organization development: Principles and practices*. Boston: Little, Brown and Company.

Butcher, D., & Clarke, M. (2002). Organizational politics, the cornerstone of organizational democracy. *Organizational Dynamics*, 31(1), 35–46.

Butz, M. R. (1997). *Chaos and complexity: Implications for psychological theory and practice*. Washington, DC: Taylor & Francis.

Capozzoli, T., & McVey, R. S. (1996). *Managing violence in the workplace*. Delray Beach, FL: St. Lucie Press.

Cavell, M. (1998). Triangulation, one's own mind, and objectivity. *International Journal of Psychoanalysis*, 55, 349–357.

Chasseguet-Smirgel, J. (1984). *Creativity and perversion*. London: Free Association Books.

Chasseguet-Smirgel, J. (1985). *The ego ideal: A psychoanalytic essay on the malady of the ideal* (P. Barrows, Trans.). New York: Norton.

Churchman, C.W. (1968). *The systems approach.* New York: Dell.

Cloke, K., & Goldsmith, J. (2002). *The end of management and the rise of organizational democracy.* New York: Wiley & Sons, Inc.

Collins, D. (1997). The ethical superiority and inevitability of participatory management as an organizational system. *Organization Science, 8*(5), 489–507.

Czander, W. (1993). *The psychodynamics of work and organizations.* New York: Guilford.

DeLeon, L., & DeLeon, P. (2002). The democratic ethos and public management. *Administration & Society, 34*(2), 229–250.

Denhardt, R. B. (1987). Images of death and slavery in organizational life. *Journal of Management, 13*(3), 529–541.

De Tocqueville, A. (1956). *Democracy in America* (1835–1839) (J. P. Moore, Ed., G. Lawrence, Trans.). New York: Doubleday. (Original work published 1840)

Diamond, M. A. (1998). The symbiotic lure: Organizations as defective containers. *Administrative Theory & Praxis, 20*(3), 315–325.

Diamond, M. A. (1999). Embracing organized disorder: The future of organizational membership. *Administrative Theory & Praxis, 21*(4), 433–440.

Diamond, M. A. (1984). Bureaucracy as externalized self-system: A view from the psychological interior. *Administration & Society, 16*(2), 195–214.

Diamond, M. A. (1988). Organizational identity: A psychoanalytic exploration of organizational meaning. *Administration & Society, 20*(2), 166–190.

Diamond, M. A. (1991). Stresses of group membership: Balancing the needs for independence and belonging. In M. F. R. Kets de Vries (Ed.), *Organizations on the Couch* (pp. 191–214). San Francisco, CA: Jossey-Bass Publishers.

Diamond, M. A. (1993). *The unconscious life of organizations.* Westport, CT: Quorum Books, Greenwood Publishing Group.

Diamond, M. A. (1997). Administrative assault: A contemporary psychoanalytic view of violence and aggression in the workplace. *American Review of Public Administration, 27*(3), 228–247.

Diamond, M. A., & Allcorn, S. (1985). Psychological responses to stress in complex organizations. *Administration & Society, 17,* 217–239.

Diamond, M. A., & Allcorn, S. (1987). The psychodynamics of regression in work groups. *Human Relations, 40*(8), 525–543.

Diamond, M. A., & Allcorn, S. (2003). The cornerstone of psychoanalytic organizational analysis: Psychological reality, transference and counter-transference in the work-place. *Human Relations, 56*(4), 491–514.

Diamond, M. A., & Allcorn, S. (2004). Moral violence in organizations: Hierarchic dominance and the absence of potential space. *Organisational & Social Dynamics, 4*(1), 22–45.

Diamond, M. A., Stein, H. F., & Allcorn, S. (2002). Organizational silos: Horizontal organizational fragmentation. *Journal for the Psychoanalysis of Culture and Society, 7*(2), 280–296.

Diamond, M. A., Allcorn, S., & Stein, H. F. (2004). The surface of organizational boundaries: A view from psychoanalytic object relations theory. *Human Relations, 57*(1), 31–53.

Driscoll, R. J., Worthington, K. A., & Hurrell, J. J., Jr. (1995). Workplace assault: An emerging job stressor. *Consulting Psychology Journal, 47*(4), 205–212.

Eagle, M. (1984). *Recent developments in psychoanalysis.* New York: McGraw-Hill.

Eigen, M. (1996). Psychic deadness. New York: Jason Aronson.

Erikson, E. (1968). *Identity, youth and crisis.* New York: W.W. Norton & Co.

Fairbairn, R. D. (1952). *An object relations theory of personality.* New York: Basic Books.

Fairbairn, W. R. D. (1952). *Psycho-analytic studies of personality.* London: Routledge and Kegan Paul.

Fairfield, S., Layton, L., & Stack, C. (Eds.). (2002). *Bringing the plague: Toward a postmodern psychoanalysis.* New York: Other Press.

Federn, E. (1952). *Ego psychology and the psychoses.* New York: Basic Books.

Field, G. A. (1974). The unconscious organization. *Psychoanalytic Review, 61*(3), 333–354.

Folger, R., & Baron, R. (1996). Violence and hostility at work: A model of reactions to perceived injustice. In G. R. VandenBos & E. Q. Bulalao (Eds.), *Violence on the Job* (pp. 51–85). Washington, DC: American Psychological Association.

Fonagy, P. (2001). *Attachment theory and psychoanalysis.* New York: Other Press.

Fonagy, P. (1991). Thinking about thinking: Some clinical and theoretical considerations in the treatment of a borderline patient. *International Journal of Psycho-Analysis, 72,* 1–18.

Foucault, M. (1977). *Discipline and punish.* New York: Pantheon.

Foucault, M. (1994). *Power, Vol 3* (James D. Faubion, Ed., Robert Hurley, Trans.). New York: The New Press.

Freud, S. (1958). *Recommendations to physicians practicing psycho-analysis,* Standard Edition, Volume 12. London: Hogarth Press. (Original work published 1912)

Freud, S. (1921). *Group psychology and the analysis of the ego.* New York: Norton & Co.

Freud, S. (1923). *The Ego and the Id.* New York: W. W. Norton & Co.

Freud, S. (1953). *The interpretation of dreams.* London: Hogarth Press. (Original work published 1900)

Fromm, E. (1941). *Escape from freedom.* New York: Avon Books.

Frost, R. (1930). Education by Poetry. In R. Poirier & M. Richardson (Eds.), *Collected Poems, Prose and Plays* (pp. 717–728). New York: Library of America.

Gabriel, Y. (1999). *Organizations in depth.* London: Sage.

Gay, P. (Ed.) (1989). *The Freud reader.* New York: W. W. Norton & Co.

Gedo, J. (1999). *The evolution of psychoanalysis: contemporary theory and practice.* New York: Other Press.

Gerson, S. (2004). The relational unconscious: A core element of intersubjectivity, thirdness, and clinical process. *The Psychoanalytic Quarterly, LXXIII*(1), 63–98.

Ghent, E. (1990). Masochism, submission, surrender. *Contemporary Psychoanalysis, 26,* 169–211.

Gill, M. (1994). *Psychoanalysis in transition.* Northvale, NJ: Analytic Press.

Gilligan, J. (1996). *Violence: Our deadly epidemic and its causes.* New York: Grosset/Putnam.

Glass, J. M. (1995). *Psychoses and power.* Ithaca, NY: Cornell University Press.

Goff, J. L., & Goff, P. J. (1991). *Organizational co-dependence*. Niwot, CO: University Press of Colorado.

Goleman, D. (1998). *Working with emotional intelligence*. New York: Bantam.

Green, A. (2004). Thirdness and psychoanalytic concepts. *The Psychoanalytic Quarterly, LXXIII*(1), 99–136.

Greenberg, J., & Mitchell, S. (1983). *Object relations in psychoanalytic theory*. Cambridge, MA: Harvard University Press.

Grinberg, L., Sor, D., & Tabak de Bianchedi, E. (1993). *New introduction to the work of Bion* (rev. ed.). Northvale, NJ: Jason Aronson.

Guntrip, H. (1969). *Schizoid phenomena, object relations and the self*. New York: International Universities Press.

Harrison, M. I. (2005). *Diagnosing organizations: Methods, models, and processes* (3rd ed.). Thousand Oaks, CA: Sage Publications.

Harrison, M. I., & Shirom, A. (1999). *Organizational diagnosis and assessment*. Thousand Oaks, CA: Sage Publications.

Harvey, M., & Cosier, R. (1995, March/April). Homicides in the workplace: Crisis or false alarm? *Business Horizons*, 11–20.

Hegel, G. W. F. (1807). *The phenomenology of mind* (J. B. Baille, Trans.). London: George Allen & Unwin/New York: Humanities Press.

Hinshelwood, R. D. (1989). *A dictionary of Kleinian thought* (2nd ed.). Northvale, NJ: Jason Aronson.

Hinshelwood, R. D. (1994). *Clinical Klein: From theory to practice*. New York: Basic Books.

Hirschhorn, L. (1988). *The workplace within*. Cambridge, MA: MIT Press.

Horney, K. (1950). *Neurosis and human growth*. New York: W. W. Norton.

Hummel, R. P. (1982). *The bureaucratic experience*. New York: St. Martin's.

Hunt, J. C. (1989). *Psychoanalytic aspects of fieldwork*. London: Sage.

Hymer, S. (1997). The analyst's use of the lost-and-found metaphor in psychoanalysis. *Psychoanalytic Review, 84*(1), 129–147.

Jacoby, H. (1973). *The bureaucratization of the world*. Berkeley: University of California Press.

Janus, I. (1982). *Group think* (2nd ed.). Boston: Houghton Mifflin.

Jaques, E. (1995). Why the psychoanalytical approach to understanding organizations is dysfunctional. *Human Relations, 48*(4), 343–349.

Jenkins, E. L. (1996). Workplace homicide: Industries and occupations at high risk. *Occupational Medicine State of Art Reviews, 11*(2), 219–225.

Jenkins, E. L., Kisner, S. M., Fosbroke, D. E., Layne, L. E., Stout, N. A., & Castillo, D. N. (1993). *Fatal injuries to workers in the United States, 1980–89. A decade of surveillance. National profile*. (DHHS [NIOSH]) Publication Number 93–108. Washington, DC: U.S. Department of Health and Human Services.

Johnson, P., & Indvik, J. (1994). Workplace violence: An issue of the nineties. *Public Personnel Management, 23*(4), 515–523.

Kaeter, M. (1993). The age of the specialized generalist. *Training, 30*(1), 48–53.

Kandel, E. R. (2006). *In search of memory: The emergence of a new science of mind*. New York: W. W. Norton & Co.

Kant, I. (1929). Critique of pure reason (N. K. Smith, Trans.). London: Macmillan.

Kernberg, O. (1980). *Internal world and external reality.* Northvale, NJ: Jason Aronson.

Kernberg, O. (1998). *Ideology, conflict, and leadership in groups and organizations.* New Haven, CT: Yale University Press.

Kets de Vries, M. F. R. (Ed.). (1984). *The irrational executive.* New York: International University Press.

Kets de Vries, M. F. R. (Ed.). (1991). *Organizations on the couch.* San Francisco: Jossey-Bass.

Kets de Vries, M. F. R. (2001). *Struggling with the demon.* Madison, CT: Psychosocial Press.

Kets de Vries, M. F. R. (2001). *The leadership mystique.* New York: Financial Times/ Prentice Hall.

Kets de Vries, M. F. R., & Miller, D. (1984). *The neurotic organization.* San Francisco: Jossey-Bass.

Kets de Vries, M. F. R., & Miller, D. (1987). Interpreting organizational texts. *Journal of Management Studies, 24*(3), 233–247.

Klein, M. (1946). Notes on some schizoid mechanisms. *International Journal of Psychoanalysis, XXVII*, 99–110.

Klein, M. (1959). Our adult world and its roots in infancy. *Human Relations, 12,* 291–303.

Klein, M. (1975). *Envy and gratitude and other works, 1946–1963.* New York: Delacorte.

Klein, M. (1975a). *Love, guilt and reparation and other works, 1921–1945.* New York: Free Press.

Klein, M. (1975b). *Envy and gratitude and other works 1946–1963.* New York: Free Press.

Klein, M., & Riviere, J. (1964). *Love, hate and reparation.* New York: W. W. Norton & Co.

Kluckhohn, F., & Strodbeck, F. (1961). *Variations in value orientations.* Evanston, IL: Row Peterson.

Kohut, H. (1972). Thoughts on narcissism and narcissistic rage. *The Psychoanalytic Study of the Child, 27*, 360–400.

Kohut, H. (1977). *The restoration of the self.* New York: International Universities Press.

Kohut, H. (1984). *How does analysis cure.* Chicago: University of Chicago.

Kunda, G. (1992). *Engineering culture.* Philadelphia: Temple University Press.

Lacan, J. (1975). *The seminar of Jacques Lacan, Book I, 1953–1954* (J. Forrester, Trans.) New York: W. W. Norton & Co.

Laplanche, J., & Pontalis, J. B. (1973). *The language of psychoanalysis.* New York: W. W. Norton & Co.

Lasch, C. (1979). *The culture of narcissism.* New York: Norton.

Lasch, C. (1984). *The minimal self.* New York: Norton.

Lasswell, H. (1930). *Psychopathology and politics.* Chicago: University of Chicago Press.

Lasswell, H. (1948). *Power and personality.* New York: W. W. Norton & Co.

Lawrence, P. R., & Lorsch, J. W. (1967). *Organization and environment*. Boston, MA: Harvard Business School Press.

Leach, E. (1976). *Culture and communication*. Cambridge: Cambridge University Press.

Levinson, H. (1957). Industrial mental health: Some observations and trends (with William C. Menninger). *Menninger Quarterly, VIII*(4), 1–31.

Levinson, H. (1972). *Organizational diagnosis*. Cambridge, MA: Harvard University Press.

Levinson, H. (1973). *The great jackass fallacy*. Boston: Harvard Business School.

Levinson, H. (1981). *Executive*. Cambridge, MA: Harvard University Press.

Levinson, H. (2002). *Organizational assessment*. Washington, DC: American Psychological Association Press.

Lewin, K. (1946). Action research and minority problems. *Journal of Social Issues 2*(4), 34–46.

Lifton, R. J. (1999). *Destroying the world to save it*. New York: Metropolitan Books.

Lissack, M. R. (1999). *A complexity: The science, its vocabulary, and its relation to organizations*. Unpublished manuscript.

Loewald, H. (1962). Internalization, separation, mourning, and the superego. *Psychoanalytic Quarterly, 31*, 483–504.

Lopez-Corvo, R. E. (2003). *The work of W. R. Bion*. London: Karnac.

Macpherson, C. B. (1962). *The political theory of possessive individualism: Hobbes to Locke*. London: Oxford University Press.

Mahler, M. S., Pine, E., & Bergman, A. (1975). *The psychological birth of the human infant*. New York: Basic Books.

March, J. G., & Simon, H. A. (1958). *Organizations*. New York: John Wiley.

Marcuse, H. (1960). *Reason and revolution: Hegel and the rise of social theory*. Boston, MA: Beacon Press.

Masterson, J. (1988). *The search for the real self*. New York: Free Press.

Mayer, R. (2001). Robert Dahl and the right to workplace democracy. *Review of Politics, 63*(2), 221–247.

Mayo, E. (1960). *The human problems of an industrial civilization*. New York: Viking. (Original work published 1933)

McManus, J. (1994, January 17). Sayonara time for silos as brand groups re-align. *Brandweek, 35*, 3.

Meltzer, D. (1975). Adhesive identification. *Contemporary Psychoanalysis, 11*, 289–310.

Merton, R., Gray, A., Hockey, B., & Selvin, H. (1952). *Reader in bureaucracy*. New York: Free Press.

Miller, M. L. (1999). Chaos, complexity, and psychoanalysis. *Psychoanalytic Psychology, 16*(3), 355–379.

Mills, J. (2000). Hegel on projective identification: Implications for Klein, Bion, and beyond. *The Psychoanalytic Review, 87*(6), 841–874.

Minolli, M., & Tricoli, M. L. (2004). Solving the problems of duality: The third and self-consciousness. *The Psychoanalytic Quarterly, LXXIII*(1), 137–166.

Mitchell, J. (Ed.). (1987). *The selected Melanie Klein*. New York: Free Press.

Mitchell, S. A. (1988). *Relational concepts in psychoanalysis: An integration.* Cambridge, MA: Harvard University Press.

Mitchell, S. A., & Aron, L. (Eds.). (1999). *Relational psychoanalysis: The emergence of a tradition.* Hillsdale, NJ: Analytic Press.

Modell, A. H. (1984). *Psychoanalysis in a new context.* New York: International Universities Press.

Modell, A. H. (1993). *The Private Self.* Cambridge, MA: Harvard University Press.

Modell, A. H. (2003). *Imagination and the Meaningful Brain.* Cambridge, MA: The MIT Press.

Monahan, J. (1995). *The clinical prediction of violent behavior.* New York: Jason Aronson.

Moore, B. E., & Fine, B. D. (1990). *Psychoanalytic terms & concepts.* New Haven, CT: Yale University Press/American Psychoanalytic Association.

Mossman, D. (1995). Violence prediction, workplace violence, and the mental health expert. *Consulting Psychology Journal, 47*(4), 223–232.

National Institute for Occupational Safety and Health (NIOSH) (1996). *Violence in the workplace: Risk factors and prevention strategies.* Current Intelligence Bulletin, 57. Washington, DC: U.S. Department of Health and Human Services.

Neebe, A. W. (1987). An improved, multiplier adjustment procedure for the segregated storage problem. *The Journal of the Operational Research Society, 38*(9), 815–825.

Nigro, L. G., & Waugh, W. L. (1996). Violence in the American workplace: Challenges to the public employer. *Public Administration Review, 56*(4), 326–333.

Noer, D. M. (1995). *Healing the wounds: Overcoming the trauma of layoffs and revitalizing downsized organizations.* San Francisco: Jossey-Bass.

Obeyesekere, G. (1980). *Medusa's hair: An essay on personal symbols and religious experience.* Chicago: University of Chicago Press.

Ogden, T. (1982). *Projective identification and psychotherapeutic technique.* Northvale, NJ: Jason Aronson.

Ogden, T. (1986). *Matrix of the mind.* Northvale, NJ: Jason Aronson.

Ogden, T. (1989). *The primitive edge of experience.* New York: Jason Aronson.

Ogden, T. (1992). The dialectically constituted/decentred subject of psychoanalysis. I. The Freudian subject. *International Journal of Psycho-Analysis, 73*, 517–526.

Ogden, T. (1994). *Subjects of analysis.* Northvale, NJ: Jason Aronson.

Ogden, T. (2004). The analytic third: Implications for psychoanalytic theory and technique. *The Psychoanalytic Quarterly, LXXIII*(1), 167–196.

O'Leary-Kelly, A. M., Griffin, R. W., & Glew, D. J. (1996). Organization-motivated aggression: A research framework. *Academy of Management Review, 21*(1), 225–253.

Paul, R. (1987). The question of applied psychoanalysis and the interpretation of cultural symbolism. *Ethos, 15*(1), 82–103.

Person, E. S. (1995). *By force of fantasy.* New York: Basic Books.

Pierce, C. (1972). *Charles S. Pierce: The essential writings* (E.C. Moore, Ed.). New York: Harper & Row.

Post, J. M. (2004). *Leaders and their followers in a dangerous world*. Ithaca, NY: Cornell University Press.

Rabinow, P. (Ed.). (1984). *The Foucault reader*. New York: Pantheon.

Resnick, P. J., & Kausch, O. (1995). Violence in the workplace: Role of the consultant. *Consulting Psychology Journal, 47*(4), 213–222.

Riviere, J. (Ed.). (1952). *Developments in psychoanalysis*. London: Hogarth.

Rice, A. K. (1963). *The enterprise and its environment*. London: Tavistock.

Rice, A. K., & Miller, E. (Eds). (1976). *Task and organization*. London: Wiley.

Ricoeur, P. (1970). *Freud and philosophy*. New Haven, CT: Yale University Press.

Riesenberg-Malcolm, R. (2001). Bion's theory of containment. In C. Bronstein (Ed.), *Kleinian theory: A contemporary perspective* (pp. 165–180). London: Whurr Publishers.

Rycroft, C. (1968). *A critical dictionary of psychoanalysis*. London: Penguin Books.

Schafer, R. (1976). *A new language for psychoanalysis*. New Haven, CT: Yale University Press.

Schafer, R. (1983). *The analytic attitude*. New York: Basic Books.

Schein, E. (1985). *Organizational culture and leadership*. San Francisco: Jossey-Bass.

Schilder, P. (1950). *The image and appearance of the human body*. New York: International Universities Press.

Schwartz, H. (1991). *Narcissistic processes and organizational decay*. New York: New York University Press.

Searles, H. F. (1960). *The nonhuman environment*. New York: International Universities Press.

Segal, H. (1957). Notes on symbol formation. *International Journal of Psycho-analysis, 38*, 391–397.

Segal, H. (1988). *Introduction to the work of Melanie Klein*. London: Karnac Books.

Shapiro, E., & Carr, A. W. (1991). *Lost in familiar places*. New Haven, CT: Yale University Press.

Sharpe, E. F. (1948). An examination of metaphor. In R. Fliess (Ed.), *The Psychoanalytic Reader: An Anthology of Essential Papers with Critical Introductions* (pp. 273–290). New York: International Universities Press.

Simon, H. A. (1961). *Administrative behavior*. New York: The Macmillan Company.

Spence, D. P. (1982). *Narrative truth and historical truth*. New York: Norton.

Spiegel, J. (1971). *Transactions: The interplay between individual, family, and society*. New York: Science House.

Stacey, R. D. (1992). *Managing the unknowable*. San Francisco: Jossey Bass.

Stacey, R. D. (1996). *Complexity and creativity in organizations*. San Francisco: Berrett Koehler Publishers.

Stapley, L. (1996). *The personality of the organization*. London: Free Association Books.

Stein, H. F. (1982). Autism and architecture: A tale of inner landscapes. *Continuing Education for the Family Physician, 16*(6), 15–16, 19.

Stein, H. F. (1985). *The psychoanthropology of American culture*. New York: Psychohistory Press.

Stein, H. F. (1987). *Developmental time, cultural space*. Norman, OK: University of Oklahoma Press.

Stein, H. F. (1992). *The culture of Oklahoma*. Norman, OK: University of Oklahoma Press.

Stein, H. F. (1994). *Listening deeply*. Boulder, CO: Westview.

Stein, H. F. (1998). *Euphemism, spin, and the crisis in organizational life*. Westport, CT: Quorum Books, Greenwood Publishing Group.

Stein, H. F. (2001). *Nothing personal, just business*. Westport, CT: Quorum Books, Greenwood Publishing Group.

Stein, H. F., & Apprey, M. (1987) *From metaphor to meaning: Papers in psychoanalytic anthropology*. Charlottesville, VA: University Press of Virginia.

Stein, H. F., & Hill, R. E. (1988). The dogma of technology. *The Psychoanalytic Study of Society, 13*, 149–179.

Stern, D. (1985). *The interpersonal world of the infant*. New York: Basic Books.

Stern, D. (2004). *The present moment in psychotherapy and everyday life*. New York: Norton & Company.

Stone, R. (1995). Workplace homicide: A time for action. *Business Horizons, 38*, 3–10.

Sullivan, H. S. (1953). *The interpersonal theory of psychiatry*. New York: W.W. Norton & Co.

Tausk, V. (1919). On the origin of the "influencing machine" in schizophrenia. In R. Fliess (Ed.), *The Psychoanalytic Reader* (pp. 31–64). New York: International Universities Press.

Thompson, J. (1967). *Organizations in action*. New York: McGraw-Hill.

Tustin, F. (1984). Autistic shapes. *International Review of Psycho-Analysis, 11*, 279–290.

Tustin, F. (1980). Autistic objects. *International Review of Psycho-Analysis, 7*, 27–40.

U.S. Government Accountability Office (GAO) (1994a).U.S. Postal Service: Labor-management problems persist on the workroom floor (Vol. 1). Report to congressional requesters.

U.S. Government Accountability Office (GAO) (1994b). U.S. Postal Service: Labor-management problems persist on the workroom floor (Vol. 2). Report to congressional requesters. Vanden Bos, G. R., & Bulatao, E. Q. (Eds.). (1996). *Violence on the job*. Washington, DC: American Psychological Association.

Van Maanen, J. (1988). *The tales of the field*. Chicago: University of Chicago Press.

Vaughan, S.C. (1997). *The talking cure: Why tradition talking therapy offers a better chance for long-term relief than any drug*. New York: Owl Books, Henry Holt and Company.

Volkan, V. (1988). *The need to have enemies and allies*. Northvale, NJ: Jason Aronson.

Volkan, V. (1997). *Bloodlines: From ethnic pride to ethnic terrorism*. New York: Farrar, Straus and Giroux.

Wallwork, E. (1991). *Psychoanalysis and ethics.* New Haven, CT: Yale University Press.

Weick, K. (1969). *The social psychology of organizing.* Reading, MA: Addison-Wesley.

Weick, K. (1995). *Sensemaking in organizations.* Thousand Oaks, CA: Sage.

Winnicott, D. W. (1965). *The maturational processes and the facilitating environment.* New York: International Universities Press.

Winnicott, D. W. (1971). *Playing and reality.* London: Tavistock.

Zaleznik, A., & Kets de Vries, M. F. R. (1975). *Power and the corporate mind.* Boston: Houghton Mifflin Co.

Zweibel, R. (2004). The third position: Reflections about the internal analytic working process. *The Psychoanalytic Quarterly, LXXIII*(1), 215–265.

About the Authors

Michael A. Diamond, PhD

Dr. Michael A. Diamond is Professor of Public Affairs, Associate Director for Academic Programs, and Director of the Center for the Study of Organizational Change at the Harry S. Truman School of Public Affairs, University of Missouri. He teaches and writes on organizational analysis and change, group dynamics and conflict resolution from a contemporary psychoanalytic perspective. He has consulted for nearly thirty years to public, private, and nonprofit organizations. Diamond was awarded the 1994 Harry Levinson Award for Excellence in Consulting from the American Psychological Association, the 1999 William T. Kemper Fellow for Excellence in Teaching, and the 2005 Faculty-Alumni Award from the University of Missouri. He is founder and past-president of the International Society for the Psychoanalytic Study of Organizations (ISPSO), a member of the International Society of Political Psychology (ISPP) since 1980, and a member of the American Political Science Association. He has authored or co-authored three books and over fifty articles in scholarly journals on the subject of the psychodynamics of organizational change.

Seth Allcorn, PhD

Dr. Seth Allcorn is Vice President for Business and Finance at the University of New England. Dr. Allcorn has twenty years of experience working with physicians, hospitals, and academic medical centers. He has served as the Assistant Dean for Health Services Management for the Texas Tech University Health Sciences Center School of Medicine and as Associate Dean for Fiscal Affairs at the Stritch School of Medicine, Loyola-Chicago. He has also been the administrator of the departments of medicine at the University of Missouri and University of Rochester schools of medicine. He has worked for twenty years as a part-time and full-time organizational consultant specializing in the management of change, strategic planning, and organizational restructuring. Dr. Allcorn is extensively published. He is the author or co-author of eleven books and over sixty papers that have appeared in scholarly and practitioner journals. He is a founding member of the International Society for the Psychoanalytic Study of Organizations.

Index

Abram, J., 124
accountability. *See* responsibility
action research, 1–3, 11
Adams, S., 54–55
"Age of the specialized Generalist, The"
    (Kaeter), 68
aggression, 5–6
  depressive organizations and, 20
  oppressive cultures and, 136, 137
  paranoid-schizoid organizations and, 23
  roots of, 138–39
  See also moral violence; violence
American culture, 53–54, 94–95, 161–62
Analytic Attitude, The (Schafer), 152
analytic third, 4–5
  Benjamin and, 78–79
  creativity and, 77
  dialectic and, 79
  Green and, 84–85
  intersubjectivity and, 79, 84
  intervention and change and, 85–89
  Minolli and Tricoli and, 82–83
  Ogden and, 79–81
  projective identification and, 79–81, 83
  psychoanalysis and, 74–77
  Winnicott and, 77–78
Argyris, C., 101
attachment, 84, 111, 112–13, 117
authority
  boundaries and, 35
  delegation of, 129
  democratic organizational cultures and, 161
  emotions and, 24
  hierarchical organizations and, 49
  narcissism and, 110–11, 119
  organizational violence and, 107
  psychological regression and, 97–98
  as sensate surface, 39
  as tool of oppression, 116
  transference and countertransference
    and, 154
autistic-contiguous mode, 8, 14, 17–18, 31,
    170–71

dialectical interplay and, 18–20
organizations and, 24–26, 173
silos and, 51, 63–64, 67–68, 69
awareness
  autistic-contiguous organizations and, 25
  of boundaries and silos, 46
  of consultant, 148
  of dialectical tension, 19
  of organizational identity, 133
  of regression, 98

Balkanizing. *See* silo mentality
Baron, R. A., 138
Being a Character (Bollas), 100
Benjamin, J., 76, 78–79, 109, 112
  autonomy and independence and, 117,
    118
  object relations theory of, 165
  subjugation of the other and, 140
"Beyond Doer and Done To: An
    Intersubjective View of Thirdness"
    (Benjamin), 78
Bion, W.
  analytic third and, 81
  collective regression and, 101
  containment and, 27, 99–100, 176–77
  psychological regression and, 95, 96, 156
Bollas, C., 63, 100–101
bonds, 84–85, 113
Bonds of Love, The (Benjamin), 140
boundaries, 4
  authority and, 35
  chaos and complexity and, 34
  collapse of dialectic tension, 19
  conflict and, 36
  crossing of, 34, 36, 41
  of culture, 36
  data collection and, 176
  democracy and, 167
  identity and, 33
  maintenance of, 33–34, 69–70, 130
  responsibility and, 69
  sensory deprivation and, 17–18

boundaries (*continued*)
  silos and, 12, 41, 51
  specialization and, 69
  surfaces and, 31–32
  types of, 35
  See also surfaces
Briskin, A., 142–43
Britton, R., 75, 76, 81–82, 93
bureaucracy, 50
Burge, F. J., 52
Butcher, D., 163
Butz, M. R., 131

Carr, A. W., 185
change, 5
  analytic third and, 85–89
  bottom-up processes and, 128
  consultants and, 177
  depressive mode and, 9
  dialectic and, 73, 132
  emotional loss and, 84–85
  moral violence and, 116
  organizations and, 167, 175
  psychological regression and, 102–4
  psychotherapies and, 7–8
  silos and, 68–71
  stress of, 8
  transference and countertransference
    and, 158
"Chaos, Complexity, and Psychoanalysis"
    (Miller), 131
chaos and complexity, 5, 127–28
  boundaries and, 34
  creativity and, 129
  dialectic interplay and, 132
  organized disorder and, 130
  psychological regression and, 129
  of transference dynamics, 155
Chasseguet-Smirgel, J., 160
Churchman, C. W., 163
Clarke, M., 163
"Clinical Research: A National Call to
    Action" (AMA), 53
Cloke, K., 162
collaterality, 53
Collins, D., 163
condensation, 45
consultation, 2, 7
  analytic third and, 85
  holding environment and, 46
  personnel changes and, 184–85
  phases of, 177–78

psychoanalytic consultants and, 149–50
  silos and, 46, 54
  surfaces and, 46
container/contained, 43–44, 99–100, 176–77
  silos and, 45–46, 62
containment, 27–28, 93
  autistic-contiguous mode and, 17, 18
  democracy and, 169
  depressive mode and, 15, 18
  depressive organizations and, 20
  of emotions, 40
  leaders and, 99, 100
  psychological regression and, 157
  See also defective containers
"Contribution to the Psychogenesis of
    Manic-Depressive States, A" (Klein),
    135
countertransference, 80
  change and, 158
  definition of, 154–55
  hierarchy and authority and, 154
  intervention and, 158
  object relational approach and, 148
  in organizational life, 155
  in organizational studies, 153
  psychological regression and, 156–57
  See also transference
creativity
  analytic third and, 77
  boundary maintenance and, 34
  chaos and complexity and, 129
  democracy and, 171
  dialectical interplay and, 171
  leaders and, 133
  moral violence and, 112
Creativity and Perversion (Chasseguet-
    Smirgel), 160
culture
  artifacts of, 139, 149
  boundaries of, 36
  cultural third and, 83–84
  democratic cultures and, 158–60, 161,
    168
  ideology and, 101
  of oppressive organizations, 107, 135–36,
    139
  of organizations, x, 20, 67–68, 95, 149
  silo mentality and, 69
  See also American culture; oppressive
    organizations
Culture of Oklahoma, The (Stein), 36
Czander, W., 33, 35

defective containers, 5, 27–28, 97–99, 108
  perversions of democracy and, 159, 160
defensive routines, 3, 6
  boundary maintenance and, 34
  collapse of dialectic tension, 19
  defective containment and, 27–28
  oppositional groups and, 166–67
  paranoid-schizoid mode and, 16–17
  paranoid-schizoid organizations and, 23
  silos and surfaces and, 43–44, 188
  See also psychological splitting
DeLeon, L., 162
DeLeon, P., 162
democracy, 6
  authority and, 161
  awareness of regression and, 98
  boundaries and, 167
  containment and, 169
  creativity and, 171
  culture of, 158–60, 161, 168
  dialectical interplay and, 171–74
  human nature and, 167
  leaders and, 161, 167–68
  perversions of, 168–69
  threats to, 102
  in workplace, 161–64
depressive mode, 9, 169, 170–71
  containment and, 15
  dialectical interplay and, 18–20
  organizations and, 20–22, 172
  responsibility and, 14, 15
diagnosis, 6–7, 28, 58
  data for, 149, 151–52, 176
  dialectical interplay and, 19
  history and, 70
  personnel changes and, 184–85
  psychodynamic assessments and, 149–51
  transference and countertransference
    and, 153
dialectic
  analytic third and, 79
  change and, 73, 132
  chaos and complexity and, 132
  creativity and, 171
  democracy and, 171–74
  between nonrational and rational, 95
  of surface experience, 39
  of three modes of experience, 18–20
"Dialectical Modes of Experience" (Ogden),
    165
"Dilbert" (Adams), 54–55

Discipline and Punish: the Birth of the Prison
    (Foucault), 164
double-loop learning, 128
duality, 82–83

"Education by Poetry" (Frost), 49
Ego and the Id, The (Freud), 17
Eigen, M., 109, 112, 119, 140
emotional abuse. *See* moral violence
emotions, 1–2
  autistic-contiguous mode and, 24
  psychological reality and, 147–48
  psychological splitting and, 119
  silos and, 51, 54
Experiences in Groups (Bion), 101

fascism, 100–101
feelings. *See* emotions
Field, G., 94
Fine, B. D., 68, 154
Folger, R., 138
Foucault, M., 164–65
fragmentation, 16
  of horizontal axis, 40, 42–43, 55
  organizations and, 52–53
  silos and, 40–41
  of vertical axis, 42–43, 55
Freud, S.
  condensation and, 68
  identification and, 45
  individual as social psychology and, 167
  instincts and, 84
  psychological regression and, 95, 96, 156
  sensations, surfaces, and boundaries
    and, 17
  symbols and, 44
Fromm, E., 98
Frost, R., 49

Gerson, S., 76, 83–84
Gilligan, J., 143
Glass, J. M., 100, 102, 158, 168
Goldsmith, J., 162
"Great Wall of China, The" (Kafka), *ix*
Green, A., 76, 84–85
Group Psychology and the Analysis of the Ego
    (Freud), 96, 167

Hegel, G. W. F., 78, 83
hierarchy
  American culture and, 54
  authority and, 49
  communication and, 51

hierarchy (*continued*)
  hierarchical structures and, 4, 110, 113, 117
  horizontal status and, 56
  leaders and, 51
  organized disorder and, 131
  paranoid-schizoid organizations and, 23
  silos and, 4
  transference and countertransference and, 154
Hill, R. E., 41
history
  depressive mode and, 15
  depressive organizations and, 20
  diagnosis and, 70
  paranoid-schizoid mode and, 16
  paranoid-schizoid organizations and, 23
holding environment, 7, 8–9, 27, 46
horizontal axis, 49–50, 55
Human Costs of a Management Failure, The (Allcorn, Baum, Diamond, and Stein), 141
human nature, *ix*, *x*, 73–74, 94, 162, 167. *See also* autistic-contiguous mode; depressive mode; paranoid-schizoid mode
Hunt, J. C., 153

idealization, 45, 122
identification, 26–28, 45, 62, 136
identity
  boundaries and, 33
  ideology and, 101
  internalization and, 142–43
  of organizations, 25, 96–97, 133
Imagination and the Meaningful Brain (Modell), 187
immersion, 176
"Improved Multiplied Adjustment Procedure for the Segregated Storage Problem, An" (Neebe), 52
individuality, 53–54, 160
integration, 39, 59–60, 69, 148–49
internalization, 27, 142–43
"Interpreting organizational texts" (Kets de Vries and Miller), 151
intersubjectivity, 75, 78, 79, 84
intervention, 58
  analytic third and, 85–89
  challenge of, 70–71
  healing organizational splits and, 167

transference and countertransference and, 158
introjection, 43, 61, 62
Irrational Executive, The (Kets de Vries), 94

Kaeter, M., 68
Kafka, F., *ix*
Kant, I., 119
Kernberg, O., 156–57
Kets de Vries, M., 94, 151–52
Klein, M., 7, 14, 166
  analytic third and, 81
  depressive mode and, 9
  impoverishment of the ego and, 119
  persecutors and, 135
  roots of adult behavior and, 8
Kluckhohn, F., 53
Kohut, H., 109, 120–21

Lasswell, H., 167
Leach, E., 35
leaders, leadership
  autistic-contiguous mode and, 24
  autistic-contiguous organizations and, 26
  consultation and, 178
  containment and, 99, 100
  creativity and, 133
  democracy and, 167–68
  democratic organizational cultures and, 161
  depressive organizations and, 20
  hierarchy and, 51
  idealization of, 45
  leader-follower relations, 117–18
  narcissism and, 110–11
  organizational identities and, 96
  paranoia and, 140
  psychological regression and, 12, 97
  resistance to change and, 191
  silos and, 52, 57
learning, 19. *See also* double-loop learning
Levinson, H., 150, 151, 176
Lewin, K., *x*
Like Subjects, Love Objects (Benjamin), 109
linearity, 53
listening deeply, 2
Listening Deeply: An Approach to Understanding and Consulting in Organizational Culture (Stein), 2

Maturational Process and the Facilitating Environment, The (Winnicott), 127
Mayer, R., 162

metaphors, 41, 49. *See also* silos
Miller, M. L., 131, 151–52
Minolli, M., 76, 82–83
Modell, A., 1, 166, 187
Moore, B. E., 68, 154
moral violence, 5, 109
    change and, 116
    creativity and, 112
    organizations and, 113–16
    origins of, 117–20
    psychological regression and, 118–21
    relational patterns of, 121–23
    stress and narcissism and, 110–11
    transitional space and, 124

narcissism, 110–11, 160
    authority and, 119
    idealization and, 45
    narcissistic rage and, 120–21
    oppressive cultures and, 136
    relational patterns of, 121–23
    silo mentality and, 62
narrative data, 151–52, 176, 187
Neebe, A., 52
Nigro, L. G., 137–38

object relations theory, 4, 7–9, 11, 14, 148, 166
Ogden, T.
    analytic third and, 75, 76, 79–81
    autistic-contiguous mode and, 17, 93
    boundaries and surfaces and, 31
    depressive mode and, 15
    dialectical interplay and, 13, 18, 19
    modes of experience and, 8, 132, 147
    object relations theory of, 14, 165
    potential space and, 77
    protective surfaces and, 44
    psychological regression and, 101
    sensory deprivation and, 18
    silos and, 63, 64
O'Leary-Kelly, A. M., 138–39
oppressive organizations, 135–37, 139,
        140–41, 142–43
"Organizational Democracy" (Butcher and
        Clark), 163
organized disorder, 130–32
"Origin of the 'Influencing Machine' in
        Schizophrenia, On the" (Tausk), 61

panopticism, 164
"Paradox of Recognition between Self and
        Object" (Benjamin), 165

paranoiagenesis, 156–57
paranoid-schizoid mode, 8, 14, 16–17, 170, 171
    dialectical interplay and, 18–20
    learning and, 19
    organizations and, 22–24, 172–73
participant observation, x, 1, 176
pattern matching, 151
Paul, R., 44
Phenomenology of Mind, The (Hegel), 83
Playing and Reality (Winnicott), 73, 77
positivism, x, 140
potential space, 77–78, 168
Primitive Edge of Experience, The (Ogden),
        31, 63, 93
Private Self, The (Modell), 1
"Problem of Domination" (Benjamin), 165
projection. *See* projective identification
projective identification, 16, 17, 61
    analytic third and, 79–81, 83
    defective containment and, 27–28
    paranoid-schizoid organizations and, 23–24
    silos and, 43
Psychic Deadness (Eigen), 140
psychoanalytic theory, ix–x, 7–9, 14
psychological anthropology, ix
psychological regression, 5, 6, 96–97
    autistic-contiguous mode and, 24
    change and, 102–4
    chaos and complexity and, 129
    defective containment and, 27–28
    dialectic tension and, 19
    fragmentation and, 40
    leaders and, 12, 97–98
    moral violence and, 118–21
    narcissism and, 110–11
    object relations theory and, 8
    paranoid-schizoid organizations and, 23
    responsibility and, 40
    silo mentality and, 62
    stress and, 8
    transference and countertransference
        and, 156–57
psychological splitting, 16, 17, 61, 98, 111, 141
    defective containment and, 27–28
    emotions and, 119
    object relations theory and, 8–9
    paranoid-schizoid organizations and, 23–24
    silo mentality and, 62
    "us *vs.* them" and, 42, 54, 56, 140
Psychosis and Power (Glass), 100, 158, 168

reification, 43, 62
"Relational Unconscious: A Core Element
      of Intersubjectivity, Thirdness, and
      Clinical Process, The" (Gerson), 83
reparation, 146, 167, 185–86
"Researchers Are Urged to Work toward
      New Treatments with Health-Care
      Providers" (Brainard), 53
responsibility
      boundaries and, 69
      depressive mode and, 14, 15
      depressive organizations and, 20
      paranoid-schizoid organizations and, 23
      psychological regression and, 40
Riesenberg-Malcolm, R., 27

Schafer, R., 152
Searles, H. F., 61
self, 1, 39, 77, 98, 164
Shapiro, E., 185
Sharpe, E. F., 60–61
silo mentality, 4, 52, 55
      narcissism and, 62
      organizational culture and, 69
      paranoid-schizoid organizations and,
            23–24
      psychological regression and splitting
            and, 62
      specialization and, 58–59
silos
      American culture and, 53–55
      as autistic organizational artifacts, 51,
            63–64, 67–68, 69, 139
      boundaries and, 12, 41, 51, 64–68
      change and, 68–71
      as condensation, 44–45
      consultation and, 46, 54
      defensive mind and, 188
      emotions and, 51, 54
      experience of, 41–43
      horizontal fragmentation and, 40–41
      images of, 52
      implicit complexity of, 59–60
      integration and, 59–60
      leaders and, 52, 57
      organizational, 4
      origins of, 50–55, 57
      paranoid-schizoid organizations and, 23
      psychological defenses and, 43–44
      specialization and, 42, 60, 68

      surface of, 41
      workplace psychodynamics of, 60–63
silo thinking. *See* silo mentality
specialization, 54
      boundaries and, 69
      silos and, 42, 58–59, 60, 68
      See also silos
Spiegel, J., 53–54
splitting. *See* psychological splitting
Stacey, R., 34–35, 172
Stapley, L., 35
Stein, H. F., 2, 36, 41, 64, 67, 149
stories. *See* narrative data
stress, 8, 9, 110
Strodbeck, F., 53
structures
      hierarchical structures and, 4, 110, 113, 117
      organizational structures and, 31, 49–50
      organizational *vs.* personality structure, 165
      organized disorder and, 131
      self-perception and, 164
      social and psychological structures and,
            13, 35, 148–49
      as a tool of oppression, 116
      See also hierarchy; horizontal axis
"Subjectivity, Objectivity, and Triangular
      Space" (Britton), 93
Subjects of Analysis (Ogden), 13, 147
Sullivan, H. S., 3
surfaces, 17–18, 36, 38–39
      authority and, 39
      autistic-contiguous mode and, 24
      autistic-contiguous organizations and, 26
      boundaries and, 31–32
      consultation and, 46
      psychological defenses and, 43–44
      of silos, 41
      See also boundaries
symbiosis, 98
symbiotic lure, 100–102
symbolism, 14, 44–45, 95

Tausk, V., 61
Thompson, J., 33
"Thoughts on Narcissism and Narcissistic
      Rage" (Kohut), 109
transference, 28, 80, 95, 113, 121–23
      change and, 158
      definition of, 153, 154
      hierarchy and authority and, 154

intervention and, 158
   object relational approach and, 148
   in organizational life, 155
   in organizational studies, 153
   psychological regression and, 156–57
   See also countertransference
transitional objects, 123–24
transitional space, 77–78, 124, 168
triangular space. See analytic third
Tricoli, M. L., 76, 82–83

"Unconscious Organization, The" (Field), 94
"Use of an Object and Relating through
   Identification, The" (Winnicott), 175

violence, 5–6, 107
   emphasis on security and training and, 138
   oppressive cultures and, 136, 137
   roots of, 138–39

See also moral violence
Violence: Our Deadly Epidemic and Its
   Causes (Gilligan), 143
"Violence and Hostility at Work: A Model
   of Reactions to Perceived Injustice"
   (Folger and Baron), 138
Volkan, V., 141

Waugh, W. L., 137–38
Winnicott, D. W.
   analytical third and, 76, 77–78
   change in patients and, 175
   cultural experience and, 73, 74
   holding environment and, 7, 8–9, 99
   infinite falling and, 127
   moral violence and, 109
   regression and, 98
   transitional phenomena and, 123–24